LOVE, SEX AND MARRIAGE IN THE MIDDLE AGES

A SOURCEBOOK

Edited by

Conor McCarthy

Routledge
Taylor & Francis Group
LONDON AND NEW YORK

First published 2004
by Routledge
11 New Fetter Lane, London EC4P 4EE

Simultaneously published in the USA and Canada
by Routledge
29 West 35th Street, New York, NY 10001

Routledge is an imprint of the Taylor and Francis Group

Typeset in Garamond and Univers by
Florence Production Ltd, Stoodleigh, Devon

Printed and bound in Great Britain by
TJ International Ltd, Padstow, Cornwall

British Library Cataloguing in Publication Data
A catalogue record for this book is available from the British Library

Library of Congress Cataloging in Publication Data
A catalogue record for this book has been requested

ISBN 0–415–30745–7 (hbk)
ISBN 0–415–30746–5 (pbk)

CONTENTS

ACKNOWLEDGEMENTS

Having spent quite a few years now studying this topic, I have accumulated a good many debts along the way, and this seems an appropriate place to acknowledge some of them. I owe most to Gerald Morgan, who supervised my postgraduate work on medieval marriage at Trinity College, Dublin, with great generosity and enthusiasm. It is a pleasure to thank him again. The examiners of that thesis, John Scattergood and Alcuin Blamires, made suggestions that have found their way into this book, for which I thank them. I am grateful also to former colleagues and students at the National University of Ireland, Galway, and the University of Durham, several of whom were interested in the subjects discussed here, or related topics, and were generous with their time and knowledge.

Personal thanks are due to my family (all of them) for their enduring support and interest: in particular my parents, Michael and Nuala McCarthy, and my brothers, Michael and David. Thanks likewise to friends for the same, particularly Niamh Walsh and Lisa Carey. My thanks also to Dario and Juliette Brollo, Darren Brollo and Emily Brollo, for hospitality, the frequent use of a computer, and what must have been hundreds of cups of tea. My biggest personal debt is to Deidre Brollo, who lived with the writing of this book over a couple of years, encouraging throughout. It would be difficult to thank her enough.

This book was written in Durham in 2001 and rewritten in Sydney in 2002, and I want to thank the Universities of Durham and Sydney for the use of their libraries and the helpfulness of their library staff. Particular debts are owed for some of the translations: I am grateful to Kathleen Coleman for her revisions of my translations of the Latin statutes in extract 15, and I am similarly grateful to Robert Carver for his revisions of the translations in extracts 10, 11 and 12. At Routledge, thanks to Vicky Peters for seeing the book past all hurdles, to Sünje Redies, editorial assistant at Routledge, and to Gillian Oliver for suggesting something like this project in the first place. Further thanks to Miranda Chaytor for copyediting, Alex Ballantine for last-minute editorial assistance and Ruth Bourne for production editing. My thanks also to several anonymous readers for any number of suggested improvements. To all of the above, named or not, many thanks.

It remains to acknowledge the debt of this book to other books, and my own fallibility. It's self evident that nobody could possibly be an expert in all of the areas discussed by a book like this, covering so broad a span of time. Chaucer describes himself in *A Treatise on the Astrolabe* as a 'lewd compilator', an unlearned compiler of the works of others. In assembling this anthology, I too may claim to be a 'lewd compilator', and, probably unlike Chaucer, to mean it. As a consequence, although I am also repeating the knowledge of others, and in some cases 'have it translatid in myn Englissh', I am sure to have introduced errors somewhere in the materials assembled here. I apologize to the reader for any that might come to notice.

Conor McCarthy
Sydney
September 2002

PERMISSIONS

The author and publishers are grateful to the following for permission to reproduce copyright material from the following publications: Penguin books for material from St Augustine, *Concerning the City of God against the Pagans*, trans. Henry Bettenson, Harmondsworth: Penguin, 1972, copyright © Henry Bettenson 1972; St Bede, *Ecclesiastical History of the English People*, trans. L. Sherley Price, R. E. Latham and D. H. Farmer, revised edn, Harmondsworth: Penguin, 1990, copyright © Leo Shirley Price 1955, 1968; *The Book of Margery Kempe*, trans. B. A. Windeatt, Harmondsworth: Penguin, 1985, copyright © B. A. Windeatt 1985; *The Letters of Abelard and Heloise*, trans. Betty Radice, Harmondsworth: Penguin, 1974, copyright © Betty Radice 1974; and *The Lais of Marie de France*, trans. G. S. Burgess and K. Busby, Harmondsworth: Penguin, 1986, copyright © Glyn S. Burgess and Keith Busby 1986, 1999, reproduced by permission of Penguin Books Ltd. Oxford University Press for *Medieval English Prose for Women,* ed. and trans. Bella Millet and Jocelyn Wogan-Browne, Oxford: Oxford University Press, 1990; *The Life of St Christina of Markyate: A Twelfth Century Recluse*, ed. and trans. C. H. Talbot, Oxford: Oxford University Press, 1959; *The Romance of the Rose*, trans. F. Horgan, Oxford: Oxford University Press, 1994; *Councils and Synods with Other Documents Relating to the English Church, AD 1205–1313*, ed. F. M. Powicke and C. R. Cheney, London: Oxford University Press, 1964; and *Paston Letters and Papers of the Fifteenth Century*, ed. Norman Davis, Oxford: Oxford University Press, 1971–1976, reprinted by permission of Oxford University Press. The Pontifical Institute of Mediaeval Studies for *The Plaint of Nature*, trans. James J. Sheridan, Toronto: Pontifical Institute of Mediaeval Studies, 1980, copyright © 1980 by the Pontifical Institute of Mediaeval Studies, Toronto; *Gawain on Marriage: The 'De Coniuge Non Ducenda'*, ed. and trans. A. G. Rigg, Toronto: Pontifical Institute of Mediaeval Studies, 1986, copyright © 1986 by the Pontifical Institute of Mediaeval Studies, Toronto; and Emil M. Fackenheim, 'A Treatise on Love by Ibn Sina', *Mediaeval Studies*

7 (1945): 208–228, copyright © 1945 by the Pontifical Institute of Mediaeval Studies, Toronto, reprinted by permission of the publisher. The Selden Society for *Select Cases from the Ecclesiastical Courts of the Province of Canterbury, c.1200–1301*, ed. Norma Adams and Charles Donahue Jr, London: Selden Society, vol. 95, 1981; and *Select Cases in Manorial Courts, 1250–1550: Property and Family Law*, ed. and trans. L. R. Poos and Lloyd Bonfield, London: Selden Society, vol. 114, 1998, reprinted by permission of the Selden Society. Professor John O'Meara for Giraldus Cambrensis, *The History and Topography of Ireland*, trans. John J. O'Meara, Harmondsworth: Penguin, 1982, copyright © 1982 John O'Meara. Harvard University Press for *Bracton: On the Laws and Customs of England*, ed. G. E. Woodbine and trans. S. E. Thorne, Cambridge, MA: Harvard University Press, copyright © 1968, 1977 by the President and Fellows of Harvard College. University of Pennsylvania Press for Mary Frances Wack, *Lovesickness in the Middle Ages: The Viaticum and its Commentaries*, Philadelphia: University of Pennsylvania Press, 1990, copyright © 1990 Mary Frances Wack, reprinted by permission of Pennsylvania University Press. Gerald Duckworth & Co. Ltd for *Andreas Capellanus, On Love*, ed. and trans. P. G. Walsh, London: Duckworth, 1982. Faber and Faber for *A Choice of Anglo-Saxon Verse*, ed. and trans. Richard Hamer, London: Faber, 1970. Orion books for *Sir Gawain and the Green Knight, Pearl, Cleanness, Patience*, ed. J. J. Anderson, London: Dent, 1996, and A. V. C. Schmidt, *The Vision of Piers Plowman*, London: Dent, 1987. Persea Books Inc. (New York) for *The Book of the City of Ladies*, Christine de Pizan © 1982, 1998. State University of New York Press for *Women's Secrets: A Translation of Pseudo-Albertus Mangus' De Secretis Mulierum with Commentaries* by Helen Rodnite Lemay, the State University of New York Press ©1992, State University of New York. All rights reserved. Robert L. A. Clark for 'Jousting without a Lance: The Condemnation of Female Homoeroticism in the Livre des Manières'. Routledge, Inc., part of The Taylor & Francis Group, for extracts from Louise Fradenburg and Carla Freccero (eds) *Premodern Sexualities* © 1996, and Emilie Amt, *Women's Lives in Medieval Europe* © 1993. The Augustinian Heritage Institute for extracts from St. Augustine, *Marriage and Virginity*, ed. D. G. Hunter, trans. Ray Kearney, *The Works of St. Augustine* © 1999. University of North Carolina Press for extracts from *La Querelle de la Rose: Letters and Documents*, ed. and trans. Joseph L. Baird and John R. Kane (1978).

Every effort has been made to contact copyright holders, although this has not been possible in every case.

INTRODUCTION

Love, sex and marriage were topics much discussed in medieval writings of all sorts: in literary works and theological discussions, in medical textbooks and private letters, in chronicles and legal manuals, in penitential guides and conduct books. This book gathers together extracts from such writings from across the entire medieval period, from the fourth century to the sixteenth. It includes selections from texts and authors whose influence was felt across medieval Christendom, such as Augustine's *City of God*, Gratian's *Decretum*, the letters of Abelard and Heloise, the *Romance of the Rose* of Guillaume de Lorris and Jean de Meun, and the medical text that circulated under the name *Trotula*. It focuses in particular on medieval England, presenting selections from texts well known to modern readers such as *Beowulf* and Chaucer's *Canterbury Tales*, alongside much less familiar material such as local ecclesiastical legislation and accounts of court cases concerning marriage and sexual behaviour. The purpose of this selection is not to offer any one, single, homogeneous view of love, sex and marriage in the medieval period. On the contrary, it is to demonstrate the varieties and differences to be found in medieval writing on these subjects.

What should we expect to find in these texts? Modern readers of the Middle Ages have seen both continuities and discontinuities between the attitudes expressed concerning love, sex and marriage in medieval times and our own. These continuities and differences can be about both actions and ideologies, ideologies being, in Louis Althusser's words, 'the imaginary relationship of individuals to their real conditions of existence' (Althusser 1984: 37). Persons in the twenty-first century, or the eighth, or the fifteenth, might carry out similar actions: a declaration of love, an act of sexual intercourse, a marriage ceremony. But although the acts in different centuries might resemble one another, the understanding of what takes place through these actions, the cultural construction of their meaning (both to the persons concerned and to the wider culture that they live in) might vary significantly across time. Familiar actions in these texts may be accompanied by very different mindsets.

Some examples of continuities, as modern readers have seen them: James Brundage has argued that discussions of sex in medieval legal theology extend into the attitudes found in some modern statute law (Brundage 1987: xx, 608–617). P. G. Walsh has pointed to a similar line of influence upon modern theological discussions of marriage, noting that Vatican II's discussions of marriage in the twentieth century cite St Augustine's writings on the subject from the fifth (Walsh 2001: v). C. S. Lewis argued many years ago that modern notions of romantic love have their roots in the eleventh century (Lewis 1936). But as an example of significant discontinuity, Michel Foucault has argued that the notion of a 'sexuality' is a modern one, whose history can be traced to the recent past: he argues that in the premodern period, the performance of sexual acts did not lead to the constitution of a sexual identity in a way that is true of contemporary society (Foucault 1981: 43). Some of these readings just cited are contested ones, to which we shall return very shortly, but they demonstrate that modern readers of medieval discussions of love, sex and marriage can expect to find points of contact with the present day, but also substantial differences.

The texts also pose difficulties of interpretation for the modern reader. One of the first obstacles to arise is that of bias. The written records surviving from the medieval period, from which we might attempt to reconstruct a picture of how life was lived in the past, are primarily ecclesiastical documents. For most of the medieval period, to be literate was to be a cleric, and the medieval Church's attitude towards sexual behaviour of any sort was a predominantly negative one. The Church attempted, with varying degrees of vigour and varying results, to impose celibacy upon its clergy and to police the sexual activities of the laity, both married and unmarried. It promoted a view of sexual behaviour which exalted virginity and chastity above even marital sex. So the written sources that provide us with our evidence about medieval sexual behaviour are problematic, in that they are often texts written by a clergy enjoined to keep celibacy about lay behaviour which they regard as sinful. Many of the texts here are at best uneasy about sexual behaviour, and many are downright hostile. We need to be able to read between the lines to recover a more balanced picture of what the realities of love, sex and married life might have been like for those outside the clergy.

But paradoxically, ecclesiastical disapproval also makes these texts quite informative. Sex as it appears in these texts is at once more public and more private than might nowadays seem the norm. In the extracts below, we can see that the sexual behaviour of ordinary individuals is subjected to several sources of inquiry: confessors, the ecclesiastical courts, local manorial courts and the municipal authorities can all be seen inquiring into sexual behaviour (see extracts 17, 18, 19, 34, 35). In the less-than-spacious living conditions of later medieval households, we discover that witnesses in court cases are able to testify concerning the conjugal relations of their friends: in the thirteenth-century case of Alice *contra* John the Blacksmith, Alice's landlady can testify that she often saw the couple in bed together, and Evelyn and Edmund, fellow lodgers, give similar testimony (extract 17). The private life of couples is a matter of general awareness to the point where witnesses can discuss it in court. On the other hand, what appears to be a taboo against nudity (on which see Brundage 1987: 161, 302, 424–425) seems to mean that even at their most intimate, there are things which married couples do not reveal to one another. 'A husband ought not to see his wife nude', says the Anglo-Saxon Penitential of Theodore (extract 7), and, in the fifteenth century, Margery Kempe's husband sleeps with her for years without noticing the hairshirt that she wears constantly beneath her clothing (extract 39.i).

Literature might seem to offer us a sort of counterbalance to the suspicion of sex found in ecclesiastical texts. The bawdy humour of the *fabliaux* appears to present a comic celebration of sexuality in antithesis to the suspicion of sex found in clerical texts (e.g. extract 61). But it is important perhaps not to take this opposition at face value. The *fabliaux* and the vernacular poems dealing with antimatrimonial satire might seem to offer a world-view directly opposite to that of the Latin writings that express suspicion of sex, but in fact all of these texts are often found to share a similar antifeminist agenda (on which see Blamires 1992). From some perspectives, they look very different. From others, they look very similar indeed.

So, while the texts quoted below offer a great variety of evidence, that evidence needs careful handling. This is partly because of authorial bias, and partly because historical change can mean that what seems familiar at first may in fact turn out to differ quite seriously from modern assumptions. Before proceeding any further, it may prove useful to briefly summarize at this point the dominant twentieth-century readings of love, sex and marriage in the Middle Ages, and to indicate how the extracts anthologized below seem to reflect on those readings.

LOVE

'Courtly love'

The defining model for twentieth-century discussions of medieval notions of love was the idea of 'courtly love', most influentially expressed in English by C. S. Lewis in his 1936 book, *The Allegory of Love*. There, Lewis argued that a new form of love had found expression in French troubadour poetry, and that this new form of love exercised a fundamental influence on the literature of the later medieval period, in France, but also in England. He also asserted that this love with which medieval literature was concerned had nothing to do with marriage, and was in fact an idealization of adultery. In Lewis's own words:

> Two things prevented the men of that age from connecting their ideal of romantic and passionate love with marriage. The first is, of course, the actual practice of feudal society. Marriages had nothing to do with love, and no 'nonsense' about marriage was tolerated. All matches were matches of interest, and, worse still, of an interest which was continually changing. When the alliance which had answered would answer no longer, the husband's object was to get rid of the lady as quickly as possible. Marriages were frequently dissolved. The same woman who was the lady and 'the dearest dread' of her vassals was often little better than a piece of property to her husband. He was master in his own house. So far from being a channel for the new kind of love, marriage was rather the drab background against which that love stood out in all the contrast of its new tenderness and delicacy. The situation is indeed a very simple one, and not peculiar to the Middle Ages. Any idealization of sexual love, in a society where marriage is purely utilitarian, must begin by being an idealization of adultery.
>
> The second factor is the medieval theory of marriage – what may be called, by a convenient modern barbarism, the 'sexology' of the medieval church. A nineteenth-century Englishman felt that same passion – romantic love – could be either virtuous or vicious according as it was directed towards marriage or not. But according to the medieval view passionate love itself was wicked, and did not cease to be wicked if the object of it were your wife. If a man had once yielded to this emotion he had no choice between 'guilty' and 'innocent' love

> before him: he had only the choice, either of repentance, or else of different forms of guilt.
>
> (Lewis 1936: 13–14)

Lewis's formulation of 'courtly love' has often been attacked, and for a number of reasons. His assertion that adultery is idealized in medieval literary discussions of love has been criticized as inaccurate, and his reading of Andreas Capellanus's book, *De Amore* (extract 55) has been seen as overliteral (Donaldson 1970). The newness of the phenomenon has been questioned: Peter Dronke finds the same sentiments found in medieval love-lyric expressed in ancient Egypt, in Byzantium, and in numerous other times and places (Dronke 1968: I, 1–56). Although the Old English poem *Wulf and Eadwacer* (extract 52) is notoriously difficult to interpret, some readings of the poem do see it as an expression of that passionate love which Lewis argues should not appear until hundreds of years later: as Christine Fell writes, the poem is 'within the romantic view of marriage rather than the practical' (Fell 1984: 70). And to say (as Lewis does, following Andreas Capellanus) that *amor* and marriage are incompatible is not to say that all forms of love are seen as incompatible with marriage in the medieval period. Rather, distinctions are made between marital and extramarital love. As Philippe Ariès puts it:

> Nowadays we tend to forget an absolutely basic phenomenon in the history of sexual behaviour, which remained quite unchanged from the earliest times up to the eighteenth century [. . .] – the distinction that men of nearly all societies and ages, except our own, have made between love within and love outside marriage.
>
> (Ariès 1985b: 130).

So, although Andreas declares *amor* to be incompatible with marriage, there is another sort of emotional bond that may exist between persons who are married, called *maritalis affectio*, 'marital affection' (on which see Brundage 1987, Kooper 1991, Sheehan 1991). Against Lewis, then, we might argue that the new phenomenon of passionate love is not new, and that the alleged incompatibility between love and marriage fundamental to his formulation of 'courtly love' is not a full and accurate account of the possibilities.

Despite this, the notion of 'courtly love' persists as a way of talking about medieval ideas about love, both by medievalists and by historians who adopt a broader scope. Theodore Zeldin, in his innovative book, *An*

Intimate History of Humanity, has a chapter on how new forms of love have been invented. In it, he writes that 'everybody knows that passionate love was given a new form by Germany's Romantic poets, and before them by the knights and troubadours of France, who themselves transformed echoes of emotions refined by the Arab conquerors of Spain' (Zeldin 1994: 76). R. Howard Bloch cites Lewis (among others) in his argument for the newness of the love expressed in twelfth-century French literature (Bloch 1991: 8–9). Admittedly, Bloch's purpose is far removed from Lewis's, arguing as he does that the idealization of the feminine in vernacular lyric and romance must be read alongside antifeminist traditions: that seemingly opposed images of women, idealization and denigration, in fact exist to similar ends. Sarah Kay uses the term 'courtly love' in the title of a recent paper called 'Courts, Clerks, and Courtly Love' (Kay 2000). As with Bloch, what Kay means by 'courtly love' is very different from what C. S. Lewis meant by it. Indeed, in another recent essay, her use of the term 'courtly love' derives not from Lewis's use of it, but from Lacan's, in a discussion of psychoanalytic criticism and medieval literature (Kay 1999). In 'Courts, Clerks, and Courtly Love', she argues that discussions of 'courtly love' have been problematic in 'their assumption that such love was susceptible of codification as a system of rules or doctrines', an assumption picked up from texts such as Andreas Capellanus's *De Amore*, who do indeed provide systems of rules and doctrines, though not always without irony. Kay argues instead that 'courtly love' is better discussed as 'a series of questions which are debated across a large number of texts, and which can be traced back to tensions within medieval court life' (Kay 2000: 81). But for all the differences between their approaches, Kay, like Lewis, seeks to establish a relationship between the discussion of love in medieval courtly romances and the realities of life in medieval courts. Even if the understanding of the topic has undergone considerable change, the boundaries for discussion of medieval ideas about love remain the walls of the court, and 'courtly love' continues to be the dominant model for understanding medieval notions about love at the end of the twentieth century.

Medieval categories of love

Medieval romances are indeed concerned with love. But so are many other medieval texts, and perhaps we need to take a wider view in order to be able to discuss medieval ideas about love in a larger perspective. Furthermore, perhaps Kay's fruitful suggestion that discussions of love in medieval texts could be seen as posing questions might be broadened to incorporate an examination of tensions not just within a single all-encompassing category labelled 'courtly love', but rather between a number of different ideas of love.

The Middle Ages has a wide range of different terms for love, and they carry a wide range of meanings (on vocabulary, see Morgan 1977, 1980, Payer 1984, Fell 1984: 68, Boswell 1996: ch. 1). This is something that the reader of this book, approaching these texts in translation, needs to be particularly conscious of. When medieval texts discuss love, they do discuss *amor*, the passionate love that C. S. Lewis labels 'courtly love', but they also discuss many other different sorts of love. In his *City of God* (extract 5), St Augustine discusses the Latin words used for love in the Bible, and discusses not only *amor*, but also *caritas* (charity – the love of God), *cupiditas* (desire) and so on. Andreas Capellanus distinguishes between *amor* and *affectio*, the latter being the sort of love more appropriate to marriage, the former being the sort of love usually found outside it. That distinction between *amor* and *affectio* can be found elsewhere – in legal texts such as *Bracton* (extract 31). St Thomas Aquinas distinguishes between natural and rational categories of love (extract 13) – the former the unerring and instinctive urge of all created things directing them towards God, the latter the very human love that involves fallible choices (on this distinction, and its importance in Dante and Chaucer, see Morgan 1977). Elsewhere, we can see love described as an ennobling force, as in Avicenna (extract 79), or as a melancholic disease, as in Constantine Africanus (extract 80). Indeed, love sometimes seems to the lover to be downright contradictory, as in the Middle English lyric which can describe love as both 'greatest bliss' and 'distress and woe', 'soft', 'sweet', but also the cause of grief and 'much care' (extract 65.ii).

Medieval ideas of love, then, cannot simply be reduced to one overarching idea of what love is. The Middle Ages has a number of sometimes overlapping and sometimes contradictory ways of discussing the subject. Therefore recognizing the many ways in which the medieval period discusses love would seem to be potentially a more fruitful approach than attempts to refine and rework Lewis's flawed formulation of a love which is supposedly normative in later medieval literature. The selection of texts given here offers writing about many different sorts of love from a number of different perspectives: including legal texts, literary texts, medical texts and so on. It is a selection intended to demonstrate that there are a great variety of ways of thinking about love across the medieval period, and that recognizing this plurality is an essential first step towards a serious understanding of the sophistication of medieval discussions of love.

SEX

As is the case with the texts that discuss love, there is a variety of evidence on offer in the texts regarding medieval sexual practice. As already mentioned, these texts present a difficulty for the modern reader in the significant amount of bias against any sort of sexual behaviour found in many of them. The second problem that we have is that it is difficult to discuss medieval sexual practices in terms of modern sexual categories.

Sexual categories, medieval and modern

In the opening volume of his *History of Sexuality*, Michel Foucault argued that the notion of a 'sexuality' is a modern one, whose history can be traced to the recent past. People in the Middle Ages, then, cannot be regarded as 'heterosexual' or 'homosexual' or 'bisexual' or 'transvestite', or labelled with any modern sexual categorization, even though we might be able to identify them as performing actions which would lead a modern person to be labelled in this way. In Foucault's view, in the premodern period the performance of sexual acts does not lead to the construction of 'sexualities' as a category of identity in the same way as is true of the modern period. Writing of the period prior to the eighteenth century, Foucault argues:

> What was taken into account in the civil and religious jurisdiction alike was a general unlawfulness. Doubtless acts 'contrary to nature' were stamped as especially abominable, but they were perceived simply as extreme forms of acts 'against the law'; they were infringements of decrees which were just as sacred as those of marriage, and which had been established for governing the order of things and the plan of beings. Prohibitions bearing on sex were essentially of a juridical nature. The 'nature' on which they were based was still a kind of law.
>
> (Foucault 1981: 38)

The person committing crimes against nature, then, differs significantly from the modern homosexual:

> As defined by the ancient civil or canonical codes, sodomy was a category of forbidden acts; their perpetrator was nothing more than the juridical subject of them. The nineteenth-century homosexual became a personage, a past, a case history, and a childhood, in addition to being a type of life, a life form, and

> a morphology, with an indiscreet anatomy and possibly a mysterious physiology. Nothing that went into his total composition was unaffected by his sexuality.
>
> (Foucault 1981: 43)

Foucault's discussion of the differences between modern and premodern constructions of sexual identity has been a focal point for discussions of sexual behaviour in the Middle Ages, despite the fact that his work had very little to say about the medieval period. Hence Allen J. Frantzen argued in a reading of Chaucer's portrait of the Pardoner from the General Prologue to the *Canterbury Tales* (extract 70) that:

> It is not necessary to insist that he is homosexual or to identify the Pardoner as gay; to do so is to assume (without evidence) that such a category constitutes medieval identity when it seems, rather, to describe acts performed by certain persons that contributed to their identity but did not define them.
>
> (Frantzen 1994: 133)

Many medievalists would now suggest that we can speak of sexual identities in the premodern period, although these are not to be indentified with contemporary sexual categories. Simon Gaunt argues that although words like 'homosexual' and 'heterosexual' in their modern senses are inappropriate to medieval culture, that sexual identity itself is not a purely modern phenomenon (Gaunt 1996: 157). Allen J. Frantzen writes that we can speak of a sexual identity based on same-sex acts in the Anglo-Saxon period: that the labelling of individuals using terms like 'sodomites' or 'molles' or other such terms contributes to a group identity based on sexual practices, although this group identity is not the same as the contemporary category of sexuality (Frantzen 1998: 174). Carolyn Dinshaw, in a recent discussion of later medieval England, argues similarly that men who engaged in acts of male–male sex were thought to be visibly marked and were, for others at least, defined by their sexual desire (Dinshaw 1999: 194–195). Indeed Dinshaw, citing David Halperin, suggests that it may be a distortion of Foucault's claims in volume one of his *History of Sexuality* to try to make an absolute distinction between sexual acts and sexual identities (Dinshaw 1999: 195).

Sodomy, as a category of sexual identity, is indeed different from homosexuality. The essential division that medieval moralists seem to make is between 'natural' and 'unnatural' categories of sexual behaviour. 'Natural' sexual acts here are those that lead to reproduction. 'Unnatural' acts are those that do not. Thomas Aquinas therefore seems to make no essential distinction between various 'unnatural' sexual acts like masturbation, bestiality and sodomy (extract 13.ii). This classification of sodomy with a range of other types of behaviour, which appear to us as very dissimilar, seems to underlie Foucault's description of the category of sodomy as 'uncertain' and 'confused' (Foucault 1981: 37).

Several of the texts presented below raise interesting questions in regard to this contemporary debate on the nature of premodern sexual identities. Chaucer's Pardoner (extract 70) is the focus of suspicion from the poem's narrator. The narrator suspects that the Pardoner is somehow deviant, but cannot quite put his finger on the *way* in which he is deviant. The Pardoner shows physical signs of effeminacy, and the narrator suspects that he is either a 'gelding' or a 'mare', conventionally translated as 'a eunuch or a homosexual', but the narrator visibly finds the Pardoner difficult to pin down, and has no easy categorizations to place the character in. The possibility that he is (in modern categories) a eunuch or homosexual sits beside his heterosexual appearance in the Wife of Bath's prologue (extract 71), where he states an intent to get married. Chaucer does seem to be suggesting that the Pardoner's sexual actions contribute importantly to his identity – why else would he give the Pardoner's sexual activities so much attention? And in Foucauldian terms, the Pardoner shares with the nineteenth-century homosexual an 'indiscreet anatomy', a 'mysterious physiology', and (like all the pilgrims in the General Prologue) being presented as a 'type of life' (Foucault 1981: 43). But the poem's suspicious narrator ultimately seems to have no way of determining what the Pardoner's sexual identity might be, or any means of expressing it. And so the Pardoner, instead of being assigned a sexual identity, seems to remain a set of unanswered questions for both narrator and audience.

Also interesting is the case of John/Eleanor Rykener (extract 35), where the court seems to have difficulties in labelling John/Eleanor with any of their available categories of sex or gender: as a prostitute, as a fornicator, as a sodomite, as a man, or as a woman, because all, and so none, of these seem appropriate. Ruth Mazo Karras and David Lorenzo Boyd argue in their discussion of the case that it is ultimately the gender transgression which is the focus of attention (Karras and Boyd 1996). But certainly what the court cannot do is to produce an identity category of transvestism to explain to themselves the circumstances described.

The three grades of chastity

Just as the study of gender does not equal the study of women (on which see Frantzen 1993), so the study of sexuality does not equal the study of same-sex couples, and in fact medieval moralists devote far more attention to heterosexual behaviour than they do to same-sex relations. The context within which these discussions of heterosexuality take place is the model of the three grades of chastity, the three grades being virginity, widowhood and marriage, in that order of merit. This model is present, either manifestly or latently, in much medieval writing about marriage. It lies behind the three treatises of St Augustine, on *The Excellence of Marriage, The Excellence of Widowhood,* and *Holy Virginity* (extracts 2, 3, and 4). A conviction that chastity in widowhood was better than remarriage lies behind ecclesiastical pressure on the secular power not to force widows to remarry, and both the coronation charter of Henry I and Magna Carta concede this (extracts 26 and 27). Throughout the medieval period, men and women could publicly vow themselves to virginity (conventionally in the context of entering religious life, or less usually while remaining in the world), or to chastity in widowhood after the death of their spouse. Although hagiographical texts often emphasize the difficulties that such vows created for individuals – the vow of virginity is often seen as under threat from the possibility of rape or family pressure to marry (see extract 36, discussion in Saunders 2001: ch. 3) – moralistic texts did not find the category of virginity inherently problematic. Widows were potentially a source of difficulty as sexually experienced independent women not under the authority of either fathers or husbands, and hence potentially a threat to masculine authority (McCarthy 1999). But the real site of anxiety is marriage because, unlike the other two categories, it conferred merit, but it also involved sex. To quote Foucault, prescriptive codes:

> were all centred on matrimonial relations; the marital obligation, the ability to fulfil it, the requirements and violence that accompanied it, the useless or unwarranted caresses for which it was a pretext, its fecundity or the way one went about making it sterile, the moments when one demanded it (dangerous periods of pregnancy or breast-feeding, forbidden times of Lent or abstinence), its frequency or infrequency, and so on. It was this domain that was especially saturated with prescription. The sex of husband and wife was beset by rules and recommendations. The marriage relation was the most intense focus of constraints; it was spoken of more than anything else; more than any other relation it was required to give a detailed accounting of itself.
>
> (Foucault 1981: 37).

The difficulty for ecclesiastical writers was in reconciling the merits of marriage with a suspicion of sex. As the thirteenth-century English text *Holy Virginity* (extract 46) puts it, sex is 'that indecent heat of the flesh, that burning itch of physical desire, that animal union, that shameless coupling, that stinking and wanton deed, full of filthiness', which is, for all that, to be tolerated to some extent within marriage. This anxiety about marital sex endures throughout the period.

Boswell and tolerance

It will be clear from what has been said so far that the view of sexual behaviour presented in these texts is not one which modern readers generally would regard as tolerant. But one historian of sexual behaviour, John Boswell, has argued in a number of studies (Boswell, 1980, 1996) that for much of the earlier medieval period there is a remarkable level of tolerance of male–male sexual behaviour. Although other medievalists have argued against his views in some detail (Brundage 1987, Johansson and Percy 1996, Frantzen 1998), two recent books have made a modified case that, although the Middle Ages is intolerant of male–male sexual acts, the early Middle Ages at least does approve of male–male love where there are no sexual implications. C. Stephen Jaeger argues that friendship and love were social ideals of the medieval aristocracy, lay, clerical and monastic, and that from antiquity to the late eleventh century this ideal was restricted to love and friendship between men. Jaeger acknowledges a debt to Boswell's studies, but rejects his argument that sex between men was tolerated (Jaeger 1999: 6–7 and n. 7). Allen J. Frantzen, discussing Anglo-Saxon society, suggests that when sex acts are not explicit, male–male affection is visibly expressed in a number of celebrated texts (including *Beowulf*) in contexts of male camaraderie, familial bonds and religious devotion (Frantzen 1998: 69).

In response to Boswell's argument for tolerance, however, it should be said that while Boswell may be correct in arguing for a rise in the degree of intolerance in the central Middle Ages and afterwards, the moralizing texts presented below from all periods show very little tolerance for any sort of sex, and that includes heterosexual as well as homosexual sex. One of the surprising exceptions comes in the poem *The Owl and the Nightingale*, which seems to cast a relatively benign eye on youthful error, as long as that error consists of heterosexual fornication between two persons who might later marry each other (extract 67). Elsewhere, praise of heterosexual sex within marriage often comes as a contrast with condemnation of homosexual sex, as in *Cleanness* (extract 68), which hardly amounts to tolerance at all.

A note on sex and heresy

Heresy is associated with sexual deviance in the accusations of the orthodox throughout the Middle Ages. Augustine's writings on marriage are, in part, concerned to attack the views put forward by the heretical Manichaeans on marriage and sexuality (Noonan 1986: ch. 4). In the central Middle Ages, the Bogomils and Cathars were likewise accused of sexual deviance (Boswell 1980: ch. 10, Noonan 1986: ch. 6, for actual sexual behaviour in a Cathar village, see Ladurie 1978). We can see the link between heresy and sodomy in Froissart's account of the execution of Hugh Despenser, accused of being 'a heretic and a sodomite' (extract 45), the two being a neat pairing. Heresy is also associated with the subversion of gender roles: hence the accusation levelled at Margery Kempe that she is a Lollard (extract 39; for the Lollards and same-sex sex, see Dinshaw 1999).

MARRIAGE

There is no single dominant model of 'medieval marriage' to match the positions occupied by Lewis and Foucault in influencing discussion of medieval love and sex respectively. In fact, the model proposed by one of the most prominent historians of medieval marriage, Georges Duby, emphasizes the lack of a single model of marriage in the Middle Ages:

> The codes by which marriage is governed . . . belong to two different orders: the profane, and what we may call the religious. Normally the two systems adapt to, and reinforce one another. But there are times when they are in conflict, and such temporary discord causes marriage practices to change and evolve towards a new equilibrium.
>
> (Duby 1983: 19)

I want to go further than Duby here, and emphasize not only conflict between the two systems, but also contradictions within them.

Marriage and the Church

The Church Fathers and the good of marriage

The extracts which open the discussion of marriage below are from two of the most influential of the Church Fathers, St Augustine and St Jerome, each writing at the end of the fourth and the beginning of the fifth century. The question which each is attempting to address concerns the good of marriage. As already discussed, marriage is seen by early Christian writers as occupying the lowest of the three grades of chastity – virginity, widowhood and matrimony. Both Augustine's writings on marriage and Jerome's are to some degree a response to the heretical writings of Jovinian, who argued that virginity was not inherently better than marriage. The difficulty was to refute Jovinian's writings without arguing that marriage was not good in itself. Jerome's *Against Jovinian* was seen by contemporaries as being excessive in its attack upon marriage in his attempts to exalt virginity. As Peter Brown puts it, 'the pamphlet was a disaster. One of his own friends, Pammachius, simply withdrew it from circulation' (Brown 1988: 377). *Against Jovinian* did survive, however, as a source for much later antifeminist and antimatrimonial writing (the two often going hand in hand). Augustine was concerned to take a more moderate line, and to put the case that marriage was good, but less so than virginity. He argued that marriage contained three goods: offspring, fidelity and the sacrament, and that marriage was inherently good because of these. But Augustine's arguments for the value of marriage are nonetheless rather equivocal because of his ambivalence about sexual intercourse, even within marriage. He argues in *The Excellence of Marriage* (extract 2) that marital intercourse for the sake of procreation is not sinful, whereas marital intercourse for other purposes is venially sinful. But this concession that intercourse within marriage for procreation is not sinful seems to be undermined a few lines later by the suggestion that even marital intercourse for procreation is inferior to abstinence from intercourse entirely. This ambiguity about sexual intercourse on the part of the Church, as already discussed, leads to an ambiguity about the value of marriage that persists throughout the medieval period.

Two marriages in particular play an important part in medieval ecclesiastical thinking about the institution. Both are biblical: the marriage of Adam and Eve, and the marriage of Mary and Joseph. Part of Augustine's concern in asserting that marriage is good is to defend the marriage of Christ's parents from criticism. And he argued in *The City of God* that if the Fall had not happened, Adam and Eve would have reproduced in Eden without sin – that sexual union was not inherently tainted, but had become so after the Fall because of the sin of lust (extract 5, discussed in Clark 1991: 19). This doublethink about marriage persists throughout the medieval period. It is seen as having been instituted twice, to different purposes. On the first occasion, it is instituted by God in Paradise as a sacrament, when he instructs Adam and Eve to increase and multiply. The second institution comes after the Fall, when marriage is conceded as a remedy for the sin of lust, for, as St Paul puts it in 1 Cor. 7, postlapsarian marital sex is permitted by way of concession, not by command. As the Second Statutes of Exeter put it in 1287, 'for avoiding the evil of this kind of desire, the sacrament of marriage was granted to man by the apostle after sin, which was instituted as a duty by God in Paradise and before sin' (extract 15.vi).

Incidentally, these early Christian arguments on the good of marriage resurface in very different form in later medieval vernacular poetry which debates the question of the good of marriage from a secular standpoint. There we see antimatrimonial perspectives coming from women, as in Marie de France's portrait of the *malmariée* in *Yonec* (extract 59), but more often from men, as the debate on marriage in late medieval vernacular poetry often serves a double purpose as a debate about women. Hence Chaucer gives Theophrastus a new twist (perhaps even a protofeminist twist, depending on your reading of the text) in his Wife of Bath's prologue (extract 71), and Dunbar in his turn reworks Chaucer's poem in his account of dissatisfied wives and widows (extract 76). There are also responses to the antifeminist tradition, though (see Blamires 1992, 1997), and they make an appearance here in the form of an extract from Christine de Pizan's *Book of the City of Ladies* and an extract from the debate on the *Romance of the Rose* which she helped to spark (extracts 62, 63).

The Church and marriage in Anglo-Saxon England

During the earlier part of the Middle Ages, the Church did not enjoy exclusive legal jurisdiction over marriage. It attempted to impose its teachings in various ways, as we can see from the penitentials (extract 7) and the evidence of ecclesiastical influence upon the secular law (extract 23). But it is only in the eleventh century when William the Conqueror separates the lay and spiritual tribunals that the Church gains control over marriage as a spiritual matter, and hence subject to its jurisdiction (Goody 1983: 150). In Anglo-Saxon England, there is difficulty in assessing the extent to which people accepted the Church's teachings on marriage, and the extent to which Germanic marriage practices which existed prior to Christianity and which might have been at odds with its teachings – on subjects such as polygamy and divorce, for example – might have survived into the conversion period and afterwards (Goody 1983: 75–76, Lucas 1983: 68, Clunies Ross 1985, Brundage 1987: 143–145).

We can see evidence in the texts below of what appears to be compromise on these issues, and we can also see contradictions between different ecclesiastical texts. The Church's prohibition on divorce, for example, is instituted by St Paul in 1 Cor. 7, and Paul's statement on divorce is quoted by Augustine in *The Excellence of Marriage* in his discussion of the goods of marriage, where he argues that marriage, as a sacrament, is indissoluble (extract 2.iv). But in the Anglo-Saxon Penitential of Theodore 2. XII, we can see various concessions on this principle of indissolubility, discussing the circumstances under which married persons separated from their spouses may remarry (extract 7). And a text as late as the eleventh-century laws of Canute still finds it necessary to insist that a man should have only one wife, and to forbid concubinage (extract 23), suggesting perhaps that practices at odds with Christian teaching survive until the very end of the Anglo-Saxon period.

As evidence of tensions between ecclesiastical views on compromise, we might look at Bede's account of the correspondence between Pope Gregory I and St Augustine of Canterbury on matters concerning marriage (extract 8). Goody notes the surprise of some contemporaries that this text should concede that marriages between Christians related in the third degree were not forbidden under the Church's incest prohibitions. Nonetheless, Pope Zachary accepts these concessions because they were offered to people undergoing the process of conversion (Goody 1983: 35). And Payer notes contradictions between other prescriptions of Gregory as reported by Bede and those found in the Penitential of Theodore (Payer 1984: 35). Indeed, the Church compromises not only on the sexual behaviour of the laity, but that of the clergy. Although the first attempt at prohibiting clerical marriage comes in the early fourth-century canons of Elvira, clerical celibacy proves a practical impossibility through the early Middle Ages (Brundage 1987: 69–70, 150–151). In the Law of the Northumbrian Priests (extract 9), we see the Church trying to ensure that their unchaste clergy are at least faithful to their sexual partners: a far cry from the ideal of clerical chastity.

All of this was to change with the Church reform movement that began in the eleventh century. Through reform, and through the development of canon law which accompanied it, a much more rigorous attitude emerged on such questions as the indissolubility of marriage, the outlawing of concubinage, the prohibition of incest (broadly defined – see extract 14), and the outlawing of clerical sex (inside or outside regular unions).

Consent as the basis for marriage in later medieval canon law

If Church reform saw a tightening of traditional, albeit neglected, prohibitions concerning marriage and sexual behaviour, it also saw the formulation of a positive theory of marriage based fundamentally on the consent of the parties to be married. The basic texts of medieval canon law were Gratian's *Decretum* (*c.*1140) and the *Liber Extra* or *Decretals* of Gregory IX (1234), which together formed the *Corpus Iuris Canonici*. Gratian's view of the role of consent in the formation of marriage was that it played a role, but that consent in itself did not establish the marital bond. Consent began marriage, but sexual intercourse confirmed it (extract 10). This view was challenged by the theologian Peter Lombard in his book, the *Sentences*. Lombard argued that consent alone made marriage (extract 11). The eventual resolution between these competing views was achieved by Pope Alexander III, whose decretals on marriage are incorporated in the *Decretals* of Gregory IX. Alexander ruled that consent expressed in the present tense made marriage, or that consent expressed in the future tense made marriage if it was followed by sexual intercourse or an expression of consent in the present tense (extract 12). This became the Church's position on how marriage was formed, and this consensual theory was the one implemented by its courts. It is a theory, as Noonan observes, that does not liberate sons and daughters from psychological or social pressure, and does not disturb the prevailing pattern of parentally arranged marriages. But in removing the ultimate decisions regarding marriage from the hands of the family, it makes them subject to the jurisdiction of the Church (Noonan 1973: 429, 433).

This view of marriage as a bond created simply by the verbal expression of the consent of the parties to be married, without requiring anything else, led to significant problems with clandestine marriages. Under the Church's consensual theory of marriage, people could (and did) contract valid secret marriages outside the control of their families and of the Church. The phenomenon is the source of a significant amount of local legislation in thirteenth- and fourteenth-century England. Section 83 of the First Statutes of Salisbury (extract 15.i) outlines Church concerns that promises made in jest, or for the purposes of seduction rather than marriage, will create binding marriages. But there is again a sort of doublethink going on throughout the local legislation attacking clandestine marriage. Section 84 of the Salisbury statutes outlines the 'correct' way to contract a marriage – in public, in the presence of a priest, with several public announcements having been made beforehand so that the Church can be reassured that the persons to be married are not married already, or that they are not too closely related to each other and so on. But the same statute embodies the consensual theory of marriage: outlining the form of words to be used in the consent spoken (the crucial issue being that they should be in the present tense), the statute admits, 'for in these words great force exists, and marriage is brought about'. So if section 84 of the First Salisbury statutes argues that there is a 'correct' way to make a marriage, it also makes it clear that there are all sorts of ways of 'incorrect' ways of making a marriage that are just as valid canonically. To quote Michael M. Sheehan on the subject:

> Whatever the theoretical priorities of the new conception of marriage might have been, it contained within itself the grave pedagogical problem of the act that is at once forbidden and possible. English legislation resolved it by a steady insistence on the publicity of marriage that completely overshadowed the quiet admission that such publicity was not essential to the union.
>
> (Sheehan 1996: 175–176)

But that 'quiet admission' causes real problems, and the English statutes return to the subject of clandestine unions again and again in the thirteenth and fourteenth centuries. An example of a clandestine marriage given below is that of Margery Paston and Richard Calle, where the daughter of the Paston family has married one of the servants without the family's consent (extract 41). The bishop of Norwich, in attempting to determine whether or not a marriage actually has been contracted between Margery and Richard, examines each of them on the form of words they spoke to each other. According to the canonical emphasis on consent, this is what is vital in determining whether or not they are married.

Inevitably, the consensual theory of marriage created a lot of business for the ecclesiastical courts. An example below of a marriage where a dispute arises regarding the formation of the bond is the marriage of Alice and John the Blacksmith (extract 17), where there have been public ceremonies before a priest and witnesses, but perhaps only of engagement. Nevertheless, engagement (consent to marry using words in the future tense) followed by intercourse is marriage, and it is clear that there has been intercourse in this case. Although all parties seem to accept that a marriage already exists, there are nevertheless references to another 'espousal' ceremony to come – perhaps a public solemnization of what all parties agree is already a marriage?

Not all medieval marriages, however, are based on free consent. The Church sometimes forced recidivist fornicators into marriage, forcing them to take matrimonial vows, often expressed in the future tense, so they would become valid if there was subsequent intercourse, or with a condition attached to the same effect (extract 15.ii, v). That this was in contradiction of the notion of free consent was not lost on contemporaries, and there is a gloss to a manuscript of the Second Statutes of Exeter pointing this out (extract 15). Interestingly, there is a Middle English poem about this very subject, where the poem's narrator is brought to the ecclesiastical court, accused of fornication, whipped and forced to marry his lover (extract 66). Although the idea of consent is fundamental to the Church's theory of marriage, then, its practice sometimes differs.

Marital sex

If consent made marriage in the later Middle Ages, what was it that people consented to in marrying? In particular, did they consent to sexual intercourse with their partners? St Paul's injunction in 1 Cor. 7 that each partner had control over his or her spouse's body (quoted by St Augustine, extract 2.iv, and Chaucer's Wife of Bath, extract 71 to very different ends) would seem to imply that consent to marriage was consent to intercourse: that it was not possible to agree to marry someone, and then refuse to have intercourse after marriage. But this issue was complicated by the Church's ambivalence about sexual intercourse, even within marriage. Augustine's statement that marital intercourse for the purpose of procreation (but not all marital intercourse) was free from sin shows a certainty unavailable to later medieval canonists, who, in the words of James Brundage, 'taught that marital sex was free from sin under some circumstances, although they failed to agree just what those circumstances might be' (Brundage 1987: 448). And if sexual intercourse within marriage might be sinful, was it perhaps not better to abstain from it? Many married people in the medieval period seem to have thought so, and some of their experiences in trying to abstain from sex within marriage are recounted in hagiographical narratives (discussed in Elliott 1993). Examples given below are Mary of Oignies and Margery Kempe, who persuade their husbands to join them in vowing chastity within marriage, and Christina of Markyate, who unsuccessfully attempts to persuade the husband forced upon her by her parents to agree to a chaste marriage, and is forced to take other measures instead (extracts 36, 37 and 39).

Also important for the Church's unease concerning the role of intercourse within marriage was the example of the marriage of Christ's parents. If consent to marriage is consent to sexual intercourse, and Mary and Joseph were married, then Mary must have consented to intercourse. But how could that be reconciled with the medieval belief that Mary had taken a vow of virginity? Gratian tries to reconcile these two positions (extract 10), but later writers such as Aquinas (extract 13.iii) take a different view, arguing that Mary did not in fact consent to sexual intercourse, unless it was pleasing to God. The anxiety on the part of medieval theologians to demonstrate that the marriage of Mary and Joseph was not in any way open to question (again, see Aquinas, extract 13.iii and Elliott 1993) played an important part in influencing their thinking on the role of intercourse within marriage.

Marriage and secular law

Marriage and property

During the Anglo-Saxon period, the lay and ecclesiastical jurisdictions do not have separate spheres of control over matters relating to marriage and sexuality as they do in the later Middle Ages. Anglo-Saxon legal texts are not generally as concerned with sexual offences in the same detail as the Penitentials are, and their focus is for the most part on offences such as adultery and rape, but this reflects perhaps not a division of jurisdictions as in the later medieval period, but a differing set of concerns regarding sexual ethics on the part of the secular and ecclesiastical jurisdictions. The laws of Canute, however, interest themselves in subjects such as fornication, incest and so on, as the penitential texts do. Canute's laws are late, and reflect ecclesiastical influence (the laws are perhaps written by Archbishop Wulfstan). But they are nonetheless secular laws prescribing a wide-ranging sexual ethic, something we do not see in the later medieval period.

In later medieval England, such questions are outside the scope of the secular jurisdiction, for spiritual matters relating to marriage (including the question of the formation of the marriage bond) are the exclusive preserve of the ecclesiastical courts. If a question arises in the secular court relating to such a matter – for example, if the court needs to know if a couple were validly married or not – the case is referred to the Church courts for a decision on the question before returning to the secular court for resolution of the original case. The secular law concerns itself only with matters relating to property – the allocation of property that a husband should make on his wedding day as dower for his wife, the inheritance of property and so on. However much the Church might view marriage as a spiritual matter, or as a way of legitimating sexual intercourse (otherwise sinful), it always served other functions as well: of making alliances between families, of settling feuds – as we see below in the extract from *Beowulf* (extract 49) – and of transmitting property from generation to generation. It is these aspects of marriage with which later medieval secular law concerns itself.

Conflicts between and within legal systems

The tensions between Christian teachings on marriage and survivals of Germanic practices in Anglo-Saxon England have already been discussed. We can also detect tensions between the viewpoints of the ecclesiastical and secular powers in the later Middle Ages. The Church's insistence upon the freedom of all Christians to contract their own marriages coexisted with the secular power's insistence that lords had economic rights (at the very least) in the marriages of noble widows or wards who held land from them (extracts 27 and 31), and in the marriages of their unfree tenants also (extract 34). The secular law insisted on the proprietary disability of married women – while they were married, they had no control over their property, all such powers being vested in their husbands (see extract 31). But although the canon law too insisted on the subordination of married women, their lack of any control over property prevented married women from making wills, which the Church insisted on as necessary for the possibility of individual salvation: medieval wills frequently contain donations to the Church to pay for prayers and masses for the departed (Sheehan 1963, Helmholz 1993). And the most obvious way in which the two systems of law differ is in the existence of two entirely separate views of what constituted legitimacy: the Church saw children as legitimate if their parents married after their birth, whereas the secular state did not (see extract 31). And since the division of juridsictions meant that each often relied upon the judgements of the other where there was some overlap of interest, the failure to reconcile their differing views on what constituted legitimate offspring resulted in a significant dispute (on which see Woodbine and Thorne 1968–1977: III, xv, Powicke and Cheney 1964: I, 198–199, Rothwell 1975: 353–354, Helmholz 1969: 203, 208).

There are also internal differences within the secular law – indeed, it is difficult to speak of 'the secular law' in any coherent sense since there is no single body of law that applies to secular matters in later medieval England. To quote S. F. C. Milsom, 'In the fourteenth century there was no law of England, no body of rules complete in itself with known limits and visible defects; or if there was it was not the property of the common law courts or any others' (Milsom 1981: 83). Statute law, the law contained in the legal manuals, and local customs with the status of law, did not form a coherent whole: and so we can find some local law stating that it is legal for a husband to sell a wife's marriage portion in the case of dire need, and other local law stating the very opposite (extract 33).

Furthermore, we have already seen that there are also internal differences in the Church's views on some of the most fundamental issues relating to marriage – the formation of the bond, the role of sexual intercourse, indeed, the very value of marriage itself as either a sacrament instituted by God or alternatively a mere remedy for the evils of lust. As Duby (1983) argues, then, marriage in the later medieval period is indeed governed by a dual system of laws. But neither the secular law nor the religious is internally coherent, and they are sometimes at odds with one another. Marriage is, in short, overdetermined.

THIS BOOK

The purpose of this book is to do two things. First, to bring together texts that discuss the emotional state of love, the physical act of sex and the social institution of marriage, from a variety of sources. Anthologizing texts that discuss these themes together suggests that these subjects and these texts are perhaps more easily understood together than separately: there is a complex interrelationship between these three topics, then as now. To assert, as C. S. Lewis did, that love and marriage could not be happy bedfellows in the Middle Ages, seems unlikely. In some ways, love, sex and marriage are disparate things, and all three are not always found together, but various combinations appear in the selections below. In these texts, along with much theorizing, we find evidence of married couples who are not having sex, and unmarried ones who are, marriages for creating alliances, marriages for love, and promises of marriage made in the hope of obtaining sex (leading to difficulties afterwards). We come across gentry who love servants, and married women who find God's love preferable to that of their husbands. So, love, sex and marriage interrelate in a wide variety of ways, and are fruitfully discussed together.

Second, to repeat the point made at the outset of this discussion, the purpose of the selection of texts given here is not to offer a single homogeneous view of love, sex and marriage in the medieval period. On the contrary, its purpose is to demonstrate the varieties and differences that exist within medieval writing on these subjects. This is true across the span of the millennium that separates St Augustine from Christine de Pizan – a lot can change in a thousand years – but it is true also at specific points in time. Contemporaries – Augustine and Jerome, the anonymous legislators who advocate the forced marriage of fornicators and the anonymous poet of *In the Ecclesiastical Court*, the various participants in the debate on the *Romance of the Rose* – all show us that these subjects can be the matter of fierce debates at different points throughout the Middle Ages.

The selection focuses on medieval England, but in saying that it is necessary to enter a caveat. There is no such place as 'medieval England', politically or geographically speaking. At various points in the millennium between the fall of the Roman Empire and the Renaissance, 'England' is a collection of small, separate Anglo-Saxon kingdoms, or one part of a Norman-ruled conglomeration including not just much of modern England and Wales, but also Normandy and Anjou to the east and Leinster to the west. Nor is there any such place as 'medieval England' linguistically speaking. The literate English contemporaries of Chaucer – trilingual in English, French and Latin – do not have an unbroken literary continuity that we can trace to the *Beowulf* poet. The two literary cultures are each stranded on opposite sides of the Norman Conquest. And 'English' in its linguistic and political senses do not always match. Marie de France writes in French, but probably in Norman England. William Dunbar writes in Middle Scots (or, as he calls it, 'oure Inglisch') but writes in independent fifteenth-century Scotland. 'Medieval England', then, as a source of history or literature, is a diverse and fragmented place, and it has never been isolated from outside influence. So while most of the material included in the selection here relates to England, some exercises its influence on 'medieval England' from outside. Augustine, Jerome, Gratian, Peter Lombard, Aquinas, Abelard and Heloise, *Trotula*, Avicenna, Alan of Lille, the *Romance of the Rose* and Christine de Pizan are important in medieval England just as they are elsewhere, and their influences are easily traced. In the few cases where this is not true, texts have been included to illustrate an aspect of medieval life for which I know of no English source (hence extract 44).

This book should demonstrate to the interested reader that the medieval period produced a diverse range of writing and opinion on the topics of love, sex and marriage. But it should also be apparent that, as with any anthology, the selection here can only scratch the surface. It is intended to work, not as a self-sufficient guide, but as an accessible introduction that can offer a general view of the scope of the subject.

Part I

ECCLESIASTICAL SOURCES

INTRODUCTION

The texts presented in Part I fall into four distinct groups, arranged chronologically. The first collection of extracts are from the writings of two of the most important of the Church Fathers, St Augustine and St Jerome. These texts are, strictly speaking, not medieval at all, but these late classical texts have such an enormous influence upon the thought of the following millennium that they seem an appropriate starting point. Their subject is the role of marriage in Christian society, and in particular the position of marriage in relation to virginity.

Of course, Augustine and Jerome are not the first Christian writers to treat these topics, and both look back specifically to the writing of St Paul on the subject of marital sex in 1 Corinthians 7.3ff, a cornerstone of Christian thinking about marriage and sexual behaviour:

> The husband should give the wife her conjugal rights, and likewise the wife to her husband. For the wife does not have authority over her own body, but the husband does; likewise the husband does not have authority over his own body, but the wife does. Do not deprive one another except perhaps by agreement at a set time to devote yourselves to prayer: and then come together again, so that Satan may not tempt you because of your lack of self-control. This I say by way of concession, not of command. I wish that all were as I myself am. But each has a different gift from God, one having one kind, and another a different kind. To the unmarried and the widows, I say that it is well for them to remain unmarried as I am. But if they are not practicing self-control, they should marry, for it is better to marry than to be aflame with passion. To the married I give this command – not I but the Lord – that the wife should not separate from her husband, but if she does separate, let her remain unmarried or else be reconciled to her husband, and that the husband should not dismiss his wife.

Augustine quotes this passage of Paul's in extracts 2.iv, 3 and 4 below, as well as in numerous other places in his writings (see the discussion in the introduction to Walsh 2001). Jerome likewise engages with the same text throughout his book *Against Jovinian*. And we can see the influence of Paul along with that of Augustine and Jerome throughout the medieval period.

The second group of texts come from Anglo-Saxon England. If Augustine and Jerome (and Paul) are concerned to formulate ideals of Christian behaviour, these texts from the Anglo-Saxon Church are much more concerned with the realities of sexual and marital behaviour in communities relatively new to Christianity whose existing customs may differ in focus from a Christian sexual ethic. Consequently, there are compromises and contradictions in these texts that might not pertain either in the formulations of Augustine or in the more rigorous regulations of the later medieval Church. This is not to suggest tolerance so much as pragmatism – the Church does not yet have the exclusive jurisdiction over these issues that it will enjoy in the later medieval period.

The third group of extracts represent theological and canon law texts from the period of Church reform during the eleventh century and afterwards. Extracts 10, 11 and 12 show the development of ecclesiastical thinking on the formation of the marital bond that was to lead to the consensual model of marriage, influenced in no small way by abstract theological issues concerning the marriage of Christ's parents as well as practical everyday realities. Extract 15 is a selection of English statutes which show the Church attempting to implement its relatively new marriage doctrines in a practical setting in the thirteenth and fourteenth centuries. The final group of extracts are concerned with canon law and actual practice in later medieval England. This material, mostly from court cases, demonstrates how the Church's thinking on marriage affected actual practice in later medieval England.

Some points to note in the texts presented here. We can see some continuities as well as some contrasts in Christian thinking on marriage and sexual behaviour across the period. The scope of Christian intervention in sexual and marital behaviour increases across the period, eventually coming to claim legal jurisdiction over all issues relating to sex and marriage except those relating to property. But we can also detect implicit lay resistance to Christian regulation of marital and sexual ethics across the Middle Ages.

THE CHURCH FATHERS

1 Augustine of Hippo, *Confessions*

St Augustine of Hippo (354–430) is the most influential of the Church Fathers to write on marriage, and he returns to the subject repeatedly across his large body of writings. Augustine's writing on marriage is subject to several influences. First, biblical writings on marriage, and in particular Genesis and 1 Cor. 7, exercise a significant influence on his conception of marriage and sexual relationships. Second, he is influenced by the writings of Ambrose on sex and marriage (Brown 1988: ch. 17). Third, his personal experiences leave their mark on his ideas about marriage and relationships: this extract from the autobiographical *Confessions* (*c*.397–401) is Augustine's personal account of his youthful relationships, and we can perhaps see its influence in extract 2.ii. Fourth, in his youth Augustine had been a Manichaean, a member of the heretical group founded by the prophet Mani (216–277), who held a dualist belief that there were two eternal first principles, God and Satan, who ruled worlds of light and darkness. The soul came from God, but the body came from Satan, and so renunciation of the body was recommended. Strict renunciation applied only to the Manichaean elect, but believers in general were to avoid procreation, which was the work of the Devil. Augustine's writings on marriage and sexuality are concerned to refute the arguments of his former colleagues, the Manichaeans, and to argue that marriage and reproduction are in fact good (Noonan 1986: ch. 4, Walsh 2001). Fifth, Augustine is writing in the context of the controversy on marriage and virginity created by the writings of Jovinian, a Christian contemporary of Augustine's who argued that marriage and virginity were equally good. Augustine is concerned to refute Jovinian's position (as he tells us in his *Retractiones*), but he is also concerned to take a more moderate line than Jerome, whose *Against Jovinian* (extract 6) was seen as going too far in its attack on marriage.

Further reading: Noonan 1986: ch. 4, Brundage 1987: ch. 3, Brown 1988: chs 17, 18, 19, Clark 1991, 1996, Augustine 1999, Walsh 2001.

Text from St Augustine (1961) *Confessions*, trans. R. S. Pine-Coffin, Harmondsworth: Penguin.

Meanwhile I was sinning more and more. The woman with whom I had been living was torn from my side as an obstacle to my marriage and this was a blow which crushed my heart to bleeding, because I loved her dearly. She went back to Africa, vowing never to give herself to any other man, and left with me the son whom she had borne me. But I was too unhappy and too weak to imitate the example set me by a woman. I was impatient at the delay of two years which had to pass before the girl whom I had asked to marry became my wife, and because I was more a slave of lust than a true lover of marriage, I took another mistress, without the sanction of wedlock. This meant that the disease of my soul would continue unabated, in fact it would be aggravated, and under the watch and ward of uninterrupted habit it would persist into the state of marriage. Furthermore the wound that I had received when my first mistress was wrenched away showed no sign of healing. At first, the pain was sharp and searing, but then the wound began to fester, and though the pain was duller there was all the less hope of a cure.

2 Augustine of Hippo, *The Excellence of Marriage*

In *The Excellence of Marriage* (*c.*401) Augustine is addressing some of the issues that continue to trouble Christian writers on marriage for the entire medieval period: in particular, to what extent can marriage be said to be good, to what extent can sexual intercourse within marriage be free from sin, and what it is that distinguishes marriages from other sorts of unions? On this question, perhaps we can see some echoes of Augustine's personal experiences as described in the extract from his *Confessions*, above.

Further reading: as extract 1.

Text: St Augustine (1999) *Marriage and Virginity*, ed. D. G. Hunter and trans. Ray Kearney, *The Works of St Augustine*, 1: 9, New York: New City Press.

(I) MARRIAGE: THE FIRST BOND OF SOCIETY

1. Every human being is part of the human race, and human nature is a social entity, and has naturally the great benefit and power of friendship. For this reason God wished to produce all persons out of one, so that they would be held together in their social relationships not only by similarity of race, but also by the bond of kinship. The first natural bond of human society, therefore, is that of husband and wife. God did not create them as separate individuals and bring them together as persons of a different race, but he created one from the other, making the side, from which the woman was taken and formed, a sign of the strength of their union. For those who walk together, and look ahead together to where they are walking, do so at each other's side. The result is the bonding of society in its children, and this is the one honorable fruit, not of the union of husband and wife, but of their sexual conjunction. For even without that kind of intimacy, there could have been between the two sexes a certain relationship of friendship and kinship where one is in charge and the other compliant.

(II) WHAT CONSTITUTES A TRUE MARRIAGE?

5. It is often asked whether one should call it a marriage when a man and a woman, neither of whom is married to anyone else, form a union solely for the purpose of giving in to their desires by sleeping together, and not for the purpose of having children, though with the understanding that neither of them will sleep with anyone else. It is not absurd perhaps to call this a marriage, provided they maintain the arrangement until the death of one or other of them, and provided they do not avoid having children either by being unwilling to have children or even by doing something wrong to prevent the birth of children. On the other hand, if one, or both, of these conditions is lacking, I do not see how we can call these marriages. If a man makes use of a woman for a time, until he finds someone else more suited to his wealth and social standing to take as his partner, that state of mind makes him an adulterer, not with regard to the woman he is on the lookout for but with regard to the one he is sleeping with without being married to her. As a consequence, if the woman is aware of this and still consents to it, then

she too is unchaste in her relationship with the man with whom she is not united in marriage. Nevertheless, if she is faithful to him, and when he takes a wife she does not also think about marrying, but sets herself entirely against such a course of action, then I would not dare to call her an adulteress, easy enough though it might be to do so. Yet who would say that she does not sin, since she knows she is involved with a man who is not her husband? Just the same, if for her part all she wants from that union is to have children, and whatever she puts up with over and above what serves the purpose of having children she puts up with unwillingly, she is certainly to be preferred to many married women. Although these are not adulteresses, they often constrain their husbands to perform their marital duty, even when they wish to abstain, not out of desire to have children but making unreasonable use of their rights because of passion. In their marriages, just the same, there is at least the good feature that they are married. It was for this reason that they married, so that by being confined to the lawful bond sensuality might not wander around ugly and degenerate. In itself sensuality has the unbridled weakness of the flesh, but from marriage it has the permanent union of fidelity; in itself it leads to uncontrolled intercourse, but from marriage it has the restraint of chaste child-bearing. Although it is a shameful thing to intend to make use of one's husband for passion, it is proper nevertheless to want to have union only with one's husband and to have children only by one's husband.

(III) MARRIAGE AS A REMEDY FOR SENSUALITY

6. [. . .] Marital intercourse for the sake of procreating is not sinful. When it is for the purpose of satisfying sensuality, but still with one's spouse, because there is marital fidelity it is a venial sin. Adultery or fornication, however, is a mortal sin. For this reason abstinence from all sexual union is better even than marital intercourse performed for the sake of procreating.

(IV) THE THREE GOODS OF MARRIAGE

32. The value of marriage, therefore, for all races and all people, lies in the objective of procreation and the faithful observance of chastity.

For the people of God, however, it lies also in the sanctity of the sacrament, and this has the consequence that it is forbidden for a woman to marry anyone else while her husband is still living, even if she has been divorced by him, and even if it is only for the purpose of having children. Although this is the only purpose there can be for a marriage, the bond of matrimony is not broken when its purpose is not achieved, but only by the death of husband or wife. It is like ordination to the priesthood, which takes place for the purpose of forming a community of the faithful, but even if the community of faithful does not eventuate, the sacrament of ordination remains in those who were ordained. If anyone is dismissed from office for some wrongdoing, he will not be deprived of the Lord's sacrament once it has been received, although it will remain as something he must answer for at the judgment. The apostle, therefore, bore witness that the purpose of marriage is procreation, when he said, 'I want the younger ones to marry.' As though someone had said, 'Why?' he immediately adds: 'To have children and be mothers of families' (1 Tim 5: 14). Concerning faithful observance of chastity, there is the text, 'The wife does not have authority over her own body, but her husband does; and likewise the husband does not have authority over his own body, but his wife does' (1 Cor 7: 4); and concerning the sanctity of the sacrament, the text, 'a wife should not leave her husband, but if she does leave him, she should either remain unmarried or be reconciled to her husband, and a husband should not divorce his wife' (1 Cor 7: 10). These things, namely, offspring, fidelity and the sacrament, are all good, and because of them marriage is good. In this age, however, it is certainly better and holier not to set out to have children physically, and so to keep oneself free from any activity of that kind, and to be subject spiritually to only one man, Christ. One must use this freedom, however, in the way scripture says, to think about 'the Lord's interests,' how to please God. In other words, celibacy will be concerned that obedience should not be diminished. Being the fundamental virtue, and, as is commonly said, the source of all the others, the ancient fathers put this virtue into actual practice. Celibacy, on the other hand, they maintained as a state of mind, and no doubt, because they were righteous and holy, if they had been commanded to abstain from all intercourse, out of obedience they would have done so. When they were capable of sacrificing the offspring which was the only reason for having intercourse, how much more readily could they have held back from intercourse if that were God's command or request?

3 Augustine of Hippo, *Holy Virginity*

In praising virginity (and arguing against the views of Jovinian that marriage and virginity are of equal merit), Augustine is careful to take a more moderate line than Jerome does (extract 6), and not to condemn marriage outright. But marriage is, as he says in *Holy Virginity* (*c.*401), discouraged in a restrained way.

Further reading: as extract 1.

Text: St Augustine (1999) *Marriage and Virginity*, ed. D. G. Hunter and trans. Ray Kearney, *The Works of St Augustine*, 1: 9, New York: New City Press.

MARRIAGE ENTAILS TROUBLESOME BURDENS

16. But then he added: 'Such people will be troubled by the flesh, but I will spare you that' (1 Cor 7: 28). In this way he was encouraging virginity and perpetual chastity, and so to some extent also discouraging marriages, but in a restrained way, to be sure, and not as something bad and forbidden, but as something burdensome and worrying. Giving in to the sins of the flesh is one thing, but being troubled by the flesh is another. In one case sin is committed, in the other a burden is endured. It is a burden that people generally do not refuse, especially in the course of duties that carry great honour. In the present age, however, when bearing children physically does not contribute towards the future physical birth of Christ, to undertake for the sake of having a marriage the burden of those afflictions of the flesh that the apostle pronounces to be the lot of those who marry would be utter foolishness. The only exception is for those who lack self-control, if there is danger they will give in to the temptation of Satan and fall into mortal sin. When, however, he says he is sparing those he feels will suffer the afflictions of the flesh, nothing more helpful occurs to me to say for the moment than that he did not want to spell out the details of that affliction of the flesh that he predicted for those who decided to marry. They relate to the jealous suspicions of husbands and wives, to having and looking after children, to the sorrows and worries of widowhood. Is there anyone, among those who have tied themselves with the bonds of marriage, who is not tossed and torn by those cares? We should not exaggerate it, however, for fear of not sparing the very persons the apostle thought to spare.

4 Augustine of Hippo, *The Excellence of Widowhood*

The Church preferred widows to maintain chastity after the death of their spouses, but recognized that remarriage was permissible, given that the prohibition of remarriage might lead, not to chastity, but to fornication or adultery. But Augustine's ambiguity about the permissibility of multiple marriages in *The Excellence of Widowhood* (414) remains the case throughout the medieval period (see the discussion of the issue in Chaucer's fourteenth-century portrait of the Wife of Bath, extract 71).

Further reading: as extract 1.

Text: St Augustine (1999) *Marriage and Virginity*, ed. D. G. Hunter and trans. Ray Kearney, *The Works of St Augustine*, 1: 9, New York: New City Press.

CONCERNING MULTIPLE MARRIAGES

15. Questions are sometimes asked about third, fourth and even more marriages. To give a quick answer to this: I would not venture to condemn any marriage, but neither would I dare to say that a plurality of them is no cause for embarrassment. If, however, anyone is upset by my answering in this brisk manner, I am prepared to listen to a fuller argument from my critic. Perhaps some reason will be given for condemning third marriages but not condemning second marriages. In accordance with the advice I gave at the beginning of this instruction, I have no ambition to know more than one ought to know. Who am I to think I must set a limit when I see the apostle did not set a limit? He said, 'A woman is bound to her husband, as long as he lives' (1 Cor. 7: 39). He did not say 'first,' or 'second,' or 'third,' or 'fourth' husband, but said, 'A woman is bound to her husband, as long as he lives; but if her husband dies, she is free again, and she may marry as she chooses, although only in the Lord. In my opinion, however, it is better for her, if she stays as she is' (1 Cor. 7: 39–40). I do not know what could be added to this statement, or taken away from it, in relation to the present matter. Then I hear our Lord and Master, and the apostles' Lord and Master, answering the Sadducees, when they brought up the case of a woman who married, not once or twice, but – is it possible? – seven times, and asked whose wife she would be after the resurrection. Rebuking them, he said, 'You are making a mistake, because you do not

understand the scriptures or the power of God. In the resurrection there will be no marrying or giving in marriage; for they will not die, but will be like God's angels' (Mt 22: 29–30). Obviously he was speaking of the resurrection of those who rise to have life, not those who rise to be punished. Therefore he could have said, 'You are making a mistake, because you do not understand the Scriptures or the power of God; in that resurrection it is not possible for there to be women who have had more than one marriage,' and then could have added, 'because no one marries there.' As we see, however, there is no way his statement can be taken as condemning even the woman who had as many husbands as that. Hence, I would not dare to say anything against the natural sense of embarrassment, and state that, if her husbands die, a woman may marry as often as she likes; but neither would I venture on the strength of my own thinking to go beyond the authority of holy scripture, and condemn any number of marriages. What I say to the widow who has had only one husband, however, I say to all widows: 'It is better for you, if you stay as you are.'

5 Augustine of Hippo, *The City of God*

The first extract from *The City of God* (begun 413, completed 426) is on the various terms that may be used to describe love, and their meanings. The second is on the evil of lust. The third is on the possibility of procreation in Paradise, if sin had not occurred. Augustine argues in 14.18 that sexual intercourse, even within marriage, carries some sense of shame. But he argues in 14.23 that procreation would have taken place in Paradise if Adam and Eve had not sinned. And so he suggests in this extract from 14.26 that procreation would have taken place in Paradise untainted by lust.

Further reading: as extract 1.

Text: St Augustine (1972) *Concerning the City of God against the Pagans*, trans. Henry Bettenson, Harmondsworth: Penguin.

(I) 14.7. THE SCRIPTURAL TERMS FOR LOVE

When a man's resolve is to love God, and to love his neighbour as himself, not according to man's standards, but according to God's, he is undoubtedly said to be a man of good will, because of this love. This attitude is more commonly called 'charity' (caritas) in holy Scripture; but it appears in the same sacred writings under the appellation 'love' (amor). For instance, when the Apostle is giving instructions about the choice of a man to rule God's people, he says that such a man should be a lover (amator) of the good. And when the Lord himself had asked the apostle Peter, 'Are you more fond (diligis) of me than those?' Peter replied 'Lord, you know that I love (amo) you' (John 21: 15 ff.). Then the Lord repeated his question, asking, not whether Peter loved him, but whether he was fond of him; and Peter again replied, 'Lord, you know that I love you.' However, when Jesus asked for the third time, he himself said, 'Do you love me?' instead of, 'Are you fond of me?' And then the evangelist goes on, 'Peter was grieved because the Lord had said to him, for the third time: "Do you love me?"' Whereas in fact it was not the third time; the Lord said, 'Do you love me?' only once, but had twice asked, 'Are you fond of me?' From this we infer that when the Lord said, 'Are you fond of me?' he meant precisely the same thing as when he asked, 'Do you love me?' Peter, in contrast, did not change the word used to express the same meaning, when he replied the third time, 'Lord, you know everything. You know that I love you.'

The reason why I thought I should mention this is that quite a number of people imagine that fondness and charity are something different from love. They say, in fact, that 'fondness' is to be taken in a good sense, 'love' in a bad sense. It is, however, well established that this was not the usage even of authors of secular literature. But the philosophers will have to decide whether they make this distinction, and on what principle. Certainly their books are sufficient evidence of the high value they place on love, when it is concerned with good things and directed towards God himself. My task, however, was to make the point that the Scriptures of our religion, whose authority we rank above all other writings, do not distinguish between 'love' and 'fondness' or 'charity.' For I have shown that 'love' also is used in a good sense.

But I should not like anyone to suppose that while 'love' can be employed in both a bad and a good sense, 'fondness' can have only a good connotation. I would draw attention to a passage in one of the psalms, 'The man that is fond of wickedness hates his own soul' (Ps. 11: 5); and to a statement of the apostle John, 'if anyone has become fond of the world, there is no fondness for him for the Father' (John 2: 15). Notice that in this one text we find 'fondness' used both in a good sense and in a bad. As for 'love', I have already shown its use in a good sense; and in case anyone should demand an example of its employment with a bad connotation, here is a quotation from Scripture: 'For men will be lovers of themselves, lovers of money' (2 Tim. 3: 2). And so a rightly directed will is love in a good sense and a perverted will is love in a bad sense. Therefore a love which strains after the possession of the loved object is desire; and the love which possesses and enjoys that object is joy. The love that shuns what opposes it is fear, while the love that feels that opposition when it happens is grief. Consequently, these feelings are bad, if the love is bad, and good if the love is good.

Let me prove this statement from Scripture. The Apostle 'desires to depart and be with Christ'; and, 'My soul has desired to long for your judgments' (Ps. 119: 20), or (to put it more appropriately), 'My soul has longed to desire your judgments'; and, 'The desire for wisdom leads to sovereignty.' (Wisd. 6: 20) All the same it is the established usage that when we use 'desire' (cupiditas or concupiscentia) without specifying its object, it can only be understood in a bad sense. 'Joy' has a good connotation: 'Have joy in the Lord, and exult, you righteous ones' (Ps. 32: 11) and 'You have put joy into my heart' (Ps. 4: 7) and 'You will fill me with joy by your countenance' (Ps. 16: 11). 'Fear' has a good sense in the place where the apostle says, 'With fear and trembling work out your own salvation' (Phil. 2: 12) and 'Do not think highly of yourself, but fear' (Rom. 11: 20) and 'I fear, however, that as the serpent seduced Eve by his craftiness, so your minds will be enticed away from the purity which is in Christ' (2 Cor. 11: 3). As for 'grief', it is a nice question whether any instance can be found of its use in a good sense. Cicero tends to use the word 'distress' (aegritudo) for this feeling, while Virgil prefers 'pain' (dolor), as in the passage, 'They feel pain and gladness' (Aeneid 6: 733). The reason why I prefer 'grief' is that 'distress' and 'pain' are more generally employed of physical sensations.

(II) 14.16 THE EVIL OF LUST, IN THE SPECIFICALLY SEXUAL MEANING

We see then that there are lusts for many things, and yet when lust is mentioned without the specification of its object the only thing that normally occurs to the mind is the lust that excites the indecent parts of the body. This lust assumes power not only over the whole body, and not only from the outside, but also internally; it disturbs the whole man, when the mental emotion combines and mingles with the physical craving, resulting in a pleasure surpassing all physical delights. So intense is the pleasure that when it reaches its climax there is an almost total extinction of mental alertness; the intellectual sentries, as it were, are overwhelmed. Now surely any friend of wisdom and holy joys who lives a married life but knows, in the words of the Apostle's warning, 'how to possess his bodily instrument in holiness and honour, not in the sickness and desire, like the Gentiles who have no knowledge of God' (1 Thess. 4: 4ff) – surely such a man would prefer, if possible, to beget children without lust of this kind. For then the parts created for this task would be the servants of his mind, even in their function of procreation, just as the other members are its servants in the various tasks to which they are assigned. They would begin their activity at the bidding of the will, instead of being stirred up by the ferment of lust.

In fact, not even the lovers of this kind of pleasure are moved, either to conjugal intercourse or to the impure indulgences of vice, just when they have willed. Sometimes the impulse is an unwanted intruder, sometimes it abandons the eager lover, and desire cools off in the body while it is at boiling heat in the mind. Thus strangely does lust refuse to be a servant not only to the will to beget but even to the lust for lascivious indulgence; and although on the whole it is totally opposed to the mind's control, it is quite often divided against itself. It arouses the mind, but does not follow its own lead by arousing the body.

(III) 14.26 GENERATION IN PARADISE WOULD HAVE OCCURRED WITHOUT THE SHAME OF LUST

We conclude then that man lived in paradise as long as his wish was at one with God's command. He lived in the enjoyment of God, and derived his goodness from God's goodness. He lived without any want, and had it in his power to live like this for ever. Food was available to prevent hunger, drink to prevent thirst, and the tree of life was there to guard against old age and dissolution. There was no trace of decay in the body, or arising from the body, to bring any distress to any of his senses. There was no risk of disease from within or of injury from without. Man enjoyed perfect health in the body, entire tranquillity in the soul.

Just as in paradise there was no extreme of heat or cold, so in its inhabitant no desire or fear intervened to hamper his good will.

There was no sadness at all, nor any frivolous jollity. But true joy flowed perpetually from God, and towards God there was a blaze of 'love from a pure heart, a good conscience, and a faith that was no pretence' (1 Tim. 1: 5). Between man and wife there was a faithful partnership based on love and mutual respect; there was a harmony and a liveliness of mind and body, and an effortless observance of the commandment. Man was at leisure, and tiredness never wearied him, and sleep never weighed him down against his will.

When mankind was in such a state of ease and plenty, blest with such felicity, let us never imagine that it was impossible for the seed of children to be sown without the morbid condition of lust. Instead, the sexual organs would have been brought into activity by the same bidding of the will as controlled the other organs. Then, without feeling the allurement of passion goading him on, the husband would have relaxed on his wife's bosom in tranquillity of mind and with no impairment of his body's integrity. Moreover, although we cannot prove this in experience, it does not therefore follow that we should not believe that when those parts of the body were not activated by the turbulent heat of passion but brought into service by deliberate use of power when the need arose, the male seed could have been dispatched into the womb, with no loss of the wife's integrity, just as the menstrual flux can now be produced from the womb of a virgin without loss of maidenhead. For the seed could be injected through the same passage by which the flux is ejected. Now just as the female womb might have been opened for parturition by a natural impulse when the time was ripe, instead of by the groans of travail, so the two sexes might have been united for impregnation and conception by an act of will, instead of by a lustful craving.

The activities I am discussing are bound to induce a feeling of shame, under present conditions. And although I am doing my best to imagine the state of affairs before these activities were shameful, nevertheless, in present circumstances, my discussion must be held in check by the restraining appeal of modesty instead of being furthered by such little eloquence as I command. The possibility that I am speaking of was not in fact experienced by those for whom it was available, because their sin happened first, and they incurred the penalty of exile from paradise before they could unite in the task of propagation as a deliberate act undisturbed by passion. The result is that the mention of this subject now suggests to the mind only the turbulent lust which we experience, not the calm act of will imagined in my speculation.

6 Jerome, *Against Jovinian*

Jerome's *Against Jovinian* (393) precedes the writings of Augustine quoted above, and it also attempts to refute Jovinian's assertion that marriage and virginity were of equal merit in the eyes of God. The vigour of Jerome's assault on Jovinian made his book a fruitful source for anti-matrimonial and antifeminist writing throughout the medieval period (on which see Blamires 1992). Although Jerome's book opens by a refusal to condemn marriage and virginity outright (1.3), it is clear from a later letter to Pammachius about the book that this is what many contemporary readers saw him as doing. Augustine's early writings on marriage are also an attempt to refute Jovinian, but the strength of Jerome's assault causes Augustine to take a more moderate line. The extract given here is from the end of Book One, and is not in fact Jerome speaking *in propria persona*. This is Theophrastus, quoted at length here by Jerome, whose work does not survive separately from its quotation in *Against Jovinian*. This material from Theophrastus was often reused by later antimatrimonial writers: compare its reappearance in extract 73.

Further reading: Brown 1988, Oppel 1993.

Text: St Jerome (1893) *The Principal Works of St Jerome*, trans W. H. Fremantle, Oxford: James Parker.

1. 47. [. . .] A book *On Marriage*, worth its weight in gold, passes under the name of Theophrastus. In it the author asks whether a wise man marries. And after laying down the conditions – that the wife must be fair, of good character, and honest parentage, the husband in good health and of ample means, and after saying that under these circumstances a wise man sometimes enters the state of matrimony, he immediately proceeds thus: 'But all these conditions are seldom satisfied in marriage. A wise man therefore must not take a wife. For in the first place, his study of philosophy will be hindered, and it is impossible for anyone to attend to his books and his wife. Matrons want many things, costly dresses, gold, jewels, great outlay, maid-servants, all kinds of furniture, litters and gilded coaches. Then come curtain-lectures the livelong night: she complains that one lady goes out better dressed than she: that another is looked up to by all: "I am a poor despised nobody at the ladies' assemblies." "Why did you ogle that creature next door?" "Why were you talking to the maid?" "What did you bring from the market?" "I am not allowed to have a single friend or companion." She suspects that her husband's love goes the same way as her hate. There may be in some neighbouring city the wisest of teachers; but if we have a wife we can neither leave

her behind, nor take the burden with us. To support a poor wife, is hard: to put up with a rich one, is torture. Notice too, that in the case of a wife you cannot pick and choose: you must take her as you find her. If she has a bad temper, or is a fool, if she has a blemish, or is proud, or has bad breath, whatever her fault may be – all this we learn after marriage. Horses, asses, cattle, even slaves of the smallest worth, clothes, kettles, wooden seats, cups, and earthenware pitchers, are first tried and then bought: a wife is the only thing that is not shown before she is married, for fear she may not give satisfaction. Our gaze must always be directed to her face, and we must always praise her beauty: if you look at another woman, she thinks that she is out of favour. She must be called my lady, her birth-day must be kept, we must swear by her health and wish that she may survive us, respect must be paid to the nurse, to the nursemaid, to the father's slave, to the foster-child, to the handsome hanger-on, to the curled darling who manages her affairs, and to the eunuch who ministers to the safe indulgence of her lust: names which are only a cloak for adultery. Upon whomsoever she sets her heart, they must have her love though they want her not. If you give her the management of the whole house, you must yourself be her slave. If you reserve something for yourself, she will not think you are loyal to her; but she will turn to strife and hatred, and unless you quickly take care, she will have the poison ready. If you introduce old women, and soothsayers, and vendors of jewels and silken clothing, you imperil her chastity; if you shut the door upon them she is injured and fancies you suspect her. But what is the good of even a careful guardian, when an unchaste wife cannot be watched, and a chaste one ought not to be? For necessity is but a faithless keeper of chastity, and she alone really deserves to be called pure, who is free to sin if she chooses. If a woman be fair, she soon finds lovers; if she be ugly, it is easy to be wanton. It is difficult to guard what many long for. It is annoying to have what no one thinks worth possessing. But the misery of having an ugly wife is less than that of watching a comely one. Nothing is safe, for which a whole people sighs and longs. One man entices with his figure, another with his brains, another with his wit, another with his open hand. Somehow, or sometime, the fortress is captured which is attacked on all sides. Men marry, indeed, so as to get a manager for the house, to solace weariness, to banish solitude; but a faithful slave is a far better manager, more submissive to the master, more observant of his ways, than a wife who thinks she proves herself mistress if she acts in opposition to her husband, that is, if she does what pleases her, not what she is commanded. But friends, and servants who are under the obligation of benefits received, are better able to wait upon us in sickness than a wife who makes us responsible for her tears (she will sell you enough to make a deluge for the hope of a legacy); who boasts of her anxiety, yet drives her sick husband to the distraction of despair. But if she herself is poorly, we must fall sick with her and never leave her bedside. Or if she be a good and agreeable wife (how rare a bird she is!), we have to share her groans in childbirth, and suffer torture when she is in danger. A wise man can never be alone. He has with him the good men of all time, and turns his mind freely wherever he chooses. What is inaccessible to him in person he can embrace in thought. And, if men are scarce, he converses with God. He is never less alone than when alone. Then again, to marry for the sake of children, so that our name may not perish, or that we may have support in old age, and leave our property without dispute, is the height of stupidity. For what is it to us when we are leaving the world if another bears our name, when even a son does not all at once take his father's title, and there are countless others who are called by the same name. Or what support in old age is he whom you bring up, and who may die before you, or turn out a reprobate? Or at all events when he reaches mature age, you may seem to him long in dying. Friends and relatives whom you can judiciously love are better and safer heirs than those whom you must make your heirs whether you like it or not. Indeed, the surest way of having a good heir is to ruin your fortune in a good cause while you live, not to leave the fruit of your labour to be used you know not how.'

ANGLO-SAXON ENGLAND

7 The Penitential of Theodore

The penitentials are guides for confessors on sin and penance. The extracts here are taken from a penitential guide (668–690, with later additions) associated with Theodore of Tarsus, archbishop of Canterbury (668–690), which has been assembled not by Theodore himself, but by an anonymous Northumbrian cleric who purports to collect together Theodore's judgements as reported by a cleric named Eoda. Payer (1984) notes the novelty of many of the penitential subjects found here for the first time, which then go on to exercise subsequent influence on later collections. Some of the material here (on remarriage, for instance) is notably at odds with general Christian teaching, and may perhaps indicate tensions between Christian and Anglo-Saxon models of marriage in the period.

Further reading: McNeill and Gamer 1938, Lucas 1983: ch. 6, Payer 1984: ch. 1, Noonan 1986: ch. 5, Brundage 1987: ch. 4, Frantzen 1998: ch. 4.

Text: McNeill, J. T. and Gamer, H. M. (ed. and trans.) (1938) *Medieval Handbooks of Penance*, New York, with some slight modifications.

BOOK ONE, II OF FORNICATION

1. If anyone commits fornication with a virgin he shall do penance for one year. If with a married woman, he shall do penance for four years, two of these entire, and in the other two during the three forty-day periods and three days a week.[1]

1 The three fasting periods are the forty days before Easter, the forty days before Christmas, and the forty days after Pentecost.

2. He judged that he who often commits fornication with a man or with a beast should do penance for ten years.
3. Another judgment is that he who is joined to beasts shall do penance for fifteen years.[2]
4. He who after his twentieth year defiles himself with a male shall do penance for fifteen years.
5. A male who commits fornication with a male shall do penance for ten years.
6. Sodomites shall do penance for seven years, and the effeminate man as an adulteress.[3]
7. Likewise he who commits this sexual offence once shall do penance for it for four years. If he has been in the habit of it, as Basil says, fifteen years; but if not, one year less as a woman. If he is a boy, two years for the first offence; if he repeats it, four years.
8. If he does this between the thighs, one year, or the three forty-day periods.
9. If he defiles himself, forty days.
10. He who desires to commit fornication, but is not able, shall do penance for forty or twenty days.
11. As for boys who mutually engage in vice, he judged that they should be whipped.
12. If a woman practices vice with a woman, she shall do penance for three years.
13. If she practices solitary vice, she shall do penance for the same period.
14. The penance of a widow and of a girl is the same. She who has a husband deserves a greater penalty if she commits fornication.
15. Whoever has emitted semen in the mouth shall do penance for seven years: this is the worst of evils. Elsewhere it was his judgment that both [participants in this offence] shall do penance to the end of life; or twelve years; or as above seven.[4]

2 This contrasts with the lesser penance of ten years offered immediately above. Frantzen (1998: 153) notes that even within a single penitential text, multiple and perhaps contradictory options are offered for penances. He argues that this could mean that confessors were offered leeway regarding penances to be imposed.

3 'The effeminate man' translates Latin *molles* (for discussion of this as a sexual category, see Payer 1984: 40–41, Frantzen 1998: ch. 4). On the punishment of 'the effeminate man' as an adulteress, Frantzen (1998: 153) argues that this shows that homosexual intercourse was thought of as a perversion of heterosexual intercourse – hence one of the sexual partners is treated like a woman. Isidore of Seville derives the word *mulier* (woman) from her *mollities* (softness) (Bullough 1973: 494–495, Jacquart and Thomasset 1988: 14).

4 Commentators differ on whether or not this should be taken as referring specifically to either heterosexual or homosexual oral sex.

16. If one commits fornication with his mother, he shall do penance for fifteen years and never change except on Sundays. But this so impious incest is likewise spoken of by him in another way – that he shall do penance for seven years, with perpetual pilgrimage.[5]
17. He who commits fornication with his sister shall do penance for fifteen years in the way in which it is stated above of his mother. But this [penalty] he also established in a canon as twelve years. Whence it is not unreasonable that the fifteen years that are written apply to the mother.
18. The first canon determined that he who often commits fornication should do penance for ten years; a second canon, seven; but on account of the weakness of man, on deliberation they said he should do penance for three years.
19. If a brother commits fornication with a natural brother, he shall abstain from all kinds of flesh for fifteen years.
20. If a mother imitates acts of fornication with her little son, she shall abstain from flesh for three years and fast one day in the week, that is until vespers.
21. He who amuses himself with libidinous imagination shall do penance until the imagination is overcome.
22. He who loves a woman in his mind shall seek pardon from God; but if he has spoken [to her], that is, of love and friendship, but is not received by her, he shall do penance for seven days.

VII OF MANY AND DIVERSE EVILS, AND WHAT NECESSARY THINGS ARE HARMLESS

1. He who has committed many evil deeds, that is, murder, adultery with a woman and with a beast, and theft, shall go into a monastery and do penance until his death.[6]
3. He who drinks blood or semen shall do penance for three years.

5 Payer (1984: 31) notes that this is the first penitential to discuss sexual incest in detail.

6 Payer (1984: 20) suggests that 'adultery' may have a wider application in these texts than it does today, including sex with nuns or with another's fiancée, sex between a priest and his spiritual daughter, and bestiality.

VIII OF VARIOUS FAILINGS OF THE SERVANTS OF GOD

1. If a priest is polluted in touching or in kissing a woman he shall do penance for forty days.
2. If a presbyter kisses a woman from desire, he shall do penance for forty days.
3. Likewise if a presbyter is polluted through imagination, he shall fast for a week.
4. For masturbation, he shall fast for three weeks.
6. A monk or holy virgin who commits fornication shall do penance for seven years.
9. For masturbation, the first time he shall do penance for twenty days, on repetition, forty days; for further offences fasts shall be added.
10. If [intercourse] between the thighs, one year or the three forty-day periods.
14. Basil gave judgment that a boy should be permitted to marry before the age of sixteen if he could not abstain; but that if he is already a monk [and marries], he is both [classed] among bigamists and shall do penance for one year.

IX OF THOSE WHO ARE DEGRADED OR CANNOT BE ORDAINED

1. A bishop, presbyter, or deacon guilty of fornication ought to be degraded and do penance at the decision of a bishop; yet they shall take communion. With loss of rank, the penance dies, the soul lives.
4. If any presbyter or deacon marries a strange woman, he shall be deposed before the people.
5. If he commits adultery with her and it comes to the knowledge of the people, he shall be cast out of the Church and shall do penance among the laymen as long as he lives.
6. If anyone has a concubine, he ought not to be ordained.
8. Likewise he who slays a man or commits fornication, shall be deposed.
10. If anyone, before or after baptism, marries a twice married woman, as in the case of twice married men, he cannot be ordained.

XIV OF THE PENANCE FOR SPECIAL IRREGULARITIES IN MARRIAGE

1. In a first marriage, the presbyter ought to perform Mass and bless them both, and afterward they shall absent themselves from church for thirty days. Having done this, they shall do penance for forty days, and absent themselves from the prayer; and afterwards they shall communicate with the oblation.
2. One who is twice married shall do penance for a year; on Wednesdays and Fridays and during the three forty-day periods he shall abstain from flesh; however, he shall not put away his wife.
3. He that is married three times, or more, that is in a fourth or fifth marriage, or beyond that number, for seven years on Wednesdays and Fridays and during the three forty-day periods they shall abstain from flesh; yet they shall not be separated. Basil so determined, but in the canon four years [are indicated].
4. If anyone finds his wife to be an adulteress and does not wish to put her away but has had her in the matrimonial relation to that time, he shall do penance for two years on two days in the week and [shall perform] the fasts of religion; or as long as she herself does penance he shall avoid the matrimonial relation with her, because she has committed adultery.
5. If any man or woman who has taken the vow of virginity is joined in marriage, he shall not set aside the marriage but shall do penance for three years.
6. Foolish vows and those incapable of being performed are to be set aside.
7. A woman may not take a vow without the consent of her husband; but if she does take a vow she can be released, and she shall do penance according to the decision of a priest.[7]
8. He who puts away his wife and marries another shall do penance with tribulation for seven years or a lighter penance for fifteen years.
9. He who defiles his neighbour's wife, deprived of his own wife, shall fast for three years two days a week and in the three forty-day periods.
10. If [the woman] is a virgin, he shall do penance for one year without meat and wine and mead.
11. If he defiles a vowed virgin, he shall do penance for three years, as we said above, whether a child is born of her or not.

7 The ineffectiveness of the vows of wives without the consent of the husband applied throughout the Middle Ages. The ban appears later in Gratian's *Decretum* (see Blamires 1992: 84).

12. If she is his slave, he shall set her free and fast for six months.
13. If the wife of anyone deserts him and returns to him undishonoured, she shall do penance for one year; otherwise for three years. If he takes another wife he shall do penance for one year.
14. An adulterous woman shall do penance for seven years. And this matter is stated in the same way in the canon.
15. A woman who commits adultery[8] shall do penance for three years as a fornicator. So also shall she do penance who takes her husband's semen in her food for the increase of love.
16. A wife who tastes her husband's blood as a remedy shall fast for forty days, more or less.
17. Moreover, women shall not in the time of impurity enter into a church, or communicate – neither nuns nor laywomen; if they presume [to do this] they shall fast for three weeks.
18. In the same way shall they do penance who enter a church before purification after childbirth, that is, forty days.
19. But he who has intercourse at these seasons shall do penance for twenty days.[9]
20. He who has intercourse on the Lord's day shall seek pardon from God and do penance for one or two or three days.
21. If a man has intercourse with his wife from behind, he shall do penance for forty days for the first time.
22. If he has intercourse in the rear he ought to do penance as one who offends with animals.[10]
23. For intercourse at the improper season he shall fast for forty days.
24. Women who commit abortion before [the foetus] has life, shall do penance for one year or for the three forty-day periods or for forty days, according to the nature of the offence; and if later, that is, more than forty days after conception, they shall do penance as murderesses, that is for three years on Wednesdays and Fridays and in the three forty-day periods. This according to the canons is judged [punishable by] ten years.

8 Or perhaps 'commits an offence with another woman', depending on the manuscript reading.

9 Cf. Bede's account of Pope Gregory's correspondence with St Augustine of Canterbury (extract 8), which differs from canons 18 and 19 here. Payer (1984: 36) comments that, assuming that Gregory's replies are genuine, either Gregory's correspondence was unknown to the compiler of the penitential, or he deliberately departed from the ruling there. On 'churching' – the ceremony of purification after childbirth – in the later Middle Ages, see Rieder 2002.

10 Payer (1984: 30) comments that anal intercourse was heavily penanced because of its similarity to either bestiality or sodomy.

BOOK TWO, XII OF MATTERS RELATING TO MARRIAGE

1. Those who are married shall abstain from intercourse for three nights before they communicate.
2. A man shall abstain from his wife for forty days before Easter, until the week of Easter. On this account, the Apostle says: 'That ye may give yourselves to prayer' (1 Cor. 7: 5).
3. When she has conceived a woman ought to abstain from her husband for three months before the birth, and afterward in the time of purgation, that is, for forty days and nights, whether she has borne a male or female child.
4. It is also fully permitted to a woman to communicate before she is to bear a child.
5. If the wife of anyone commits fornication, he may put her away and take another; that is, if a man puts away his wife on account of fornication, if she was his first, he is permitted to take another; but if she wishes to do penance for her sins, she may take another husband after five years.[11]
6. A woman may not put away her husband, even if he is a fornicator, unless, perchance, for [the purpose of his entering] a monastery. Basil so decided.
7. A legal marriage may not be broken without the consent of both parties.
8. But either, according to the Greeks, may give the other permission to join a monastery for the service of God, and [as it were] marry it, if he [or she] was in a first marriage; yet this is not canonical. But if such is not the case [but they are] in a second marriage, this is not permitted while the husband or wife is alive.
9. If a husband makes himself a slave through theft or fornication or any sin, the wife, if she has not been married before, has the right to take another husband after a year. This is not permitted to one who has been twice married.
10. When his wife is dead, a man may take another wife after a month. If her husband is dead, the woman may take another husband after a year.

11 On divorce, Brundage (1987: 143) argues that divorce by mutual consent remained common in seventh- and eighth-century Gaul, and probably elsewhere too. This changed at the end of the eighth century, when adultery remains a reason for couples to part, but not to remarry.

11. If a woman is an adulteress and her husband does not wish to live with her, if she decides to enter a monastery she shall retain the fourth part of her inheritance. If she decides otherwise, she shall have nothing.
12. Any woman who commits adultery is in the power of her husband if he wishes to be reconciled to an adulterous woman. If he makes a reconciliation, her punishment does not concern the clergy, it belongs to her own husband.
13. In the case of a man and a woman who are married, if he wishes to serve God and she does not, or if she wishes to do so and he does not, or if either of them is broken in health, they may still be completely separated with the consent of both.
14. A woman who vows not to take another husband after her husband's death and when he is dead, false to her word, takes another and is married a second time, when she is moved by penitence and wishes to fulfill her vow, it is in the power of her husband [to determine] whether she shall fulfill it or not.
15. Therefore, to one woman who after eleven years confessed [such] a vow, Theodore gave permission to cohabit with the man.
16. And if anyone in a secular habit takes a vow without the consent of the bishop, the bishop himself has power to change the decision if he wishes.
17. A legal marriage may take place equally in the day and in the night, as it is written, 'Thine is the day and thine is the night' (Ps. 73: 16).
18. If a pagan puts away his pagan wife, after baptism it shall be in his power to have her or not to have her.
19. In the same way, if one of them is baptized, the other a pagan, as saith the Apostle, 'If the unbeliever depart, let him depart' (1 Cor. 7: 15); therefore, if the wife of any man is an unbeliever and a pagan and cannot be converted, she shall be put away.
20. If a woman leaves her husband, despising him, and is unwilling to return and be reconciled to her husband, after five years, with the bishop's consent, he shall be permitted to take another wife.
21. If she has been taken into captivity by force and cannot be redeemed, [he may] take another after a year.
22. Again, if she has been taken into captivity her husband shall wait five years; so also shall a woman do if such things have happened to the man.
23. If, therefore, a man has taken another wife, he shall receive the former wife when she returns from captivity and put away the later

one; so also shall she do, as we have said above, if such things have happened to her husband.

24. If an enemy carries away any man's wife, and he cannot get her again, he may take another. To do this is better than acts of fornication.

25. If after this the former wife comes again to him, she ought not to be received by him, if he has another, but she may take to herself another husband, if she has had [only] one before. The same ruling stands in the case of slaves from over the sea.

26. According to the Greeks it is permitted to marry in the third degree of consanguinity, as it is written in the Law; according to the Romans, in the fifth degree; however, in the fourth degree they do not dissolve [a marriage] after it has taken place. Hence they are to be united in the fifth degree; in the fourth, if they are found [already married] they are not to be separated; in the third, they are to be separated.

27. Nevertheless, it is not permitted to take the wife of another after his death [if he was related] in the third degree.[12]

28. On the same conditions a man is joined in matrimony to those who are related to him, and to his wife's relatives after her death.

29. Two brothers may also have two sisters in marriage, and a father and son [respectively] a mother and her daughter.

30. A husband who sleeps with his wife shall wash himself before he goes into a church.

31. A husband ought not to see his wife nude.

32. If anyone has illicit connection or illicit marriage, it is nevertheless permissible to eat the food which they have, for the prophet has said: 'The earth is the Lord's and the fullness thereof' (Ps. 23: 1).

33. If a man and a woman have united in marriage, and afterward the woman says of the man that he is impotent, if anyone can prove that this is true, she may take another [husband].

34. Parents may not give a betrothed girl to another man unless she flatly refuses [to marry the original suitor]; but she may go to a monastery if she wishes.

35. But if she who is betrothed refuses to live with the man to whom she is betrothed, the money which he gave for her shall be paid back to him, and a third part shall be added; if, however, it is he that refuses, he shall lose the money which he gave for her.[13]

12 On the permitted degrees, see the discussion in Bede (extract 8).

13 On the payment of money, see also extracts 24 and 25 (the issue is discussed in Goody 1983: appendix 2).

36. But a girl of seventeen[14] years has the power of her own body.
37. Until he is fifteen years old a boy shall be in the power of his father, then he can make himself a monk; but a girl of sixteen or seventeen years who was before in the power of her parents [can become a nun]. After that age a father may not bestow his daughter in marriage against her will.

8 Bede, *Ecclesiastical History of the English People*

The following extracts from Bede's Ecclesiastical History (731) are from an account of the correspondence between St Augustine of Canterbury (d. 604/5) and Pope Gregory (*c*.550–604, pope from 590) on matters concerning the English Church. Augustine was sent to England by Gregory in 596, arriving in 597, and welcomed by King Æthelbert of Kent (for whose laws, see extract 20). Bede (*c*.673–735), a Northumbrian monk and historian, is writing at a remove of almost a century and a half from the events described. Farmer (in Bede 1990: 77, n.) comments that 'the authenticity of these replies has been much controverted, but current opinion generally favours authenticity except for V (on marriage concessions)'. In favour of the genuineness of these marriage concessions, however, Goody (1983: 35) notes the existence of a manuscript tradition independent of Bede, and contemporary reaction judging the concessions genuine. He relates that Pope Zachary reports having heard that Gregory had allowed marriages in the fourth degree, and that this was widely reported in 'the lands of the Germans'. Zachary is prepared to believe that Gregory had allowed this because the persons concerned were undergoing conversion.

Text: St Bede (1990) *Ecclesiastical History of the English People*, trans. L. Sherley Price, R. E. Latham and D. H. Farmer, revised edn, Harmondsworth: Penguin.

IV. Augustine's fourth question: Is it permissible for two brothers to marry two sisters, provided that there be no blood ties between the families?

Pope Gregory's reply: This is quite permissible. There is nothing in holy Scripture that seems to forbid it.

V. Augustine's fifth question: To what degree may the faithful marry with their kindred? And is it lawful for a man to marry his step-mother or sister-in-law?

14 Manuscripts also read thirteen, fourteen, and sixteen years.

Pope Gregory's reply: An earthly law of the Roman state permits first-cousins to marry. But experience shows that such unions do not result in children, and sacred law forbids a man to 'uncover the nakedness of his kindred.' Necessity therefore forbids a closer marriage than that between the third or fourth generation, while the second generation, as we have said, should wholly abstain from marriage. But to wed one's step-mother is a grave sin, for the Law says: 'Thou shalt not uncover the nakedness of thy father.' Now the son cannot uncover the nakedness of his father; but since it says, 'They shall be one flesh', whosoever presumes to wed his step-mother, who was one flesh with his father, thereby commits this offence. It is also forbidden to marry a sister-in-law, since by a former union she had become one with his own brother: it was for denouncing this sin that John the Baptist was beheaded and met his holy martyrdom. For John was not ordered to deny Christ, but was in fact put to death as a confessor of Christ. For since our Lord Jesus Christ said: 'I am the Truth,' John shed his blood for Christ in that he gave his life for the truth.

But since there are many among the English who, while they were still heathen, are said to have contracted these unlawful marriages, when they accept the Faith they are to be instructed that this is a grave offence and that they must abstain from it. Warn them of the terrible judgement of God lest for their bodily desires they incur the pains of eternal punishment. Nevertheless, they are not on that account to be deprived of the Communion of the Body and Blood of Christ, lest they appear to be punished for sins committed unknowingly before they received the purification of Baptism. For in these days the Church corrects some things strictly, and allows others out of leniency; others again she deliberately glosses over and tolerates and by so doing often succeeds in checking an evil of which she disapproves. But all who come to the Faith are to be warned against doing these things, and should any subsequently be guilty of them, they are to be forbidden to receive the Communion of the Body and Blood of our Lord. For while these offences may to some extent be condoned in those who acted in ignorance, they must be severely punished in those who presume to sin knowingly.

VIII. Augustine's eighth question: May an expectant mother be baptized? How soon after childbirth may she enter church? And how soon after birth may a child be baptized if in danger of death? How soon after childbirth may a husband have relations with his wife? And may a woman properly enter church at the time of menstruation? And may she receive Communion at these times? And may a man enter church after relations with his wife before he has washed? Or receive the sacred mystery of Communion? These uncouth English people require guidance on all these matters.

Pope Gregory's reply: I have no doubt, my brother, that questions such as these have arisen, and I think I have already answered you; but doubtless you desire my support for your statements and rulings. Why should not an expectant mother be baptized? – the fruitfulness of the flesh is no offence in the sight of Almighty God. For when our first parents sinned in the Garden, they justly forfeited God's gift of immortality. But although God deprived man of immortality for that sin, he did not destroy the human race on that account, but of his merciful goodness left man his ability to continue the race. On what grounds, then, can Almighty God's free gift to man be excluded from the grace of Holy Baptism? For it would be foolish to suppose that his gift of grace is contrary to the sacred mystery by which all guilt is washed away.

As to the interval that must elapse after childbirth before a woman may enter church, you are familiar with the Old Testament rule: that is, for a male child thirty-three days and for a female, sixty-six. But this is to be understood as an allegory, for were a woman to enter church and return thanks in the very hour of her delivery, she would do nothing wrong. The fault lies in the bodily pleasure, not in the pain; the pleasure is the bodily union, the pain is in the birth, so that Eve, the mother of us all, was told: 'In sorrow thou shalt bring forth children.' If, then, we forbid a woman who is delivered of a child to enter church, we make this penalty into a sin. There is no obstacle to the Baptism either of a woman who has been delivered, or of a newborn babe, even if it is administered to her in the very hour of her delivery, or to the child at the hour of its birth, provided that there be danger of death. For as the grace of this sacred mystery is to be offered with great deliberation to the living and the conscious, so is it to be administered without delay to the dying; for if we wait to offer them this mystery of redemption, it may be too late to find the one to be redeemed.[15]

A man should not approach his wife until her child is weaned. But a bad custom has arisen in the behaviour of married people that women disdain to suckle their own children, and hand them over to other people to nurse. This custom seems to have arisen

15 Cf. *The Penitential of Theodore* (extract 7) and discussion in Payer (1984: 36).

solely through incontinency; for when women are unwilling to be continent, they refuse to suckle their children. So those who observe this bad custom of giving their children to others to nurse must not approach their husbands until the time of their purification has elapsed. For even apart from childbirth, women are forbidden to do so during their monthly courses, and the Old Law prescribed death for any man who approached a woman during this time. But a woman should not be forbidden to enter church during these times; for the workings of nature cannot be considered culpable, and it is not just that she should be refused admittance, since her condition is beyond her control. We know that the woman who suffered an issue of blood, humbly approaching behind our Lord, touched the hem of his robe and was at once healed of her sickness. If, therefore, this woman was right to touch our Lord's robe, why may not one who suffers nature's courses be permitted to enter the church of God? And if it is objected that the woman in the gospels was compelled by disease while these latter are bound by custom, then remember, my brother, that everything that we suffer in this mortal body through the infirmity of its nature is justly ordained by God since the Fall of man. For hunger, thirst, heat, cold, and weariness originate in this infirmity of our nature; and our search for food against hunger, drink against thirst, coolness against heat, clothing against cold, and rest against weariness is only our attempt to obtain some remedy in our weakness. In this sense the menstrual flow in a woman is an illness. So, if it was a laudable presumption in the woman who, in her disease, touched our Lord's robe, why may not the same concession be granted to all women who endure the weakness of their nature?

A woman, therefore, should not be forbidden to receive the mystery of Communion at these times. If any out of a deep sense of reverence do not presume to do so, this is commendable; but if they do so, they do nothing blameworthy. Sincere people often acknowledge their faults even when there is no actual fault, because a blameless action may often spring from a fault. For instance, eating when we are hungry is no fault, but being hungry originates in Adam's sin; similarly, the monthly courses of women are no fault, because nature causes them. But the defilement of our nature is apparent even when we have no deliberate intention to do evil, and this defilement springs from sin; so we may recognize the judgement that our sin has brought on us. And so may man, who sinned willingly, bear the punishment of his sin unwillingly. Therefore, when women after due consideration do not presume to approach the Sacrament of the Body and Blood of the Lord during their courses, they are to be commended. But if they are moved by devout love of this holy mystery to receive it as pious custom suggests, they are not to be discouraged. For while the Old Testament makes outward observances important, the New Testament does not regard these things so highly as the inward disposition, which is the sole true criterion for allotting punishment. For instance, the Law forbids the eating of many things as unclean, but in the Gospel our Lord says: 'Not that which goeth into the mouth defileth a man; but that which cometh out of the mouth, this defileth a man.' He also said: 'Out of the mouth proceed evil thoughts.' Here Almighty God clearly shows us that evil actions spring from the root of evil thoughts. Similarly, Saint Paul says: 'Unto the pure all things are pure; but unto them that are defiled and unbelieving is nothing pure.' And later, he indicates the cause of this corruption, adding: 'For even their mind and conscience is defiled.' If, therefore, no food is unclean to one of a pure mind, how can a woman who endures the laws of nature with a pure mind be considered impure?

It is not fitting that a man who has approached his wife should enter church before he has washed, nor is he to enter at once, though washed. The ancient Law prescribed that a man in such cases should wash, and forbade him to enter a holy place before sunset. But this may be understood spiritually; for when a man's mind is attracted to those pleasures by lawless desire, he should not regard himself as fitted to join in Christian worship until these heated desires cool in the mind, and he has ceased to labour under wrongful passions. And although various nations have differing views on this matter and observe different customs, it was always the ancient Roman usage for such a man to seek purification and out of reverence to refrain awhile from entering a holy place. In making this observation, we do not condemn marriage itself, but since lawful intercourse must be accompanied by bodily desire, it is fitting to refrain from entering a holy place, since this desire itself is not blameless. For David, who said: 'Behold, I was shapen in iniquity, and in sin did my mother conceive me,' was not himself born of any illicit union, but in lawful wedlock. But knowing himself to have been conceived in iniquity, he grieved that he had been born in sin, like a tree bearing in its branches the sap of evil drawn up from its root. In saying this, he does not term the bodily union of married people iniquity, but the desire of such union. For there are many things which are lawful and legitimate, and yet in the doing of them we are to some extent contaminated. For example, we often correct faults under stress of anger and thereby disturb our peace of mind; and though we are right to do so, it is not good that we should lose our peace of mind in the process. He who said: 'Mine eye is troubled because of anger' had been roused by the crimes of evil men, and because only a quiet mind can rest in the light of contemplation, he regretted that his eye was troubled by anger, so that he was disquieted and prevented from contemplating heavenly things so long as he was distracted by indignation at the wicked doings of men. So while anger against evil is commendable, it is harmful to a man because in being disturbed by it he is conscious of some guilt. Lawful intercourse should be for the procreation of offspring, and not for mere pleasure; to obtain children, and not to satisfy lust. But if any man is not moved by a desire for pleasure, but only for a desire for children, he is to be left to his own judgement either as to entering church, or to receiving the Communion of the Body and Blood of our Lord; for we have no right to debar one who does not yield to the fires of temptation. But when lust takes the place of desire for children, the mere act of union becomes something the pair have cause to regret; and although the holy teachings give them permission, yet this carries a warning with it. For when the Apostle Paul said: 'If they cannot contain, let them marry,' he at once added, 'I speak this by permission, and not of commandment.' This concession makes it lawful, yet not good; so when he spoke of permission, he indicated that it was not blameless.

It should be carefully considered that, when God was about to speak to the people on Mount Sinai, he first ordered them to abstain from women. And if such a degree of bodily purity was required in those who were to hear the word of God when he spoke to men through a subject creature, how much the more should women preserve themselves in purity of body when about to receive the Body of Almighty God himself, lest they be overwhelmed by the very greatness of this inestimable mystery? For this reason the priest instructed David that, if his men were clean in this respect, they might be given the shewbread, which would have been entirely forbidden had not David first certified that they had kept themselves from women. Similarly the man who has cleansed himself with water after intercourse with his wife is allowed to approach the mystery of Holy Communion, since he may enter church in accordance with this decision.

IX. Augustine's ninth question: May a man receive communion after a sexual illusion in a dream; or, if a priest, may he celebrate the holy mysteries?

Pope Gregory's reply: The Testament of the Old Law, as I have already mentioned, speaks of such a man as unclean and does not permit him to enter church until evening and after purification. But this is to be understood spiritually in another sense; for a man may be under a delusion and tempted to impurity in a dream, because, having yielded to temptation, he is defiled by real sexual imaginings. Then he must cleanse himself with water, thus washing away his sinful thoughts with tears. And, unless the fire of temptation dies earlier, he should regard himself as unclean until evening. But we should carefully examine the origin of such illusion in the mind of a sleeper; for sometimes they arise from over-eating, sometimes for excess or lack of bodily vigour, and sometimes from impure thoughts. When such an illusion occurs through excess or lack of bodily vigour, it need not be feared, because it is to be deplored rather as something the mind has unwittingly suffered than as something it has done. But when a greedy appetite runs riot and overloads the repositories of the bodily fluids, the mind is to blame, although not to the extent that a man must be forbidden to receive the holy mystery, or to say mass when a feast-day requires it, or when necessity demands that he administer the sacrament in the absence of another priest. But if there are others who can perform this ministry, then this illusion caused by greed need not debar a man from receiving the holy mystery unless the mind of the sleeper has been excited by impure thought; but I think that humility should move him to refrain from offering the holy mysteries under these circumstances. For there are some who are not mentally disturbed by impure thoughts, although subject to these illusions. In these things there is just one thing that shows the mind is not innocent even in its own judgement: although it remembers nothing that occurs during sleep, yet it does remember its greedy appetites. But if the sleeper's illusion springs from indecent thoughts when awake, his guilt stands clear in his mind and he recognizes the source of his sin, because he has unconsciously experienced what has been in his conscious thoughts. But the question arises whether an evil thought merely suggests itself to a man, or whether he proceeds to take pleasure in it, or, worse still, to assent to it. For all sin is consummated in three ways, that is, by suggestion, pleasure, and consent. Suggestion comes through the devil, pleasure through the flesh, and consent through the will. The Serpent suggests the first sin, and Eve, as flesh, took physical pleasure in it, while Adam, as spirit, consented; and great discernment is needed if the mind, in judging itself, is to distinguish between suggestion and pleasure, and between pleasure and consent. For when the Evil Spirit suggests a sin, no sin is committed unless the flesh takes pleasure in it; but when the flesh begins to take pleasure, then sin is born; and if deliberate consent is given, sin is complete. The seed of sin, therefore, is in suggestion, its growth in pleasure, and its completion in consent. It often happens, however, that what the Evil Spirit sows in the mind and flesh anticipates with pleasure, the soul rejects. And although the body cannot experience pleasure without the mind, yet the mind, in contending against the desires of the body, is to some extent unwillingly chained to them, having to oppose them for conscience sake, and strongly regretting its bondage to bodily desires. It was for this reason that Paul, that great soldier in God's army, confessed with sorrow: 'I see another law in my members warring against the law of my mind, and bringing me into captivity to the law of sin, which is in my members.' Now if he was a captive, he fought but little; yet he did fight. So he was both captive and also fighting with the law of the mind, to which the law of the body is opposed. And if he fought thus, he was no captive. So one may say that a man is both captive and free; free through the law of right which he loves, and captive through the law of bodily pleasure, of which he is an unwilling victim.

9 The Law of the Northumbrian Priests

This brief reference from an early eleventh-century ecclesiastical text (1020–1023?) shows the tolerance of clerical marriage in England prior to the reform papacy's campaign against clerical marriage and concubinage later in the eleventh century.

Further reading: on clerical concubinage in Anglo-Saxon England, see Clunies Ross 1985.

Text: Dorothy Whitelock (ed.) (1979) *English Historical Documents, 500–1042*, 2nd edn, London: Eyre Methuen.

35. If a priest leaves a woman and takes another, let him be anathema!

THEOLOGY AND CANON LAW

10 Gratian, *Decretum*

Gratian's *Decretum* (*c.*1140) is a compilation of canonical decisions, and is one of the fundamental texts of the medieval canon law, along with the *Decretals* of Gregory IX. Part 2, causa 27, from which the two extracts below are taken, discusses the formation of the marriage bond. Gratian's difficulty is to reconcile the respective roles of consent and intercourse in forming the marriage bond. The difficulty in allowing intercourse a formative role is that this might imply that chaste marriages (and Gratian has the marriage of Christ's parents in mind here) are not marriages at all. The first extract shows him discussing the marriage of Christ's parents, the second his judgement on the relative roles of consent and intercourse in making a marriage.

Further reading: Dauviller 1933, Noonan 1973, Brundage 1987: ch. 6. On the identity of Gratian, Noonan 1997. On canon law generally, Owen 1990, Brundage 1995. On extract i, Elliott 1993.

Text: Latin: E. Friedberg (ed.) (1879), *Corpus Iuris Canonici*, Leipzig. English: extract i from Dyan Elliott (1993) *Spiritual Marriage: Sexual Abstinence in Medieval Wedlock*, Princeton: Princeton University Press, p. 178; extract ii is my translation.

(I)

The Blessed Mary proposed that she would preserve a vow of virginity in her heart, but she did not express that vow of virginity with her mouth. She subjected herself to divine disposition when she proposed that she would preserve virginity, unless God revealed to her otherwise. Therefore, committing her virginity to divine disposition, she consented to carnal union, not by seeking it, but by obeying divine inspiration in both the one case and the other. But it was after she bore a son that she expressed with her lips what she had conceived with her heart, together with her husband, and each remained in virginity.

(II)

[Gratian is discussing the difference between engagement (*sponsalia*) and marriage.]
It is apparent, therefore, that she was not a wife, since she is not denied permission to marry someone else by the mere fact of her betrothed being alive. How therefore are engaged people referred to as spouses by Ambrose and the other Fathers, and from all of these arguments they are not to be regarded as spouses? Because it must be understood that betrothal begins marriage, sexual union completes it. Therefore between a betrothed man and a betrothed woman there is marriage, but begun; between those who have had intercourse, marriage is established.

11 Peter Lombard, *Sentences*

Peter Lombard's *Sentences* is a theological work rather than a canon law text like Gratian's or the *Decretals* of Gregory IX, but it exercises a considerable influence on the history of the canon law of marriage. Peter Lombard (*c.*1095–1160), later bishop of Paris, differs from Gratian's view of the formation of the marriage bond in insisting that it is consent alone that makes a marriage, as seen in this extract. Where Gratian had reserved a role for intercourse in the creation of a marriage, here sex has no formative role to play. In Peter Lombard's formulation here, it is outward actions not inward intentions that are of importance in judging whether or not a marital union has been formed: so, if someone agrees to be married, without being forced, then they are married whether they like it or not. This becomes the dominant view in the later medieval canon law of marriage.

Further reading: Brundage 1987: ch. 7.

Text: Latin: Peter Lombard (1971–1981) *Sententiae in IV Libris Distinctae*, ed. Pontificale Collegium S. Bonaventurae Ad Claras Aquas, Rome: Grottaferrata. English: my translation.

CONCERNING CONSENT WHICH MAKES MARRIAGE

But the efficient cause of marriage[16] is consent, not any consent, but expressed in words; not concerning the future, but in the present tense. For if by consent in the future tense, saying: I will accept you as my husband, and I you as my wife, this consent does not effect marriage. Likewise, if they consent mentally, and they do not express consent through words or other clear signs, neither does such consent effect marriage. But if it is expressed in words, which nonetheless are not heartfelt, provided there is no duress or deceit present, that pledge of words through which they consent, saying: 'I accept you as my husband and I you as my wife', makes marriage.

12 *Decretals* of Gregory IX

The *Decretals* (1234) also known as the *Liber Extra*, a collection of judgements assembled and promulgated by Pope Gregory IX (1155–1241) are the second part of the medieval canon law. They include the marriage judgements of Pope Alexander III (*c.*1105–1181), a professor of canon law at Bologna before he became pope, which give the definitive canonical judgement on how the marriage bond is formed. Brundage (1987: 334) describes the decretal 'Veniens ad nos' (1170s) as the clearest expression of Alexander's mature marriage theory, and that is the decretal given here. It is a complicated case, in which a man has made two pledges of marriage to different women. Alexander's decision holds that the first pledge (made in the future tense) is a marriage if there was subsequent intercourse. If so, then the second pledge of marriage, in the present tense, does not count. But if that first pledge is not followed by intercourse, then the second pledge of marriage, in the present tense, is valid and binding.

Further reading: Dauviller 1933, Noonan 1973, Brundage 1987.

Text: Latin: E. Friedberg (ed.) (1879), *Corpus Iuris Canonici*, Leipzig. English: my translation.

Coming to us, G. the bringer of the present case, revealed to us by his account, that in his house he received a certain woman, from whom he had offspring, and to whom in the presence of many he gave his faith, that he would take her as his wife. But meanwhile, he spent

16 i.e. what actually creates a marriage.

the night at the house of his neighbour, whose daughter slept with him that night. The father of the girl, coming across them together in one bed, forced the man to betroth himself to her through words of present consent. Having recently been brought before us, he has consulted us on which of them he ought rather to stay with. Because truly by no means has it become known to us whether after the manifest pledge of faith he knew the first person, therefore we hand him over to you, to the extent that you inquire diligently into the truth of the matter, and, if you shall have found out that he knew the first person after the manifest pledge of faith, make him remain with her; but if you find that, being in a position to settle into the role of constant husband (and not being forced by fear),[17] he contracted himself to her, make him cling to the second woman as his wife.

13 Thomas Aquinas, *Summa Theologiae*

The *Summa Theologiae* (thirteenth century) of St Thomas Aquinas (1224–1274) is the greatest of the encyclopaedic discussions of theology produced by medieval scholasticism. In the first extract given here, Aquinas is discussing the nature of love, in discussing the question of whether or not angels choose to love: in this discussion he makes a distinction between natural love and rational love. The second extract is Aquinas's definition of 'unnatural vice', a broad categorization of sexual activities that meet with disapproval, which includes masturbation, bestiality and sodomy. The third extract is Aquinas's full discussion of whether or not there was a complete marriage between Christ's parents.

Further reading: on extract i, Morgan 1977. On extract ii, Jordan 1997: ch. 7, and on 'sodomy' generally, Foucault 1981, Johansson and Percy 1996, Frantzen 1998. On extract iii, Elliott 1993.

Text: St Thomas Aquinas (1964–1981) *Summa Theologiae*, ed. T. Gilby and others, London: Blackfriars.

(I)

Reply: In the angels is both a natural love and a love by choice; and the latter takes its origin from the former; for this is the universal rule – what is primary in a being is the starting-point of whatever

17 Noonan (1973: 432) translates this as meaning if the compulsion was by fear such as 'could fall on a steady man'.

else may be found in it; and nature is always primary in this sense. We can see this in ourselves, both as to our thinking and our willing. Our intelligence has by nature an apprehension of certain principles; and from these we reason to conclusions which, for their part, are not the product of mere nature but of a process of discovery or teaching. And the working of the will is similar: it stands in the same relation to an end as the intellect to a first principle, as Aristotle says. Hence by nature it tends to a final end; every man naturally wants happiness. And that natural willing is the cause of every other; we will nothing except for the end's sake. Hence the distinction between natural love and the love that involves choice: the former is of the good which man desires as his end; the latter, deriving from it, is of goods man may desire in view of that end.

But bear in mind a distinction already noted between intellect and will. Knowledge occurs in so far as objects known exist in the knower; but owing to man's low place in the scale of intellectual being, he cannot by nature possess from the start all that he is capable of understanding, but only certain starting points whence he moves on to further knowledge. But in appetition the relation is reversed; by it a subject is orientated to things as these are in themselves. Now things are either good in themselves – desirable for their own sake; or good and desirable in view of something else. Hence it argues no imperfection on the side of the desiring subject if he has a prior and natural desire for something as an end in itself, and then a subsequent desire, expressed in choice, for another thing in view of that end already desired. As knowers, then, the angels have only natural knowledge, not that which comes by reasoning; the intellectual nature being realized to the full in them. As lovers, on the other hand, they act indeed by nature, but also through choice (IX, 189, 191).

(II)

It may happen variously. First, outside intercourse when an orgasm is procured for the sake of venereal pleasure; this belongs to the sin of self-abuse, which some call unchaste softness. Second, by intercourse with a thing of another species, and this is called bestiality. Third, with a person of the same sex, male with male and female with female, to which the Apostle refers,[18] and this is called sodomy. Fourth, if the natural style of intercourse is not observed, as regards

18 Romans 1: 26.

the proper organ or according to other rather beastly and monstrous techniques.

(III) DID A TRUE MARRIAGE EXIST BETWEEN MARY AND JOSEPH?

The second point: 1. It would seem that a true marriage did not exist between Mary and Joseph. Now Jerome explains that Joseph was Mary's guardian rather than her husband. If they were truly married, however, he would have been her husband. They were not then truly married.[19]

2. Again, on the text, 'Jacob was the father of Joseph, the husband of Mary,' Jerome comments, 'When you read "husband" do not read in "marriage" but keep in mind that scripture usually refers to the betrothed as husband and wife.' A true marriage, however, takes place at the wedding not at the betrothal. So then Mary and Joseph were not truly married.

3. Moreover, the Gospel says, 'Her husband Joseph, being a just man and not wanting to lead her away (i.e. to his house to live with her) was minded to put her away privately.' Remigius says he did this 'to postpone the wedding.' It would seem then that since the wedding had not taken place they were not truly married. This would be confirmed by the fact that it was not lawful to divorce anyone, even informally, after the contract of marriage had been made.

On the other hand, Augustine asserts, 'We cannot admit the Evangelist thought that Joseph should break off his union with Mary (the Gospel does state that Joseph was the husband of Mary) to show that Christ would be born of a virgin who was not married. Rather it tells us that even if after marriage they remained virginal by mutual consent they were still, and can be truly called, married.'

Reply: A marriage or nuptial is called true when it is complete. There are, however, two kinds of completion, the first and the second. The first kind is through the form which gives the specific character. The second is through the operation by which, in some way, the thing achieves its purpose. The form of matrimony then is an inseparable union of souls in which husband and wife are pledged in an unbreakable bond of mutual faith,[20] and the purpose is the birth and

19 Aquinas refutes these interpretations at the end of his argument.

20 The English text has 'love' but the Latin is *fidem*, 'faith'.

training of children. Obviously the birth of children is started through sexual intercourse, but their training is carried through by other functions of the husband and the wife as when they help each other to bring up the children.

We must say, then, in regard to the first kind of completion, that the marriage of the Virgin mother of God and Joseph was absolutely true. Both consented to the marital bond but not expressly to sexual union except under the condition that it was pleasing to God.[21] That is why the angel calls Mary the wife of Joseph, saying to him, 'Do not be afraid to take Mary home as your wife.' Augustine comments, 'She is called a wife by reason of the first promise of her fidelity. But he did not know her nor ever was to know her by sexual intercourse.'

In regard to the second kind of completion achieved through marital operation, if it refers to sexual intercourse and what that does for the begetting of children, then their marriage was not consummated. Ambrose comments on Luke, 'Don't be put out by scripture calling Mary a wife. Her marriage is asserted not to imply loss of virginity, but to witness the reality of the union.'

Their marriage did enjoy the other kind of completion, regarding the training of children. Augustine notes, 'Each marital good is found in the marriage of Christ's parents; the child, fidelity and the sacrament.[22] The child is the Lord Jesus, as we know; there was no adultery to destroy fidelity; or divorce to destroy the sacrament. The only element missing was sexual intercourse.'

1. Jerome uses the word 'husband' in reference to the sexual consummation of marriage.
2. By 'marriage' Jerome means sexual intercourse.
3. Chrysostom writes that the betrothal of Mary to Joseph meant that she lived with him in his house. 'If she who conceives in her husband's house is thought to have conceived by him, so she who conceives elsewhere is suspect.' Thus sufficient precaution would not have been taken to keep the name of Mary fair if she had not had the entry of her husband's house. So then the phrase 'not wanting to lead her away' is better understood as 'not wishing to expose her to reproach' than as 'bringing her to his home.' For this reason the text goes on to say that 'he was minded to put her away privately.'

21 Cf. Gratian's argument above, extract 10.i, on the same issue. Aquinas's position here is indebted to Peter Lombard.

22 The English text translates *sacramentum* as 'sacred element' so as to distinguish Augustine's meaning from the later meaning of the word 'sacrament'.

Still, even though by reason of her first promises Mary had entry to his house, the solemnizing of the wedding had not taken place. So then the marriage had not yet been consummated. Chrysostom says, 'The Evangelist does not say, "before she was led to her husband's house" since she already was in the house. It was an ancient custom for a betrothed girl to have frequent entry to her man's home.' The angel thus adds, 'Do not be afraid to take Mary home as your wife', i.e. to solemnize the wedding.

Another opinion is that she did not have entry to the house but was simply betrothed to him without privileges. The first opinion seems to be more in line with the Gospel account.

14 The Fourth Lateran Council

These are three canons dealing with marriage from the Fourth Lateran Council (1215). The most important are canon 50, which reduces the extent of the Church's incest prohibitions, and canon 51, which attempts to prohibit clandestine marriage, a recurrent problem through the later medieval period. The influence of the Lateran canons can be seen in the way that it is echoed by the local English statutes that follow them (extract 15): Sheehan (1996: 123) remarks on the flurry of legislative activity in the Western Church in the fifty years after the Fourth Lateran Council. These are the last major modifications of the Church's marital theory during the Middle Ages.

Text: Harry Rothwell (ed.) (1975) *English Historical Documents, 1189–1327*, London: Eyre and Spottiswoode.

50 ON THE RESTRICTION OF PROHIBITIONS TO MATRIMONY

It should not be judged reprehensible if man's decrees are varied at some time or other in accordance with changing circumstances, especially when urgent necessity or evident advantage requires it, since God himself, of the things he decreed in the Old Testament, has changed some in the New. Since therefore the prohibitions about contracting marriage in the second and third degree of affinity and about uniting the offspring of a second marriage with the kindred of the first husband, frequently lead to difficulty and sometimes endanger souls, we, inasmuch as when the prohibition ceases the effect ceases, revoke with the approval of the holy council decrees published on this subject and by this present constitution decree that contracting parties connected in these ways may in future be freely united. Also the prohibition of marriage shall not in future exceed the fourth degree of consanguinity and of affinity, since in grades beyond that such prohibition cannot now be generally complied with without grave harm. The number four agrees well with the bodily marriage – of which the Apostle says, 'The husband hath not power of his own body, but the wife, neither has the wife power over her own body, but the husband' (1 Cor. 7: 4) – because there are four humours in the body, which is composed of the four elements. As the prohibition of marriage is now restricted to the fourth degree, it is our will that it should be unqualified, notwithstanding decrees published before on this subject whether by others or by us, so that if any presume to be united contrary to this prohibition they shall not be protected by length of time, since lapse of time does not diminish a sin but increases it, and the graver offences are, the longer they keep the unfortunate soul in bondage.[23]

23 Consanguinity is relationship by blood, affinity is relationship by marriage. Goody (1983: 136–137) argues that from the eleventh century onwards, the method used for calculating degrees of kinship was the Germanic, rather than the Roman. In the Germanic system, each degree was equated with a generation, so brother and sister are related in the first degree, uncle and niece in the second. If marriage was prohibited within seven degrees of consanguinity according to the Germanic system, then no two people sharing an ancestor in the previous seven generations were permitted to marry. Hence the reduction in the number of grades in 4 Lateran 50 – now only those who have a great-grandparent in common are forbidden to marry. Pollock and Maitland (1898: II, 405) explain the relaxation of the rules of affinity as follows:

> All my wife's or my mistress's blood kinswomen are connected with me by way of affinity. I am related to her sister in the first degree, to her first cousin in the second, to her second cousin in the third, and the doctrine of the twelfth century is that I may not marry in the seventh degree of this affinity. This is affinity of the first genus. But if I and my wife are really one, it follows that I must be related by way of affinity to the wives of her kinsmen. This is the second genus of affinity. To the wife of my wife's brother I am related in the first degree of this second genus of affinity; to the wife of my wife's first cousin the second degree of this second genus, and so forth. But we can not stop here; for we can apply the axiom over and over again. . . . The council of 1215, which confined the impediment of consanguinity within the first four degrees, put the same boundary to the impediment of affinity of the first genus, while it decreed that affinity of the second or third genus might for the future be disregarded.

51 ON THE PUNISHMENT OF THOSE WHO CONTRACT CLANDESTINE MARRIAGES[24]

As the prohibition against marriage in the three remotest degrees is repealed, we wish it to be strictly observed in the others. Hence, following in the footsteps of our predecessors, we absolutely prohibit clandestine marriages, forbidding also any priest to presume to be present at such. For which reason we extend the particular custom of certain countries to countries generally, decreeing that when marriages are to be contracted they shall be published in the churches by the priests, a suitable time being fixed beforehand within which whoever wants and is able may adduce a lawful impediment. Those priests shall nevertheless find out whether any impediment exists. When it seems probable that there is an impediment to contracting the union, the contract shall be expressly forbidden until it is clear from documents produced what ought to be done about it. If any presume to enter into such clandestine marriages, or forbidden marriages in a prohibited degree, even in ignorance, the issue begotten of such union shall be reckoned truly illegitimate with no help to be had from the ignorance of their parents, since they by contracting such unions could be considered as not devoid of knowledge, or at least as affecting ignorance. Likewise the offspring shall be reckoned illegitimate if both parents, knowing of a lawful impediment, presume to contract a marriage in the presence of the church, contrary to every prohibition. Certainly a parish priest who does not trouble to forbid such unions, or any regular also, whatever his order, who ventures to be present at them, shall be suspended from office for three years and more severely

24 What is 'clandestine marriage'? English statutes (extract 15) seem to deal with four potential types: (1) The exchange of consent between two parties outside of any ceremonial setting, possibly with few or no witnesses. (2) The contracting of marriage without a public announcement beforehand (the reading of the banns). (3) The celebration of marriage ceremonies in secret circumstances or locations. (4) The celebration of marriage ceremonies where the persons to be married are unknown.

The Lateran canons here specifically include this second type as clandestine marriages. The problem with clandestine unions is that they can cause problems with multiple marriages, or with persons who should not be married because of an impediment. The impediments to marriage in Gratian are that believers could not marry non-believers, those publicly vowed to celibacy could not marry at all, children under seven were unable to contract, and those related within seven degrees by blood, affinity, or baptism could not contract. This last category is modified by 4 Lateran 50, above. For further impediments, see 1 Salisbury 86 (extract 15).

punished if the offence demands it. And for those too who presume to be united in such fashion, even in a permitted degree, an adequate penance shall be enjoined. If however anyone, to impede a legitimate union, alleges out of wickedness an impediment, he shall not escape ecclesiastical punishment.

52 ON REJECTING EVIDENCE FROM HEARSAY IN A MATRIMONIAL SUIT

Although contrary to normal practice, it was at one time out of a certain necessity decided that in reckoning degrees of consanguinity and affinity hearsay evidence should be valid, seeing that owing to the short life of man witnesses cannot testify from personal knowledge in a reckoning as far as the seventh degree, nevertheless, because from numerous instances and definite proofs we have learnt that many dangers for lawful unions have arisen from this, we decree that in this matter witnesses from hearsay are not to be admitted in the future (since the prohibition does not now go beyond the fourth degree) unless there exist persons of weight who are trustworthy and who testified before the cause was begun to things they learnt from their elders: not merely from one of them, since he alone if he were alive would not suffice, but from at least two, and they are not of bad repute and suspect, but trustworthy and quite unexceptionable, since it would appear rather absurd to admit those whose actions would be rejected; nor if one got from a number what he testifies to, or if a number with bad reputations got what they testify to from men with good, should he be admitted as if he were more than one, or they as if they were suitable witnesses, since, according to normal legal practice, the assertion of a single witness is not sufficient, even if he were resplendent with authority, and legal actions are forbidden to those of bad repute. Such witnesses shall declare on oath that in bearing witness in the cause they do not act from hate or fear or love or for advantage; they shall indicate the persons by their exact names or by gesture or by sufficient description; shall distinguish by clear reckoning every degree of relationship on either side; and, finally, shall include in their oath the statement that what they depose in evidence they got from their forefathers and they believe it to be correct. Still, they shall not be sufficient unless they declare on oath that to their knowledge the persons belonging to at least one of the aforesaid degrees regard each other as blood-relations. For it is preferable to allow some unions that are contrary to the laws of man than to contravene the law of God by parting those lawfully joined.

15 English Ecclesiastical Statutes

Michael M. Sheehan (1996: 123) comments on these thirteenth- and fourteenth-century local English statutes that:

> it is well known that the fifty years after the publication of the Lateran constitutions were a time of unusual synodal activity throughout the Western Church; England was one of the leaders in this effort at reform. Many of the English synods saw the promulgation of sets of regulations that implemented general church law with the detail that was only possible on the local level and that, to a considerable extent, instructed the parish clergy on the theology that lay behind the rules which they were expected to enforce. These synodal regulations and other collections published directly by the bishops were to provide one of the major means by which important developments in the understanding and practice of marriage were implemented during the thirteenth century.

If the statutes implement canon law on a detailed, local scale, they also narrow the focus of the larger canonical collections. To quote R. H. Helmholz, 'much of the scope of the jurisdiction exercised by the English Church was based immediately upon local custom and synodal legislation. In fact, this appears to have been true in many parts of Western Europe. The ecclesiastical courts did not always enforce all the law found in the *Corpus Iuris Canonici*' (Helmholz 1987a: ix). These statutes are a guide to everyday marital and sexual practice only in a negative sense. As David Aers comments in another context, repetition and elaboration of regulations implies resistance rather than domination (Aers 1988: 8). These are regulations that are intervening in marriage practices, rather than recording them, and they need to be read as such, and perhaps contrasted with the evidence from actual cases, as in extracts 17, 18 and 19 below.

Further reading: Cheney 1935, Helmholz 1974, 1987a, Sheehan 1974, 1978a, 1996.

Texts: extracts 1–7, Latin text: F. M. Powicke and C. R. Cheney (eds) (1964) *Councils and Synods with Other Documents Relating to the*

English Church, AD 1205–1313, London: Oxford University Press. English: my translation. Extract 8, Latin text: David Wilkins (ed.) (1737) *Concilia Magnae Brittaniae et Hiberniae*, London. English: my translation.

(I) FIRST STATUTES OF SALISBURY (BETWEEN 1217 AND 1219)[25]

9 (Concerning the penance of priests' concubines)

The concubines of priests should be frequently warned by archdeacons and especially by the priests in whose parishes they stay that they should contract or that they should enter a cloister, or on the grounds that they have sinned publicly, they should perform public penance. But a person who in contravention of this salutary warning through the pretext of money or friendship has been found to be negligent will suffer the penalty mentioned above. But if they can be led to none of these through warning, when they have been banned first from the kiss of peace and the bread blessed in church, if they should persevere in obstinacy, they and those who communicate with them are excommunicated, to be handed over to secular justice if they have not recovered their senses in this case.

35 A warning concerning legitimate marriage

The laity should often be inculcated through confessions and sermons, and through the more important rites, that all intercourse between man and woman, if not excused through marriage, is a mortal sin. And if a priest has been negligent in expounding this healthy doctrine, he should be punished in accordance with canon law like a fornicator or one conspiring with fornicators.

79 Concerning prohibited marriage

Priests are to warn and forbid anyone to marry a woman whom he defiled through adultery while her husband was alive; and likewise if an adulterer has promised the adulteress that he would marry her while her husband was still alive, and also if the adulteress herself or the adulterer plotted the death of the husband.

25 On the importance of 1 Salisbury and the influence of the statutes, see Sheehan (1978a).

82 Concerning the commendation of marriage

Priests should try to commend marriage as vigorously and in as many ways as is possible through the dignity and goods of marriage itself, by making fornicators' embraces repulsive by contrast, confidently asserting that marriage was first among the sacraments in origin and was instituted first by the Lord himself in Paradise. And since the goods of marriage are security, offspring, and the sacrament, security of the bed, offspring for the worship of God, and the sacrament of Christ and his Church,[26] it appears that in this life the most desirable, good and privileged thing is marriage. For only children born of a legitimate marriage are not excluded from ecclesiastical and civil honours, when children born in any other situation are rejected as if they were bastards.

83 Concerning the reverence of marriage

On account of this we command that marriages are to be celebrated with honour and reverence, not with laughter and ribaldry, not in taverns, with public drinking and eating together. Nor should anyone bind women's hands with a noose made of reed or any other material, be it cheap or expensive, so as to fornicate with them more freely, for fear that while he considers himself to be joking, he binds himself with the rites of marriage. Nor should a promise be given to anyone from now on if not in the presence of a priest and three or four persons of good faith who have been called together for this purpose. (But if it has happened differently, a promise is not deemed to have been made to any woman, even if copulation has occurred.)[27] Nevertheless, since people entering into unions in this way trouble the church of God not a little and inflict dangers on souls, we have decided that such people should be handed over to us, and we will hand them on to the Holy See, as disturbers of the ecclesiastical peace and despisers of ecclesiastical orders. And we order this statute to be read out to the people every Sunday.

84 Concerning the (correct) form of contracting a marriage

Similarly we command that priests should teach the persons contracting a marriage this form of words in French or English: I N.

26 Cf. St Augustine, extract 2.iv.

27 Cancelled sentence in one manuscript.

accept you as mine. And similarly the woman must say: I N. accept you as mine.[28] For in these words great force exists and marriage is brought about. A priest should not presume to join any persons matrimonially without making an announcement three times, publicly and solemnly in the church; for making these announcements no fee should be demanded. And if either of the persons to be married is entirely unknown, in no way ought the priest to be responsible for the authorization of such a marriage unless it was legally proved beforehand that they were legitimate persons for the purpose of being married. Similarly, if one of them was unknown, he must have a letter of testimony that he can legally get married, and that a threefold announcement has been made in his parish.

85 Concerning clandestine marriages[29]

We similarly prohibit clandestine marriages, ordering that they shall be made in public in front of the church, in the presence of a priest who has been called for this purpose. If it has actually been done otherwise, it is not to be approved, except by our special authority. A priest who has refused to prevent unions of such a kind or who has presumed to be present at such, or any other person subject to a rule, according to the statutes of the council is suspended from office for three years, and must be more harshly punished if the size of the fault demands it. But a suitable penance must be demanded of those who have presumed to couple in this manner, even in the permitted grades.

86 That sorcery or wickedness are not made in relation to marriage

In relation to marriage is always to be forbidden the practice of sorcery and witchcraft, under threat of excommunication, and under such a penalty are to be included all those who conceal impediments to matrimony: vows, orders, consanguinity, affinity, disparity of cult, sponsorship. And this excludes only four sorts of people from marriage: godfathers, godmothers, godchildren, and spiritual brothers and sisters, that is to say, the sons and daughters of godparents. And that prohibition should be read aloud frequently in each parish.

28 The point here seems to be not that this exact form of words should be used, but that the words should be in the present tense, as here. For actual marriage vows, see extract 16.

29 On the question of what constitutes a clandestine marriage, see notes to extract 14, and also subsequent statutes below.

91 *(Concerning the appropriate end of marriage)*

Similarly, when marriages are contracted in churches, they are to be declared publicly by priests, with an appropriate time limit fixed, so that within this limit, whoever wishes and is able may oppose a lawful impediment, and the priests nevertheless investigate whether any impediment stands in the way. But when a likely objection is raised against the contracting of the union, the marriage must be expressly forbidden until it is established by documentary proofs what is to be done about it. But offspring who have been conceived in the forbidden degree, even unknowingly, are to be considered utterly illegitimate, and they will not earn a reprieve by arguing that their parents did not know what they were doing, in that by contracting such a union they seemed not to lack knowledge but to be professing ignorance. In the same way offspring are regarded as illegitimate if both parents while knowing of a legitimate impediment contrary to every interdict have still presumed to contract in the sight of the church. But if someone raises a malicious impediment to hinder a legitimate union, he will not escape the revenge of the church.

(II) FIRST STATUTES OF WINCHESTER (1224)

54. That laypersons who keep their mistresses or concubines publicly should be compelled by their priest to betroth or give a pledge to each other in the presence of several people, under this condition that if after this they shall be carnally joined that they will consider themselves just as married persons in perpetuity.[30]

58. If anyone has intimacy with a woman and this should become public, his priest should commit him under threat of excommunication to one of the following courses of action: namely that in the presence of four or five witnesses, the same woman being present, he should give his pledge that he will always *have* her as a wife if he should henceforth know her carnally, and the woman should likewise on her

30 This practice of forcing recidivist fornicators to marry is called abjuration *sub pena nubendi* – i.e. the persons concerned are required to part or are forced to marry. See Sheehan 1974, Helmholz 1987b, subsequent statutes on the same subject, and also the Middle English poem *In the Ecclesiastical Court* (extract 66). The Second Statutes of Exeter (extract 15.vi below) contain a gloss in one manuscript objecting to the practice.

part truly promise this in public; but if it is not possible to induce them to this, through a pledge and persons giving security they should promise a financial penalty according to their means if henceforth they should meet in the same house. And if they are found in one house, and this can be proved by evidence of the deed or through legitimate witnesses, the penalty is to be immediately demanded. But secret fornicators are to be punished with secret correction. When, in truth, fornication has become clear through offspring or other means, and was not habitual, with respect to the aforementioned the fornicators should not be compelled but only warned, and the woman's safety is to be ensured in other ways as has seemed appropriate.

59. We strictly forbid that there should be any settlement in a dispute which has arisen between a man and a woman about a contract of matrimony or betrothal, unless it takes the form of the man having the woman as his wife as long as it is agreed that they are persons legally allowed to marry; seeing that if separation of such a kind has to happen, it is proper that it should be made through judgment and not through settlement. Moreover, when a question has arisen about impediments to marriage, no settlement is to be fully implemented but it must be superseded by judgment.

(III) STATUTES OF COVENTRY. TRACT ON CONFESSION AND PENANCE (BETWEEN 1224 AND 1237)

And likewise concerning married persons there must be an enquiry concerning sins of the flesh which they committed before marriage, and it must be ascertained whether they use their own wives in accordance with the natural debt, otherwise they sin in marriage. About the hazards of the flesh inquest should be made briefly in this way: either you knew that the woman whom you approached was unattached, or you did not know. If you knew, a lesser penalty is to be imposed; if you did not know, then a greater penance is to be imposed; because she could have happened to be a married woman, a nun, a relation by marriage, a relative of your parents. Likewise, prostitutes have the habit of submitting themselves to lepers, and as a result there could be a risk in giving birth and in their own body.[31] Similarly, if with widows, who are ecclesiastical persons, if with

31 Medieval medicine fails to distinguish between leprosy and venereal disease (see Jacquart and Thomasset 1988: 183ff).

virgins, if with married women, if with nuns, and thereupon it is to be enquired if it was a blessed nun, and such persons are to be sent to the bishop, because the bishop is accustomed to excommunicate such persons. If by any chance they refuse to go to the bishop, the priest should go to the bishop and have his authorization. Similarly, if with those related by consanguinity or affinity, it is to be inquired in what grade, remotely or closely. If in pregnancy or during menstruation, where there is danger on account of offspring, because corrupted offspring arise from corrupted semen.[32] Similarly if with a woman near childbirth, because thus there is danger; for it is possible to kill the child. Likewise if with men. If with beasts of burden. And there is this penalty imposed upon those who have sex with beasts of burden, besides others that are bound to be imposed, which is never to eat of that flesh. And, to conclude briefly, whatever way semen is emitted except while asleep or with one's own wife, and this should happen lawfully in accordance with the natural debt, is a mortal sin, and in accordance with diverse circumstances, diverse penalties are to be imposed. It is not proper to ask all these questions of all persons, but in accordance with what God has inspired the priest ought to make an enquiry. But there is one general rule: people who condone mortal sins, whatever they are, sin mortally, although not as heavily at any time as while acting thus. But if he asks to be reinstated, the person taking part in the sin ought to be restored, and consenters to fornication, whether male or female, ought to be punished as if in revenge for a mortal sin.

(IV) THIRD STATUTES OF WORCESTER (1240)

22 Concerning marriage and betrothal

Because truly to the sons of Adam, cleansed from sin, baptized in the water, strengthened by the Holy Spirit in confirmation, and sustained by the holy eucharist, the law of fatal lust applies without which there is to be no sexual union, because of this evil principle of generation which was certainly totally corrupt, marriage was

32 On the corruption of offspring due to intercourse during menstruation, see Jacquart and Thomasset (1988: 183ff) and the comments in Pseudo-Albertus Magnus below (extract 78).

allowed as a remedy, which had originally been instituted as a duty.[33] But, this sacrament, which signifies the sacrament which is between Christ and his Church, is certainly worthy of all veneration and must be celebrated by the faithful, after all precautionary measures have been taken, especially since execrable lawsuits arise as a result of error on the part of those contracting the marriage and those assisting them, because of which along with the statutes of the council we command that there shall be no marriage unless a solemn announcement has been made three times previously in church. And priests who presume to violate this statute are to know that they must be suspended from office for three years. But we do not only think this concerning marriages which have been solemnly celebrated, but also concerning those which happen by other means, provided that there was still a contract of marriage by present consent.

(V) STATUTES OF WELLS (1258?)

13 Rubric. Concerning the form of oaths

But oaths that are made for fornication we forbid altogether under financial penalties; but transgressors, having made an oath, bind themselves, but if they happen to admit in court or are convicted of having a relapse afterwards, they must be exposed to corporal punishment in accordance with the condition of their persons and the type of crime they have committed, without contradiction in any way they will undergo it. But if they have incurred that penalty and have been convicted of a third lapse of this type or they have acknowledged their guilt, then the man and the woman by taking an oath contract a marriage under this formula: I accept you as mine from now, if I know you carnally from now on, and: I accept you as mine, if from now on I have carnal knowledge of you. And so that there can be a more definite procedure in cases of this kind, we order what has been done to be recorded faithfully in writing; we order that this formula of marriage, without having any conditions attached, be observed in actual contracts.

33 This is a reference to the dual institution of marriage – first by God in Paradise, but later as a remedy for lust after the Fall.

(VI) SECOND STATUTES OF EXETER (1287)

7 *Concerning marriage*

The vice of desire of the flesh, having been contracted from the disobedience of our first parents, thus passed on towards posterity so that, although man is renewed by the grace of baptism, reinforced by the strength of confirmation, and restored through the sacred meal, nevertheless he is not restored to former innocence in all respects; on the contrary the tinder of former desire while still remaining does not cease to disturb the person himself, through which he is buffeted by the incitement of Satan, constantly struggling through this as through other ways of doing harm to lead man towards destruction. Nevertheless, if man shall have been rightly restored on account of victory in this kind of struggle, he will achieve a greater reward. Therefore, for avoiding the evil of this kind of desire, the sacrament of marriage was granted to man by the apostle after sin, which was instituted as a duty by God in Paradise and before sin.

[. . .]

In respect of the oaths of fornicators, we order this form to be used from now on, that transgressors are bound together, having given an oath, but if they happen to suffer a relapse afterwards they will undergo corporal punishment without any contradiction, which will be imposed on them by the decision of their own judge; if afterwards they incur this and concerning this are convicted or have confessed, then the transgressors without an oath being exacted, are to to contract in this way: I accept you as mine from now on if henceforth I know you carnally, and, I you as mine if from now on I am known carnally by you. Certainly we order this form of contract to be committed to writing, that the truth should be proved through it in dubious claims. [One manuscript has a gloss as follows: Note that this regulation is against the law and the just claim of nature, because by law marriage and betrothal should be free, as having been noted from (quotation unclear).]

(VII) SECOND STATUTES OF DURHAM (BETWEEN 1241 AND 1249)

Likewise, a man or a woman passing into bigamy should not be blessed by a priest, because, since they have been blessed on another occasion, it is not fitting for their blessing to be repeated.[34]

34 'Bigamy' here refers to the remarriage of widows or widowers.

(VIII) THE COUNCIL OF LONDON (1342)

11 Concerning those who celebrate clandestine marriages in churches, oratories, or chapels

Human desire, always inclined towards evil, frequently desires more ardently what is forbidden than what is allowed: whence different people, who on account of consanguinity, or affinity, or another impediment are unable to contract mutually by law a legal marriage, oftentimes desire it *de facto*, that under the veil of a concealed marriage they are able more freely to perform the destructive and illicit work of the flesh; such people, knowing that their impediments will be known in the parishes in which they live, because on account of such notorious impediments or a strong rumour of an impediment they cannot find parish priests ready to solemnize marriage between such persons, such people move temporarily to a remote place, and especially to cities and well populated towns in which they do not have an advance reputation; and to that place at some time, without banns having been given publicly, at inappropriate times and on inappropriate dates, several times in churches, sometimes in chapels or oratories, they manage *de facto* to solemnize marriage between them; and lingering in the same place, or afterwards returning to their own place, and cohabiting like married persons because the ordinaries of those places and the rest of the population, on account of fear of ill treatment and expense, do not desire or would not dare to challenge them concerning their illicit connection, or, by denouncing them, publicize their crimes – they remain mutually joined illicitly, to the ruin of their souls. Therefore desiring to eradicate this very common vice, we order through the authority of the present council, that from now on those contracting matrimony, and having it solemnized between them, knowing such impediments, or having plausible suspicion of the same, and priests solemnizing such forbidden marriages, or even knowingly contracting legal marriages between persons other than their own parishioners, without having obtained a licence concerning this from their diocesans, or their curates, also clandestine marriages in churches, oratories or chapels being solemnized henceforward through force or fear, and those being present at the solemnization of marriages of this kind, conscious of what has already been mentioned, are to incur the penalty of greater excommunication as a result of their action; and four times in each year generally those to be excommunicated are to be publicly denounced; and they are not to be protected by law from other penalties directed against those celebrating marriage without publication of the banns having been given, or by means of other clandestine statutes.

Indeed, because, the constitution of Simon of fond memory, formerly archbishop of Canterbury, our immediate predecessor, which begins 'Likewise, from contracts',[35] etc., near the surface of his words, in the opinion of many, in his without doubt or obscurity, desiring to render this very constitution unambiguous for the future, we declare that thus it will have to be understood, through the approval of this council, that whatever priest, secular or regular, who dares to participate in the solemnization of marriage outside his parish, his church, or chapel having to itself suitable parochial rights of old, must undergo the penalty incurred by his deed.

35 Simon Mepham's constitutions of 1328.

CANON LAW AND ACTUAL PRACTICE

16 Late Medieval Marriage Vows

Note the difference between the vows for each partner: in addition to the form of the husband's vow, the wife vows to be 'cheerful and obedient in bed and at board'.

Text: *Manuale et Processionale ad Usum Insignis Ecclesiae Eboracensis* (1875) Surtees Society, vol. 63, London: Quaritch. With modernized spelling and some words translated.

[THE HUSBAND'S PLEDGE]

I N. take thee N. to my wedded wife, to have and to hold from this day forward, for better, for worse, for richer, for poorer, in sickness, and in health, till death do us part, if holy church will ordain it: And thereto I pledge thee my faith.

[THE WIFE'S PLEDGE]

I N. take thee N. to my wedded husband, to have and to hold from this day, for better, for worse, for richer, for poorer, in sickness, and in health, to be cheerful and obedient, in bed and at board, till death do us part, if holy church will ordain it: And thereto I pledge thee my faith.

17 An Ecclesiastical Court Case from the Province of Canterbury

These extracts are witness depositions, the only documents surviving in the case of Alice against John the Blacksmith, in which Alice apparently wishes to have the court enforce the promises of marriage that John has made to her but subsequently ignored. Cases to enforce marriage vows are the most common sort of case involving marriage to appear in the ecclesiastical courts of later medieval England (Helmholz 1974: 25). These documents suggest that John has repeatedly agreed to marry Alice, once in a formal Church ceremony, but that difficulties continue. The date of this case (*c.*1200) places this case prior to the large body of English statute legislation (extract 15) emphasizing how marriage should take place. It is later than 'Veniens ad nos' (extract 12), which expresses the position which becomes the Church's basic ruling on marital consent. But it is difficult to judge to what extent the Church's judgement on the formation of the bond has stabilized at this point.

Further reading: Woodcock 1952, Helmholz 1974.

Text: Norma Adams and Charles Donahue Jr (eds) (1981) *Select Cases from the Ecclesiastical Courts of the Province of Canterbury, c.*1200–1301, London: Selden Society.

DEPOSITIONS ON BEHALF OF ALICE

[Endorsed] Attestations of Alice against John, the blacksmith. First production of Alice against John, the blacksmith, for the purpose of proving it (the marriage) notorious.

Roger, a priest, sworn, says that around the feast of the apostles Peter and Paul (29 June) just past, three years ago, a certain friend of his, Ralph, a baker, asked him if he would be present at a certain marriage to be contracted between a certain young man and a certain niece of his, who, as he said, had already been joined, faith having been given before lay people, but for greater security he wished that this be confirmed before a priest. One day the same Ralph brought them before the same priest in his church of Fenchurch with many laymen, and the priest asked who was the young man who was to marry (*ducere*) the niece of the baker. They said John, a blacksmith. And because he knew him before, he exhorted him, and he took as much care as he could, warning him not to take any woman as wife without consulting his friends or at least give his faith under any condition with a fixed penalty attached [. . .].[36] The same John replied that he would put no penalty on it, and he would never

36 Ellipses in the text here indicate small holes in the manuscript.

change his mind nor ever dismiss her for another so long as they lived. And thus, the same priest dictating the words, the same John received Alice, the niece of the said Ralph, as wife, and she him as husband, by words of the present tense, and both gave faith in the hand of the other that they would keep the marriage faithfully. And the same John promised Alice by way of dower one half of all his goods, what he had and what he would get. After this, both of them offered a halfpenny on the altar, and afterwards they lived together for a year, as the same priest heard by the relation of many. Asked on what day these things were done, he says that he does not remember. He says also that John was dressed in a cloak of blue and that Alice was dressed in a cape with sleeves of blue. He says also that these things took place in the church of Fenchurch within the chancel of the same church.

Alice, wife of Alphedge, a baker, sworn, says that she was in the church of Fenchurch where she saw and heard John, the blacksmith, take Alice as his, and the same Alice took him as her husband by words of the present tense, faith being given, and she understood that everything that pertains to a marriage took place, except the solemnity of a mass. Concerning the time, the place, and their clothes, she agrees with Roger. She knows nothing about a named dower, but she says that the same John offered a penny and Alice a halfpenny. She adds also that they had a party the same day.

Agnes, sworn, says that she was not present at this marriage but she heard from many who were present that John, the blacksmith, contracted with Alice by words of the present tense.

Beatrice agrees with Agnes in all respects.

Edith, wife of Henry, sworn, agrees with Roger the priest concerning the contract, the time, the place and what they wore, but she says that he offered a penny and she a halfpenny. She adds also that she knew that John had intercourse with her in the house of R., the baker, after the contract.

Gervase, a servant of Ralph, the baker, says that John, the blacksmith, asked him to come with him to Fenchurch and to see how he pledged faith to Alice, his lady friend, there. And when the same Gervase was setting out for the church with him, he turned back at the command of his lord R., and when the same John and Alice had returned from the church, he heard John calling her his wife, and he saw them many times thereafter together in table and bed.

Aeldrita, the widow of Ralph, the baker, sworn, says that Alice was lodging with her, and came with her to the church of Fenchurch in the first week after the past feast of the apostles Peter and Paul (29 June), three years ago, and she saw and heard that John took Alice as his to have her as a wife for as long as he would live from that hour, Roger, the priest who now ministers in the church of St Botolph, dictating the ritual words. And some people wanted to add a penalty, but John replied that it was not fitting, because he would not, as long as he lived, put her away, for a prettier or for an uglier one, and Alice took John as hers, and both gave faith in the hand of the other that they would faithfully observe the marriage. She says also that John offered on the altar one penny and Alice a halfpenny. She says that this was done in the chancel of the church of Fenchurch before the altar and before dinner. But she does not remember on what day, but, as she believes, it was on a certain Sunday. She says also that John was dressed in a blue cloak and Alice in John's cape of blue cloth. Asked if John afterwards knew her carnally, she says that she often saw John and Alice lying in one bed, and she says that John supported Alice for a long time in his house and returned to her as a wife.

Evelyn, wife of Edmund, a baker, says that she had a room in the house of Ralph, the baker, with whom Alice was then staying, and she was called to the church at Fenchurch where she saw a marriage contracted between John and Alice by words of the present tense, an oath having been taken; she agrees with Roger, the chaplain, about the other circumstances. She adds also that she saw John support Alice in table and in bed, publicly, as his wife, and after Evelyn left the house of Ralph and rented another house John returned to his house for half a year, to the said [. . .] in the marital fashion, so that the bed of John and Alice was near the bed of Evelyn, and she says that she saw them often lying in one bed.

Edmund, sworn, says the same in every respect as Evelyn about the contract made between John and Alice in the church of Fenchurch, and he says that he saw John return to his house and support Alice in his house as his wife for half a year, and he saw them often lying in one bed, as he says.

Albert, a deacon, sworn, says that he was the clerk ministering in the church of Fenchurch, and he saw in the first week after the feast of the apostles Peter and Paul, three years ago, on a feast day, as he believes, John, the blacksmith, take Alice as his by words of the present tense and she him in like manner, and both of them gave faith to faithfully observe the contract. And he says that Roger, the priest, asked if John wished that there be a pecuniary penalty. He said 'no', and that he would not put her away for any other as long as he lived. He adds also that the priest read the gospel, and John and Alice and many others offered their offerings to the priest. Asked about the other circumstances, he says that he does not remember.

DEPOSTIONS (CONTINUED)

Second production of Alice against John concerning the marriage.

Solomon, the dean of Arches, sworn, says that around Christmas Alice made a complaint to him that John, her husband, had repudiated her, and John was then in his jurisdiction. And the same John, cited, came with his friends to the church of Arches with Hugh, his lord, and many other friends of his. Hugh then said that they would not plead because they knew that Alice had made a just complaint. He says that John solemnly took Alice as his by words of the present tense and she him as husband before all who were there, and John swore in the hand of Solomon that from that hour he would support Alice and treat her as his wife, and she swore that she would not compel or trouble him about making that solemnity before the feast of St Michael, if only he treated her as he ought, as he saw and heard. Asked on what day this was done, he says he does not remember but he says that many were present at this contract.

Godman, sworn, says that before Christmas just past, after the feast of St Andrew (30 November), at the request of John, the blacksmith, he came to the church of St Mary at the Arches, and he heard John confess that he was bound to Alice, an oath having been given that he would espouse her, and afterwards he gave faith in the hand of Solomon, the dean, that within the year he would espouse her, or if he could not do it within this term, with the consent of both of them it would be deferred to another certain time, and that in the meantime he would return to her as his, and she swore that if he returned to her, she would not vex him about that espousal within the aforesaid term.

Hugh, a blacksmith, sworn, agrees with Godman in every respect. He adds also that he understood by the confession of John that so much had taken place between John and Alice that he could not take another wife while she lived.

Roger, a blacksmith, sworn, agrees in every respect with Hugh except that he says that if John did not wish or was not able to espouse her within the aforesaid term, he would make amends to Alice as she wished.

18 Two Cases from an Episcopal Visitation of Canterbury Diocese

The first case from this visitation (1292–1294) is interesting because it shows the class discrimination operated by the Church in imposing penance. It is not seen as appropriate for a knight to be whipped around the marketplace and the church as his mistresses are. The second shows the realities of the Church's difficulties in enforcing clerical celibacy.

Further reading: Helmholz 1974.

Text: Harry Rothwell (ed.) (1975) *English Historical Documents, 1189–1327*, London: Eyre & Spottiswoode.

(I)

Thomas de Marynes knight keeps in adultery a certain Elanor de Elmstede daughter of John de Wadesole, and earlier he kept another, Agnes Soppestre by name, whom he still supports, and he ill-treats and has long ill-treated his wife. The knight appeared on Thursday before the lord [commissary] and confesses that he sinned with each and with the said Ellen and he renounced both and suspect places on pain of forty marks to be spent at the will of the lord archbishop of Canterbury if they are incurred and because it is not seemly for a knight to do public penance he is commanded on the orders of the lord [commissary] to pay or cause to be paid twenty marks to poor villeins of the district, to which the said knight agreed.

And on the same day the said Agnes Soppestere appears and on oath confesses that she cohabited with the said knight for nine years or so and given birth twice for him and says that it is a year and more since the man last knew her and renounced the said knight and suspect places and she will be whipped five times through the market-place and five times round the church in a chemise as is customary and because the said Ellen is pregnant . . . herself this time and it is decreed that the said knight and his wife are to appear before the lord [commissary] on the morrow of the next feast of St Luke the

Evangelist and receive for the dissension that has arisen between them what is right and the same knight agreed that he could be forced both to the aforesaid penance if incurred and to payment of the said marks to be paid on that account as aforementioned as touched on above by any ecclesiastical censures whatsoever without any remedy in lay law.

(II)

Aylward vicar of West Hythe kept in his house long ago a certain woman by whom he had ever so many children and who died in his house as if she were his wife, and at length he took a certain Chima Tukkyld a woman whom he keeps openly and he enfeoffed her with a certain house and he often knows her in a hut and on banks to the scandal of the whole [priestly] order. The said vicar confesses in the visitation that he has indeed a bad reputation where Chima Tuckyld is concerned, though he is blameless concerning her as he says. He appears and sworn to speak the truth confesses that at some time or other he had two children by the one who is dead and eight years have elapsed since he last knew her, and a year since she died in his house. He says also on oath that he has no connection with the surviving woman mentioned, and on this he submitted himself to an inquisition to be made on Friday, and the said survivor, Chima, appears, denies on oath the fact and says that the said chaplain never enfeoffed her with any house and submitted herself to inquisition . . . afterwards that Aylward was deprived and the woman renounced her sin and suspect places and was whipped three times though Hythe market-place and three times round the church of West Hythe.

19 A Rural Dean's Court

This is a selection of the sorts of offences concerning sex and marriage that the ecclesiastical courts dealt with in rural localities: for the most part, fornication, adultery, and the mistreatment of spouses.

Text: Harry Rothwell (ed.) (1975) *English Historical Documents, 1189–1327*, London: Eyre & Spottiswoode.

[Chapter held in the church] of Dodderhill on the Friday before the feast of the Ascension in the year 1300 [Friday, 13 May] and there will be another at Salwarp on the Wednesday after the feast of St Barnabas in the aforesaid year [Wednesday, 15 June 1300].

. . . of . . . fornicated with . . . and confesses and is whipped in the usual way. The woman did [penance]. The man is not subject to the jurisdiction [of this court].

Henry son of John fornicated with Lucy de (Wych) Coker. Each appears and confesses and renounces his sin and is whipped in the usual way. They are doing [penance]. They did [penance].

Roger le Gardiner fornicated for the seventh time with Lucy de la Lynde. Each appears and confesses and renounces his sin and is whipped in the usual way. Each withdrew.

Henry le coupere of Birmingham fornicated repeatedly with Isabella daughter of Richard le potter. Each is suspended for contumacy.[37] Each is excommunicated. Each is reconciled and is whipped once for contumacy and confesses and is whipped in the usual way. They did [penance].

John of Hodscote fornicated with Julia daughter of Thomas de Colemor. The man is not found. Purgation six-handed is decreed for the woman.[38] The woman withdrew for four compurgators.[39]

Roger de la Berne fornicated with Christine daughter of Roger clerk. Each is suspended for contumacy. The woman did [penance]. The man withdrew.

Peter de la Holyok fornicated with Isabella Ketel. The man appears and confesses and is whipped in the usual way. The woman is infirm.

(Hanbury) Nicholas Veredarius fornicated for the second time with Evette Pinyng. The woman appears and confesses and renounces her sin and is whipped in the usual way once through the market place. The man confesses and is whipped in the usual way. He did [penance]. The woman withdrew.

Richard Suel fornicated with Margery le Senegar. Purgation six-handed is decreed for the man. The man makes his purgation. The woman is not subject to the jurisdiction.[40]

37 Contempt of court for non-attendance?

38 i.e. she needs to find six people to testify that she is innocent.

39 i.e. four people to testify.

40 Probably because she is not local.

(Bromsgrove) John son of William le Foler fornicated with Matilda le Koubestere. Each is suspended for contumacy. Each is reconciled and confesses and is whipped in the usual way once for contumacy. They withdrew.

Adam Blouerd fornicated with Alice le beggestere. Each is suspended for contumacy. Each is excommunicated. Each is excommunicated *cum communi*. They withdrew.

(Stoke Prior) Richard le coupere committed adultery with Lucy the daughter of Christopher. The woman is suspended. She is not cited. Purgation nine-handed is decreed for the man. The man makes his purgation.[41] The woman is suspended for contumacy. The woman is reconciled. Purgation ten-handed is decreed for the woman . . . William whose surname she does not know and whom she renounces and is whipped in the usual way three times through the market place. The woman is doing [penance]. The woman did [penance].

(St Nicholas's) Richard the servant of John Elliott fornicated with Christine Louchard. Each appears and confesses and is whipped in the usual way. They withdrew.

Thomas Louchard ill-treats his wife and this with the rod. The man appears and confesses and is whipped in the usual way once through the market place. He withdrew.

Thomas Tenor of Criche fornicated with Julia Thorn of Hampton. They renounce [their sin] with each other and are whipped in the usual way. Each withdrew.

John Colines a married man committed adultery with Agnes Smal. The man is suspended for contumacy. The woman appears and confesses and renounces her sin and is whipped in the usual way twice through the market place. They did [penance].

(Elmbridge) Richard Green chaplain committed adultery with Christine Brudeneburi of Bromyard. Purgation nine-handed by compurgators of the same status is decreed for the man. The man withdrew for four compurgators.

(King's Norton) John son of William John fornicated with Isabella daughter of Adam de Lega. Each appears and confesses and is whipped in the usual way. Each withdrew.

41 i.e. he is found innocent, having found enough people to testify to the fact. Lucy does seem to have committed adultery, but with the mysterious William, not Richard?

Richard the servant of Henry de Wrodenhal fornicated repeatedly with Isabella daughter of Sontasse. Purgation six-handed is decreed for each. The man is not cleared by compurgation. The woman makes her purgation.

(Upton) Thomas Colier fornicated with Julia Godmon. Each appears and confesses and is whipped in the usual way. The woman withdrew. The man did {penance}.

Part II

LEGAL SOURCES

INTRODUCTION

Part II is composed of extracts from legal texts issued by secular jurisdictions in England that relate to sexual behaviour or to marriage. For the most part, these texts are not particularly concerned with sex or marriage in themselves. Anglo-Saxon laws are generally concerned with the financial consequences of the making and breaking of marriages, with questions of inheritance, and with sexual offences that have financial penalties attached to them, such as adultery, rape, or intercourse with another's slave. The laws of Canute are an exception, taking a much broader perspective (possibly due to ecclesiastical influence). In the later medieval period, when the Church enjoys exclusive jurisdiction over marriage as a spiritual matter, the king's courts deal only with issues of property, such as dower and inheritance, which are nonetheless of great importance in the making of marriages. As already discussed in the Introduction at the beginning of the book, the financial motivation for marriage evident in the secular law sometimes caused friction with the Church's emphasis upon free consent for all Christians, for the secular power insisted that lords had economic rights (at the very least) in the marriages of noble widows or wards who held land from them (extracts 27 and 31), and in the marriages of their unfree tenants also (extract 34). Whereas the texts in Part I were interested in the regulation of sex and marriage for spiritual and moral reasons, the focus of the texts here is property and money.

The texts divide into two subgroups. The first consists of legal texts from the Anglo-Saxon kingdoms, from Æthelbert of Kent in the seventh century to Canute in the eleventh. The second section contains legal texts from after the eleventh-century Norman conquest of England. Law in later medieval England was a matter of local and private jurisdictions existing alongside the jurisdictions of the king and the Church, and so we have texts here from a number of different types of source. Statute legislation and manuals of the common law discuss law applicable throughout the country in the king's courts. But we also have local customary law from towns where custom had the status of law, and cases from manorial courts where the peasantry were subject to their lord's jurisdiction and had to account for themselves at the lord's courts.

These texts may not be as useful as they appear as evidence for legal practice. Commenting on Anglo-Saxon legal texts, Carole Hough writes that 'modern historians have established that the purpose of much early medieval legislation was not for practical use in a court of law but to enhance the public image of the king' (Hough 1997a: 2). Later medieval legal texts are complicated by the question of multiple jurisdictions. Customary law may contradict and override the common law, as we see in extract 33 on the legal status of married women. But what we also see there is that customary law varies from place to place. Nor is medieval statute law the same as modern. In the early fourteenth century, for instance, judges would allow the king's writ to override a statute (Sayles 1984: xviii). Legal manuals such as Bracton (extract 31) might appear to offer some overall view, but Milsom warns that the preconceptions of Bracton, with his knowledge of Roman and canon law, were not those of the courts of the fourteenth century, which lacked such scope (Milsom 1981: 41–42). Individually, then, these legal texts offer us a very partial view. But taken together, and read alongside other contemporary documents, a broader picture appears.

We do see secular courts take an interest in something outside of the financial side of marriage in the last two extracts. In extract 34, we see cases from manorial courts where fines are extracted for sexual misbehaviour (again, perhaps this is a way to raise income rather than an attempt at moral regulation – effectively a sort of tax). And in extract 35, the case of John/Eleanor Rykener, we see a case where a transvestite prostitute is brought to court in London. But, generally speaking, the secular law is interested for the most part in the close relationship between marriage and property.

ANGLO-SAXON LAW

20 Laws of Æthelbert of Kent

Æthelbert of Kent (d. 616) ruled from 560 to 616, and was the first Anglo-Saxon king to be converted to Christianity. Bede comments on these early seventh-century laws as inspired by Roman example and remaining in force to his own day (Bede 1990: II.5). They are, for the most part, concerned with fixing financial penalties to be paid in the case of various offences (the size of the penalties depending upon the status of the person involved), and with the financial aspects of marriage arrangements.

Further reading: Goody 1983, Lucas 1983, Fell 1984, Clunies Ross 1985, Brundage 1987: ch. 4, Frantzen 1998, Hough 1999, 2001, Saunders 2001: ch. 1. Cf. the Germanic laws in Amt 1993: part 1 section C.

Text: F. L. Attenborough (ed. and trans.) (1922) *The Laws of the Earliest English Kings*, Cambridge: Cambridge University Press.

10. If a man lies with a maiden belonging to the king, he shall pay 50 shillings compensation.[1]
11. If she is a grinding slave, he shall pay 25 shillings compensation. [If she is of the] third [class], [he shall pay] 12 shillings compensation.
14. If a man lies with a nobleman's serving maid, he shall pay 12 shillings compensation.

1 This and the following provisions concern the compensation to be paid to slave-owners by anyone having sex with one of their slaves.

16. If a man lies with a commoner's serving maid, he shall pay 6 shillings compensation; [if he lies] with a slave of the second class, [he shall pay] 50 sceattas [compensation]; if with one of the third class, 30 sceattas.
64. If anyone destroys the generative organ, he shall pay for it with three times the wergeld.[2]
64. 1. If he pierces it right through, he shall pay 6 shillings compensation.
64. 2. If he pierces it partially, he shall pay 6 shillings compensation.
73. If a freeborn woman, carrying the keys, misconducts herself, she shall pay 30 shillings as compensation.[3]
74. Compensation [for injury] to be paid to an unmarried woman, shall be on the same scale as that paid to a freeman.[4]
75. The compensation to be paid for violation of the mund of a widow of the best class, [that is, of a widow] of the nobility, shall be 50 shillings.
75. 1. For violation of the mund of a widow of the second class, 20 shillings; of the third class, 12 shillings; of the fourth class, 6 shillings.
76. If a man takes a widow who does not [of right] belong to him, double the value of the mund shall be paid.[5]

2 Compensation payment, literally the 'man-price'.

3 The text is adapted here to follow the argument of Fell (1984: 60–61) but cf. the argument in Clunies Ross (1985: 10) that this refers to an unmarried noblewoman, a 'freewoman with long hair', rather than 'a freeborn woman, carrying the keys'. In a recent article, Hough (2001: 578) argues that 73 and 74 should read 'If a free woman in a position of responsibility commits any violence, she is to pay 20 shillings compensation' and 'The compensation payable by an unmarried girl is to be the same as that payable by a free woman'.

4 Saunders (2001: 37–38) argues that 74, 75 and 76, and 82 to 84 respectively address crimes of force against women of different status: virgins, widows and slaves.

5 *Mund* means 'protection'. Hough (1999) argues that the consensus of scholarly opinion is that clauses 75 and 76 deal with the abduction of widows, who apparently occupied a subordinate position under the protection or guardianship of members of their kin. She argues that the situation is the reverse of that, and that it was the widows who extended protection to their household (p. 1). Hough translates (1999: 16) as follows:

> 75. The right of protection of a widow of the highest class of the nobility is to be compensated for at 50 shillings. 75.1. That of one of the second class, at 20 shillings; of one of the third class, at 12 shillings; of one of the fourth class, at 6 shillings. 76. If anyone takes a widow who is not his own [legal wife], [the penalty] is twice the value of the right of protection.

77. If a man buys a maiden, the bargain shall stand, if there is no dishonesty.[6]
77. 1. If however there is dishonesty, she shall be taken back to her home, and the money shall be returned to him.
78. If she bears a living child, she shall have half the goods left by her husband, if he dies first.
79. If she wishes to depart with her children, she shall have half the goods.
80. If the husband wishes to keep [the children], she shall have a share of the goods equal to a child's.
81. If she does not bear a child, [her] father's relatives shall have her goods, and the 'morning gift'.[7]
82. If a man forcibly carries off a maiden, [he shall pay] 50 shillings to her owner, and afterwards buy from the owner his consent.
83. If she is betrothed, at a price, to another man, 20 shillings shall be paid as compensation.
84. If she is brought back, 35 shillings shall be paid, and 15 shillings to the king.
85. If a man lies with the woman of a servant, during the lifetime of the husband, he shall pay a twofold compensation.

21 Laws of Ine of Wessex

Ine was king of Wessex from 688 to 726. As Frantzen points out (1998: 141), his laws survive as part of the laws of Alfred (which incorporated several earlier legal collections), but have traditionally been extracted from them and edited as a separate text.

Further reading: Goody 1983, Lucas 1983, Fell 1984, Clunies Ross 1985, Brundage 1987: ch. 4, Frantzen 1998. Cf. the Germanic laws in Amt 1993: part 1, section C.

6 It is difficult to know how literally the word 'buy', *gebigeð*, is to be taken. Hough (1999: 13 and n. 37) argues that the semantic range of Old English *gebigan* is not the same as modern English 'to buy' and so this interpretation may be inappropriate. Cf. extract 24 (admittedly a later text) which prescribes the correct way of betrothing a woman, and which refers to 'remuneration for rearing' – potentially a payment to go to the bride's father. Goody (1983: appendix 2) argues that this might represent a payment to the bride via the father. For the argument that bride purchase existed in early Germanic societies, see Lucas 1983: 62.

7 Fell (1984: 74) points to this clause as evidence that a married woman retains a position in her family of birth: if she is childless, all her property, including the 'morning gift' given by her husband when they marry, reverts to her family of birth.

Text: F. L. Attenborough (ed. and trans.) (1922) *The Laws of the Earliest English Kings*, Cambridge: Cambridge University Press.

27. He who begets an illegitimate child and disowns it shall not have the wergeld at its death, but its lord and the king shall [have it].
31. If anyone buys a wife and the marriage does not take place, he [the bride's guardian] shall return the bridal price and pay [the bridegroom] as much again, and he shall compensate the trustee of the marriage according to the amount he is entitled to for infraction of his surety.
38. If a husband has a child by his wife and the husband dies, the mother shall have her child and rear it, and [every year] 6 shillings shall be given for its maintenance – a cow in summer and an ox in winter; the relatives shall keep the family home until the child reaches maturity.

22 Laws of King Alfred

King Alfred of Wessex (849–899) claims to have utilized several earlier legal codes in the compilation of his laws, including those of Offa of Mercia, Æthelbert of Kent and Ine of Wessex, but contemporary historians have questioned the practical utility of the laws (Hough 1997a: 2). These statutes contain several discussions of the penalties and consequences of rape and abduction, whether of nuns, slaves or freewomen.

Further reading: Goody 1983, Lucas 1983, Fell 1984, Clunies Ross 1985, Brundage 1987: ch. 4, Frantzen 1998, Hough 1997a, 1997b, Saunders 2001: ch. 1. Cf. the Germanic laws in Amt 1993: part 1, section C.

Text: F. L. Attenborough (ed. and trans.) (1922) *The Laws of the Earliest English Kings*, Cambridge: Cambridge University Press.

8. If anyone takes a nun from a nunnery without the permission of the king or bishop, he shall pay 120 shillings, half to the king, and half to the bishop and the lord of the church, under whose charge the nun is.
8. 1. If she lives longer than he who abducted her, she shall inherit nothing of his property.[8]

8 Saunders (2001: 39) notes that this and subsequent clauses imply that the nun may consent to her own abduction.

8. 2. If she bears a child, it shall inherit no more of the property than its mother.
8. 3. If her child is slain, the share of the wergeld due to the mother's kindred shall be paid to the king, but the father's kindred shall be paid the share due to them.
9. If anyone slays a woman with child, while the child is in her womb, he shall pay full wergeld for the woman, and half the wergeld for the child, [which shall be] in accordance with the wergeld of the father's kindred.
[. . .]
10. If anyone lies with the wife of a man whose wergeld is 1200 shillings, he shall pay 120 shillings compensation to the husband; to a husband whose wergeld is 600 shillings, he shall pay 100 shillings compensation; to a commoner he shall pay 40 shillings compensation [for a similar offence].
11. If anyone seizes by the breast a young woman belonging to the commons, he shall pay her 5 shillings compensation.[9]
11. 1. If he throws her down but does not lie with her, he shall pay [her] 10 shillings compensation.
11. 2. If he lies with her, he shall pay [her] 60 shillings compensation.[10]
11. 3. If another man has previously lain with her, then the compensation shall be half this [amount].
11. 4. If she is accused [of having previously lain with a man], she shall clear herself by [an oath of] 60 hides, or lose half the compensation due to her.
11. 5. If this [outrage] is done to a woman of higher birth, the compensation to be paid shall increase according to the wergeld.
18. If anyone lustfully seizes a nun, either by her clothes or by her breast, without her permission, he shall pay as compensation twice the sum we have fixed in the case of a woman belonging to the laity.

9 Hough (1997a) notes that 5 shillings is also the compensation for loss of a little toe or a thumbnail, i.e. a small but sometimes permanent injury (p. 5). Furthermore, compensation payment is usually accompanied by a fine in the early laws – a fine of 60 shillings where the compensation is less than 30 shillings, and a fine of 120 shillings if the compensation is larger (p. 9).

10 Hough (1997a: 7) notes a lack of consensus on whether or not this refers to rape. Compensation is required elsewhere for consensual sex with slaves, as in Æthelbert 10, 11, 14 and 16 (extract 20 above), where compensation is paid to the slaveowner (Hough 1997a: 3–4) and Alfred 10 provides for payment to the husband in cases of adultery. But compensation here is paid to the woman herself, implying an injury done to her?

18. 1. If a young woman who is betrothed commits fornication, she shall pay compensation to the amount of 60 shillings to the surety [of the marriage] if she is a commoner. This sum shall be [paid] in livestock, cattle being the property tendered, and no slave shall be given in such a payment.
18. 2. If her wergeld is 600 shillings, she shall pay 100 shillings to the surety [of the marriage].
18. 3. If her wergeld is 1200 shillings, she shall pay 120 shillings to the surety [of the marriage].
25. If anyone rapes the slave of a commoner, he shall pay 5 shillings to the commoner, and a fine of 60 shillings.
25. 1. If a slave rapes a slave, castration shall be required as compensation.
29. If anyone rapes a girl who is not of age, the same compensation shall be paid to her as is paid to an adult.[11]
65. If a man is so badly wounded in the testicles that he cannot beget children, 80 shillings shall be paid to him as compensation for it.

23 Laws of King Canute

Canute II (*c.*995–1035) was king of Denmark, England and Norway. His laws (1020–1023) seem to show significant ecclesiastical influence from one of his advisers, Wulfstan, archbishop of York and bishop of Worcester (Frantzen 1998: 143): Whitelock argues for Wulfstan's authorship of the laws (Whitelock 1948, 1970). They have a far wider scope than secular law has in the later medieval period, where matters such as marriage and the regulation of sexual behaviour are for the most part left to the Church, but the statutes here look like a king implementing Christian doctrine. Some of the statutes here again seem to suggest the survival of practices at odds with Christian marriage ideals: 54.1 and 55 are suggestive of the existence of concubinage, and 73a.2 suggests forced marriage. Cf. the discussion in the Anglo-Saxon penitentials (extract 7, above). Number 74 affirms the right of women to choose for themselves in marriage, and plays down the importance of financial transactions.

Further reading: Whitelock 1948, 1970, Goody 1983, Lucas 1983, Fell 1984, Clunies Ross 1985, Brundage 1987: ch. 4, Frantzen 1998, Saunders 2001: ch. 1. Cf. the Germanic laws in Amt 1993: part 1, section C.

11 Hough (1997b) argues that the correct translation is: 'If anyone rapes a girl not of age, that is to be the same compensation as for a woman past child-bearing age.'

Text: A. J. Robertson (ed. and trans.) (1925) *The Laws of the Kings of England from Edmund to Henry I*, Cambridge: Cambridge University Press.

I CANUTE

7. And we instruct and pray and enjoin, in the name of God, that no Christian man shall ever marry among his own kin within six degrees of relationship, or with the widow of a man as nearly related to him as that, or with a near relative of his first wife's.
7. 1. And no Christian man shall ever marry his god-mother or a professed nun or a divorced woman.
7. 2. And he shall never commit adultery anywhere.
7. 3. And he shall have no more wives than one, and that shall be his wedded wife, and he who seeks to observe God's law aright and to save his soul from hell-fire shall remain with the one as long as she lives.
24. And we enjoin that foul lasciviousness and illicit unions and every [kind of] adultery be zealously abhorred.

II CANUTE

50. Concerning adultery. If anyone commits adultery, he shall make amends according to the nature of the offence.
50. 1. It is wicked adultery for a pious man to commit fornication with an unmarried woman, and much worse [for him to do so] with the wife of another man or with any woman who has taken religious vows.
51. Concerning incest. If anyone commits incest, he shall make amends according to the degree of relationship [between them], either by the payment of wergeld or of a fine, or by the forfeiture of all his possessions.
51. 1. The cases are not alike if incest is committed with a sister or with a distant relation.
52. Concerning widows. If anyone does violence to a widow, he shall make amends by the payment of his wergeld.
52. 1. Maidens. If anyone does violence to a maiden he shall make amends by the payment of his wergeld.
53. No woman shall commit adultery. If, while her husband is still alive, a woman commits adultery with another man and it is

discovered, she shall bring disgrace upon herself, and her lawful husband shall have all that she possesses, and she shall then lose both her nose and her ears.[12]

53. 1. And if a charge is brought and the attempt to refute it fails, the decision shall then rest with the bishop, and his judgement shall be strict.

54. If a married man commits adultery with his own slave, he shall lose her and make amends for himself both to God and to men.

54. 1. And if anyone has a lawful wife and also a concubine, no priest shall perform for him any of the offices which must be performed for a Christian man, until he desists and makes amends as thoroughly as the bishop shall direct him, and ever afterwards desists from such [evildoing].

55. Foreigners, if they will not regularize their unions, shall be driven from the land with their possessions, and shall depart in sin.

73. Concerning widows, that they remain a year without a husband. And every widow shall remain twelve months without a husband, and she shall afterwards choose what she herself desires.

73a. And if then, within the space of the year, she chooses a husband, she shall lose her morning-gift and all the property which she had from her first husband, and his nearest relatives shall take the land and the property which she had held.

73a. 1. And he (the second husband) shall forfeit his wergeld to the king or to the lord to whom it has been granted.

73a. 2. And although she has been married to him by force, she shall lose her possessions, unless she is willing to leave the man and return home and never afterwards be his.

73a. 3. And no widow shall be too hastily consecrated as a nun.

73a. 4. And every widow shall pay the heriots within twelve months without incurring a fine, if it has not been convenient for her to pay earlier.

74. And no woman or maiden shall ever be forced to marry a man whom she dislikes, nor shall she be given for money, except the suitor desires of his own freewill to give something.[13]

12 Frantzen (1998: 143) comments that this penalty was new to Anglo-Saxon law, and that other evidence suggests that financial penalties were normal for adultery. Fell (1984: 64) agrees. But the idea persists: a letter of 1444 from Margaret Paston to her son John tells of a man who suspects his wife of giving birth to another man's child threatening to cut off her nose if she comes into his presence (Davis 1971–1976: I, 220).

13 Clunies Ross (1985: 8) comments on the importance of consent here, and compares 'Concerning the Betrothal of a Woman' (extract 24).

24 Concerning the Betrothal of a Woman

This discussion of betrothal shows how consent (if 'it so pleases her and her kinsmen') and financial issues all play a part in making a marriage. The last two sections indicate the Church's influence in matrimonial matters.

Further reading: Goody 1983: 254–255, Fell 1984: 58.

Text: Dorothy Whitelock (ed.) (1979) *English Historical Documents, 500–1042*, 2nd edition, London: Eyre Methuen.

How a man shall betroth a maiden, and what agreement there ought to be.

1. If a man wishes to betroth a maiden or a widow, and it so pleases her and her kinsmen, then it is right that the bridegroom first according to God's law and proper secular custom should promise and pledge to those who are her advocates, that he desires her in such a way that he will maintain her according to God's law as a man should maintain his wife; and his friends are to stand surety for it.
2. Next, it must be known to whom belongs the remuneration for rearing her. The bridegroom is then to pledge this, and his friends are to stand surety for it.
3. Then afterwards the bridgegroom is to announce what he grants her in return for her acceptance of his suit, and what he grants her if she should live longer than he.
4. If it is thus contracted, then it is right that she should be entitled to half the goods – and to all, if they have a child together – unless she marries again.
5. He is to strengthen all that he promises with a pledge, and his friends are to stand surety for it.
6. If they then reach agreement about everything, then the kinsmen are to set about betrothing their kinswoman as wife and in lawful matrimony to him who has asked for her, and he who is leader of the betrothal is to receive the security.
7. If, however, one wishes to take her away from that district into that of another thegn,[14] then it is to her interest that her friends have the assurance that no wrong will be done to her, and that if she commits an offence, they may be allowed to stand next in paying compensation, if she possesses nothing with which she can pay.[15]

14 A 'thegn' is a nobleman.

15 Lucas (1983: 79–80) contrasts this clause with the situation described in the Anglo-Saxon poem *The Wife's Lament* (extract 50).

8. At the marriage there should by rights be a mass-priest, who shall unite them together with God's blessing in all prosperity.
9. It is also well to take care that one knows that they are not too closely related, lest one afterwards put asunder what was previously wrongly joined together.

25 Old English Marriage Agreements

These are from the early eleventh century, 1014–1016 for the first document, 1016–1020 for the second.

Further reading: as extract 24.

Text: Dorothy Whitelock (ed.) (1979) *English Historical Documents, 500–1042*, 2nd edition, London: Eyre Methuen.

OLD ENGLISH MARRIAGE AGREEMENT BETWEEN WULFRIC AND ARCHBISHOP WULFSTAN'S SISTER[16]

+ Here in this document it is made known about the terms which Wulfric and the archbishop made when he obtained the archbishop's sister as his wife, namely that he promised her the land at Orleton and Ribbesford for her lifetime, and promised her the land at Knightwick, that he would obtain it for her from the community of Winchcombe for three men's lives; and he gave her the land at Alton to give and to grant to whomsoever she pleased during her lifetime or after her death; and he promised her 50 mancuses of gold and 30 men and 30 horses.

Now these were witnesses that these terms were thus made: Archbishop Wulfstan and Ealdorman Leofwine and Bishop Athelstan and Abbot Ælfweard and Brihtheah the monk, and many good men besides them, both ecclesiastics and laymen. Now there are two copies of these terms. One is with the archbishop in Worcester, and the other with Archbishop Athelstan in Hereford.

16 Wulfstan is adviser to King Canute.

OLD ENGLISH MARRIAGE AGREEMENT FROM KENT

+ Here in this document is made known the agreement which Godwine made with Brihtria when he wooed her daughter; first, namely, that he gave her a pound's weight of gold in return for her acceptance of his suit, and he granted her the land at Street with everything that belongs to it, and 150 acres at Burmarsh and in addition 30 oxen and 20 cows, and 10 horses and 10 slaves.[17]

This was agreed at Kingston in King Cnut's[18] presence in the witness of Archbishop Lifing and of the community of Christ Church, and of Abbot Ælfmar and the community of St Augustine's, and of Æthelwine the sheriff, and Sigered the Old, and Godwine, Wulfheah's son, and Ælfsige Child, and Eadmær of Burham, and Godwine, Wulfstan's son, and Karl the king's retainer.

And when the maiden was fetched from Brightling, there acted as surety for all this Ælfgar, Sigered's son, and Frerth, the priest of Folkestone, and Leofwine the priest of Dover, and Wulfsige the priest, and Eadred, Eadhelm's son, and Leofwine, Wærhelm's son, and Cenwold Rust, and Leofwine, son of Godwine of Horton, and Leofwine the Red, and Godwine, Eadgifu's son, and Leofsunu his brother; and whichever of them shall live the longer is to succeed to all the possessions both in land which I have given them and in all things. Every trustworthy man in Kent and Sussex, thegn or ceorl,[19] is aware of these terms.

And there are three of these documents; one is at Christ Church, the second at St Augustine's, the third Brihtric has himself.

17 Fell (1984: 58) argues that it is clear here that we are dealing with the acceptance of the suit by the woman herself, not by her kinsmen on her behalf.

18 Or 'Canute'.

19 i.e. noble or not.

NORMAN LAW

26 Coronation Charter of Henry I

The view of marriage offered in this charter (1100), issued at the beginning of the reign of Henry I (1068–1135), is one that upholds the principle of freedom of choice in marriage, advocated by the Church, but also by some of the Anglo-Saxon laws quoted above (the laws of Canute, for example). It also upholds the right of widows to remain unmarried, again something encouraged by the Church, which regarded chaste widowhood as preferable to remarriage. Essentially the king agrees not to abuse his feudal (and economic) rights in the marriages of those who hold land from him. But it nevertheless recognizes the *Realpolitik* of marriage as a way of forging alliances within the European nobility, and it consequently requires the nobles to consult the king on their intentions for their female relatives.

Further reading: on secular law generally in later medieval England, see Pollock and Maitland 1898, Plucknett 1956, Milsom 1981. On widows and provision for widows, see Mirrer 1992 and Walker 1993b.

Text: A. J. Robertson (ed. and trans.) (1925) *The Laws of the Kings of England from Edmund to Henry I*, Cambridge: Cambridge University Press.

3. And if any of my barons or my other vassals wishes to bestow in marriage his daughter or his sister or his niece or any [other] female relative he shall consult me on the matter, but I shall not take anything from him in return for my permission, nor shall I forbid him to bestow her in marriage, unless he desires to marry her to an enemy of mine. And if, on the death of a baron or any other vassal of mine, his daughter is left as heiress, I shall bestow her in marriage,

with the consent of my barons, along with her land. And if, on the death of her husband, a wife is left and has no children, she shall have her marriage-settlement and dowry, and I shall not bestow her in marriage except in accordance with her wishes.

4. But if the wife is left with children, she shall have her marriage settlement and dowry as long as she observes continence, and I shall not bestow her in marriage except in accordance with her wishes. And the guardian of the land and children shall be either the wife or some other relative who has a better right. And I enjoin upon my barons to act with like moderation towards the sons and daughters and the wives of their vassals.

27 Magna Carta

Magna Carta (1215) is famously issued by King John (1167–1216, king from 1199) at the insistence of his barons. These are some clauses dealing with wardship and widowhood, taking a similar line to those in the previous charter quoted. The assertion that heirs should be married without disparagement refers to those who have inherited land while under age and unmarried (see the discussion of wardship in Bracton, extract 31). Their lords have the right to arrange their marriages, and the clause here insists that they should not be disparaged – i.e. married to their social inferiors.

Text: Harry Rothwell (ed.) (1975) *English Historical Documents, 1189–1327*, London: Eyre & Spottiswoode.

6. Heirs shall be married without disparagement, yet so that before the marriage is contracted those nearest in blood to the heir shall have notice.
7. A widow shall have her marriage portion and inheritance forthwith and without difficulty after the death of her husband; nor shall she pay anything to have her dower or her marriage portion or the inheritance which she and her husband held on the day of her husband's death; and she may remain in her husband's house for forty days after his death, within which time her dower shall be assigned to her.
8. No widow shall be forced to marry so long as she wishes to live without a husband, provided that she gives security not to marry without our consent if she holds of us, or without the consent of her lord of whom she holds, if she holds of another.

28 Statute of Westminster I

Saunders (2001: ch. 1, and on this statute, 59–61) argues that rape and abduction are clearly distinguished in Anglo-Saxon law, instancing the laws of Alfred in particular, but that abduction and rape are collapsed in later medieval law, where abduction becomes the key issue, as in this statute (1275). The law of *raptus* as expressed here is superseded by Westminster II ten years later, where the focus on abduction is again emphasized.

Text: *The Statutes at Large* (1758), 6 vols, London. With modernized spelling.

13. And the king prohibits that none do ravish, nor take away by force, any maiden within age (neither by her own consent, nor without), nor any wife or maiden of full age, nor any other woman, against her will; and if any do, at his suit that will sue within forty days, the king shall do common right; and if none commence his suit within forty days, the king shall sue; and such as be found culpable shall have two years' imprisonment, and after shall fine at the king's pleasure, and if they have not whereof, they shall be punished by longer imprisonment, according as the trespass requires.

29 Statute of Westminster II

This statute (1285) deals with the granting of property to married couples, with a condition attached that the property would revert to the original donor if the line of descent petered out before a third heir. The assumption inherent in such grants is that if the direct line of inheritance survives as far as a third heir that it will continue to survive, and that reversion to the original donors (or their heirs) is unlikely. This statute is an attempt to prevent those who receive such property from disposing of it before that event: of selling it for immediate gain rather than take the risk that they might not have descendants to inherit.

Text: Harry Rothwell (ed.) (1975) *English Historical Documents, 1189–1327*, London: Eyre & Spottiswoode.

1. First, concerning tenements which are often given upon condition, that is, when someone gives his land to some man and his wife and the heirs begotten of the same man and woman with the added condition expressed that, if the man and woman should die without heir begotten of them, the land so given should revert to the donor

or his heir; also in the case where someone gives a tenement in frank marriage,[20] which gift has a condition attached, though it is not expressed in the deed of gift, which is, that if the man and woman should die without heir begotten of them, the tenement so given should revert to the donor or his heir; also in the case when someone gives a tenement to somebody and to the heirs issuing of his body: it seemed, and still seems, hard to such donors and heirs of donors that their wish expressed in their gifts has not heretofore been observed and still is not observed. For in all these cases, after offspring begotten and issuing from those to whom the tenement was thus conditionally given, these feoffees[21] have hitherto had power to alienate the tenement so given and to disinherit their own issue contrary to the wish of the donors and the form expressed in the gift. And further, when on the failure of the issue of such feoffees the tenement so given ought to have reverted to the donor or his heirs by the form expressed in the deed of such a gift, notwithstanding the issue, if any there were, had died, they [the donors] have heretofore been barred from the reversion of the tenements by the deed and feoffment of those to whom the tenements were thus given upon condition, which was manifestly against the form of their gift. Wherefore the lord king, perceiving that it is necessary and useful to provide a remedy in the aforesaid cases, has enacted that the wish of the donor, according to the form manifestly expressed in his deed of gift, is henceforth to be observed, in such wise that those to whom the tenement was thus given upon condition shall not have the power of alienating the tenement so given and thereby preventing it from remaining after their death to their issue, or to the donor or his heir if issue fail either because there was no issue at all or because if there was issue it has failed by death, the heir of such issue failing. Neither shall, henceforth, the second husband of such woman have anything by the curtesy[22] after the death of his wife in a tenement so given upon condition, or the issue of the woman and second husband have hereditary succession, but instead immediately after the death of the man and the woman to whom the tenement was so given, it shall revert after their death either to their issue or to the donor or to his heir as is aforesaid. And because in a new case a new remedy must be provided, the following writ is to be made as required:
[The text of the writ follows.]

20 Frank-marriage refers to a marriage gift of property given under these conditions: see also extract 30.iii.

21 Feoffees are those holding land by feudal tenure.

22 Land held in 'curtesy' is land held by a widower that formerly belonged to his wife.

30 *Glanvill*

There are two sorts of property transfer that take place at marriage ceremonies in medieval England, both, confusingly, called *dos*. *Glanvill*, a legal manual, distinguishes between them here by calling one *dos* ('dower' in English): this is the property that a husband agrees that his wife will receive for her support if he should predecease her. The second type of property transfer is property given to the couple, and *Glanvill* calls this *maritagium*, a marriage portion.

Text: G. D. G. Hall (ed. and trans.) (1965) *The Treatise on the Laws and Customs of the Realm of England Commonly Called Glanvill*, Oxford: Clarendon Press.

(I)

6. 1 Pleas of dower

The word 'dos' has two meanings. In common English law usage it means that which a free man gives to his wife at the church door at the time of his marriage. For every man is bound both by ecclesiastical and by secular law to endow his wife at the time of his marriage. When a man endows his wife either he nominates certain property as dower, or he does not. If he does not nominate dower, then one third of the whole of his free tenement is deemed to be her dower, and the reasonable dower of any woman is one third of the whole of the free tenement of which her husband was seised in demesne[23] at the time of her marriage. If, however, the husband nominates dower and it amounts to more than one third, it cannot stand at such a level, but will be measured up to one third; for a man can give less but not more than one third of his tenement in dower.

6. 2 Increase in dower as a result of later acquisitions

It sometimes happens that a husband who has a little land can increase the dower by adding one third or less of his later acquisitions. However, if nothing was said about acquisitions when the dower was originally assigned, then, even if the husband had little land at the time of the marriage and afterwards acquired much land, no more can be claimed in dower than one third of the land which he held at

23 Possessed for his own use.

the time of the marriage.[24] I state the same rule when a man who has no land endows his wife with money or other chattels and afterwards acquires many lands and tenements, for nothing can in future lawfully be claimed as dower from these acquisitions. For it is a general rule that however much dower and of whatever kind is assigned to a woman, if she consents to this assignment of dower at the church door she cannot in future lawfully claim any more as dower.

It should be known that a woman cannot alienate any of her dower during the life of her husband. For since legally a woman is completely in the power of her husband, it is not surprising that her dower and all her other property are clearly deemed to be at his disposal. Therefore any married man may give or sell or alienate in whatever way he pleases his wife's dower during her life, and his wife is bound to consent to this as to all other acts of his which do not offend against God. Indeed, to such an extent is a woman bound to obey her husband that if he wishes to sell her dower and she opposes him, and afterwards the dower is in fact sold and purchased, she cannot when her husband is dead claim the dower from the purchaser if she confesses, or it is proved against her, in court that it was sold by her husband against her will.

When a woman's husband dies and dower has been nominated, either it lies vacant or it does not. If it is vacant, the woman may enter on the dower and remain in seisin[25] with the consent of the heir. If, however, it is not vacant, then either none is vacant, or else some part is vacant and some is not; in the latter case she may enter on the vacant part in the manner stated above, and in respect of the rest she shall have a writ of right to her warrantor,[26] directing him to do full right to her concerning certain land which she claims as belonging to her reasonable dower.

(II)

7. *1 Marriage Portions*

In Roman law the word 'dos' has a different meaning: there 'dos' is properly used for that which is given with a woman to her husband,

24 The amount of one-third is prescribed by the common law, but in practice the amount varies according to local custom, and can be a half or even all of the husband's property.

25 Possession.

26 i.e. the heir.

which is commonly called 'maritagium', a marriage-portion. Every free man who has land can give a certain part of his land with his daughter, or with any other woman, as a marriage-portion, whether he has an heir or not, and whether the heir if he has one is willing or not, and even if he is opposed to it and protests. For he can give a certain part of his free tenement to whom he pleases in recompense for his service, or to a religious place as alms. If seisin follows the gift, the land will remain for ever with the donee and his heirs, if it was given to them heritably; however, if no seisin follows such a gift, then after the donor's death nothing can be claimed in reliance on such a gift against the will of the heir, because, according to the interpretation customary in the realm, it is deemed to be a naked promise rather than a true gift.

(III)

7. 18 The kinds of marriage-portion

A marriage-portion may be called free (frank-marriage), or liable to service. It is called frank-marriage when a free man gives some part of his land to another with a certain woman in marriage, on condition that the land shall be free of all service, which shall be discharged by the donor and his heirs to the chief lords. The land shall remain free in this way until the third heir, nor shall the heirs meanwhile be bound to do homage for it.[27] However, after the second heir the land shall again be liable for the service due from it, and homage shall be taken for it; and, if it is part of a military fee, it will bear the service of the fee in proportion to its size.

Sometimes, however, land is given in marriage, saving and reserving to the lord the service due, in which case the woman's husband and his heirs are bound to do that service, but without homage until the third heir; he will be the first to do homage for it, and all his heirs subsequently shall do it. Yet a kind of fealty, in which a solemn promise or oath is inserted, ought until then to be sworn by the women or their heirs, in nearly the same form and words as are used in the doing of homage.

When anyone received land as a marriage-portion with his wife and has by that wife an heir, whether son or daughter, who is heard

27 This is the sort of tenure discussed in the Statutes of Westminster II, above. To do homage is to accept another person as your lord and to hold property as a fief from them.

to cry within the four walls, then, if the husband survives his wife, he shall keep that marriage-portion for the rest of his life, whether the heir survives or not; after the husband's death it shall revert to the donor or his heirs. But if he had at no time any heir by his wife, then the marriage-portion reverts to the donor or his heirs immediately on the death of the wife. This partly explains why homage is not taken for such a marriage-portion, because if homage were taken for land given as a marriage-portion or in any other way, then it could never lawfully revert in the future to the donor or his heirs in the way stated above. If the woman has a second husband, the same rule applies to him as was given above for the first husband, whether the latter left an heir or not.

31 *Bracton*

The first extract here from the thirteenth-century legal manual named after Henry de Bracton (d. 1268) concerns the property rights of women within marriage. The husband has complete control over all property, his and his wife's, while he lives, but he can only dispose of her property or their joint property for the length of his lifetime: she can generally reclaim it after his death (an exception, not mentioned here, is when she consents to his permanent disposal of the property in the king's court).

The second extract asks whether gifts can be made between married persons, and concludes that they cannot. The discussion of the possible motivation for such gifts perhaps makes a distinction between *amor* and *maritalis affectio* as sorts of love appropriate and inappropriate within marriage (cf. Andreas Capellanus, extract 55). The third extract concerns the different definitions of legitimacy by the ecclesiastical law and the secular law (as discussed in the Introduction). The fourth concerns the right of lords to sell the marriages of those noble heirs who have inherited property underage and are consequently in their wardship. In fact, the statute of Merton (1236) states that the wards may not be married against their will, and Sue Sheridan Walker suggests that in practice wardship operates as a sort of taxation (Walker 1982: 123, 125, but cf. Menuge 2001: ch. 4). The fifth extract concerns the definition of dower, and the sixth how widows may lose their dower – sexual suspicion of widows as independent women appears here and in other texts that insist that widows must remain chaste to retain their property.

Text: G. E. Woodbine (ed.) and S. E. Thorne (trans.) (1968–1977) *Bracton: On the Laws and Customs of England*, Cambridge, MA: Harvard University Press.

(I)

If the wife makes a gift of her husband's property without his assent, restitution lies for the husband by the assize of novel disseisin or by writ of entry, just as it does for any other person, that is, 'she aliened without his consent.' But conversely, if the husband makes a gift of his wife's property, it will never be revoked during the lifetime of the husband, since a wife may not dispute her husband's acts. If the husband gives a thing given them both, the wife may not recall her husband's gift during his lifetime, but if she makes a gift of such property, the husband may revoke it at once.

(II)

Whether a husband may make a gift to his wife during marriage

It may be asked whether, during marriage, a husband may make a gift to his wife or a wife to her husband. An arrangement may be taken to be a marriage whether it has been publicly contracted or faith has been so pledged that the partied may not be separated, and in truth, gifts between husband and wife in marriage ought not to be good, and the reason is lest they be made because of the lust or the excessive poverty of one of the parties. That such gifts are invalid is proved in the roll[28] of Michaelmas term in the fifteenth year of king Henry in the county of Lincoln, a case from the eyre, an assise of mortdancestor, beginning 'if Helewisa', to whom a certain Eudo had made a gift after he had promised to marry her and with whom he later publicly contracted marriage, where the heirs of Helewisa took nothing by an assise of mortdancestor brought on the seisin of the said Helewisa. To the same intent in the roll of Trinity term in the seventeenth year of king Henry in the county of Norfolk, the case of Petronilla, wife of William of St Martin, who, after her husband's death was ejected from a tenement so given her and could not recover seisin by an assise of novel disseisin because the gift and the feoffment were void by the law itself. To the same intent in the roll of Hilary term in the eighth year of king Henry in the county of Nottingham, the case of Robert of Wallegha and Joanna his wife, where it is said that such a gift is invalid, particularly because

28 Court records.

the wife to whom it was made never had seisin before espousals and because her husband died seised and because the land never was separated from the land of her said husband. But what if such a gift is made after divorce? It is good and valid. But if a gift of this kind may not be made directly by a husband to a wife during marriage, or conversely, suppose it is made indirectly, the husband giving the land to a stranger that he may give it to the wife, either at once or after the husband's death, or conversely, if it is the wife who wishes to make a gift to her husband. It ought not to be valid, for in that way a fraud is perpetrated against the constitution of dower; it is just as if the gift were made directly, for it does not matter whether what is done is precisely what is prohibited or amounts to the same. The contrary, however, was held, erroneously and by mistake of the court, and, so to speak, by counsel of the court, in the case of Godfrey of Crowecombe, who gave land to Robert of Mucegros so that after the death of Godfrey the same Robert might give it to Godfrey's wife. Suppose that gifts are made before espousals and before marriage: we must see whether they ought to be good. At first sight it seems that they ought to be, for gifts made to a concubine may not be revoked, nor, if marriage is afterwards contracted by one of the parties, may what was formerly valid by law become of no force and effect. But a distinction must be made, for it makes a difference whether it is made because of affection[29] and the marriage to follow or not, for if a marriage was afterwards contracted between such persons it appears that marital honor and affection already existed, the persons being taken into account and the union of their lives considered. But suppose the prospective husband and wife betake themselves to other vows and adopt another course; such gift cannot be revoked if it is absolute and wholly unconditional. But if it is conditional, as where it is contracted thus, 'I give that you do', it may be revoked, because given for a purpose that did not follow. Simple gifts are not to be made, either before espousals, before marriage or during marriage, but only gifts because of marriage, as where a constitution of dower is made, and provided they do not exceed the amount of dower, that is, the third part, which is called rightful dower, as C. 5.3.20.3[30] where it is said that if a gift differs neither in name nor in substance from dower before marriage given by the husband, why may it not

29 In referring to marital affection here as a motivation, Bracton seems to be distinguishing between it and *amor* (mentioned later) as sorts of love appropriate and inappropriate within marriage.

30 Reference is to the *Codex Iustinianus*.

in like manner be given after marriage? We ordain that all persons, before or after they contract marriages, shall be permitted to make gifts to their wives because of dower, that is, that a man may settle dower before marriage, during the marriage or after it, provided that simple gifts are not understood but gifts made because of dower and on account of the marriage. For simple gifts are not made because of marriage, but forbidden because of it, because of lust, perhaps, or the poverty of one of the parties, and not because of the affection growing out of the marriage itself, as was touched upon above. And if such gifts could be made because of love[31] between husband and wife, one of them might be destroyed by want and poverty, which cannot be tolerated. Hence a gift between husband and wife is invalid from the beginning and cannot later become valid, unless after the death of one or the other a confirmation is made by the heirs who can confirm such a gift. The confirmation of such heirs makes valid a gift that was invalid earlier and cures every defect.

(III)

It is clear that if a man has natural children by a woman and then marries her, such children are legitimized by the subsequent marriage and considered fit for all lawful acts. But only for acts that pertain to the spiritual sphere. In secular matters they are not legitimate, nor, because of a custom of the realm to the contrary, are they regarded as heirs capable of succeeding their parents.

(IV)

When the heir is within age[32] and unmarried and in the wardship of the lord, that is, of a military fee,[33] whether the heir is male or female the marriage will belong in full right to the chief lord in whose wardship he is; he may give the heir in marriage when and where he wishes, provided he is married in the lifetime of the vendor; indeed he may give him in marriage not only once but several times, as often as he is within age and without a wife.

31 Latin '*ob amorem*' – *amor* contrasted here with *affectio.*

32 i.e. under twenty-one.

33 Land held by a feudal tenure involving the giving of homage to a lord.

(V)

What dower is

Dower is that which a free man gives his spouse at the church door on the marriage day, because of the burden of matrimony and the future marriage, for the maintenance of the wife and the nurture of the children when they are born, should the husband predecease her.

What rightful dower is

The rightful dower of every woman is the third part of each tenement, of all the lands and tenements her husband held in his demesne and so in fee that he could endow her on the day he married her.

Who can constitute dower

Who can constitute dower? Any male, whether he is a minor or of full age. To whom? To any wife, of full age or a minor. For he who is under age may endow his wife though she is under age, provided that she may merit dower and is mature enough to take a husband; and though the husband dies within age, his wife will have her dower whether she is within age or not. On this matter may be found in the roll of Easter term in the ninth year of king Henry in the county of Devon, the case of Sarah wife of William Burnel.

When and where

When? Before the marriage, at the beginning of the marriage. Where? In the face of the church and at the church door. A constitution of dower made on the death bed or in a private chamber is invalid, or elsewhere when the marriage is clandestine, for if secret nuptials are sufficient for heirs with respect to succession, they will never suffice to provide dower for wives, and it therefore must be made publicly and with a ceremony at the church door. Where there is no marriage at all there is no dower, which is true if the marriage is contracted in the face of the church. A valid constitution of dower may be made at the church door between any persons whatever, those related by blood or affinity as well as strangers, provided the marriage is not challenged or dissolved in the lifetime of the parties; if it is challenged and dissolved, for whatever reason, dower ceases to exist, since the marriage comes to an end, and any claim for dower fails: one need never answer in an action of dower to two wives claiming through one husband.

Of the two kinds of dos

Dos is of two kinds, profectitious and adventitious: profectitious is that given by a father or mother or other parent when the agreement for marrying a daughter is made. The land so given, which may be called her *maritagium* or patrimony, sometimes falls into the pot among female co-heirs, if the daughter so provided for wishes to have a share of the inheritance, as above. An absolute gift made without a matrimonial cause is not called a maritagium, adventitious, given by a person other than the father or mother or parent, whether a relative or a stranger. *Parapherna* is the same as *dos*, made besides or in addition to *dos*, even if it is made before marriage or during marriage, whether to the husband and wife together or to the wife alone, and it does not fall into the pot, though made by parents, because the gift is absolute and not made for a matrimonial cause, as above. There is also a gift on account of the marriage made by the husband to the wife on the marriage day, what the bridegroom gives the bride at the church door. That is properly called the wife's *dos* according to English custom, and it is that with which we deal here. The husband gains it if the wife predeceases him and it remains to the wife for life if her husband predeceases her. He sometimes gains it by law in his wife's lifetime, when a divorce is solemnized between them for some reason, but not if there is only a separation from bed and board.[34] Sometimes the heir gains the dower after the death of the husband, though it has been assigned, by the custom of cities and counties, as in Kent, London, Lincoln and elsewhere. It is clear that a *maritagium* given because of marriage always remains to the wife and her heirs, if she has heirs of her body. If she does not, it reverts for failure of heirs. In the same way *paraphernalia* remains to her heirs, of whatever kind.

(VI)

How a woman may lose her dower after she is in possession and for what reasons

When a woman has obtained her dower she may lose it in many ways, as by custom, which is observed as law in divers places, as in the

34 Both sorts of 'divorce' here are decided upon by the ecclesiastical courts: one declares the marriage invalid from the beginning, and annuls it; the second, a divorce from bed and board, is a separation of the couple but without effect on the marital bond – neither can remarry.

county of Kent, where if she remarries after her dower has been assigned, or before the assignment, she immediately loses the gavelkind[35] land she holds in the name of dower. On this matter may be found in the roll of Michaelmas term in the second year of king Henry after the war, in the county of Kent. The same custom is observed in the city of London, with respect to lands and tenements in that city, and elsewhere in many other places. Whether she has had seisin or not, if after the death of her husband she is found to be with child by someone other than her husband, whether she is married or not, that is, if a husband is found, or a child, or both, she will lose her dower. She will also lose her dower by felony and the like. [. . .]

32 *Britton*

This extract from the legal manual *Britton* shows that in its allocation of dower to widows the secular law is unwilling to accept marriage reconciliations enforced by the ecclesiastical courts as being entirely genuine.

Text: F. M. Nichols (ed. and trans.) *Britton*, London: Macmillan, 1865.

Again, the tenant may say that the plaintiff has forfeited and lost dower by adultery, inasmuch as she left her husband after he married her for the bed of another, by which act she forfeited her dower. If to this the wife replies that it ought not to bar or affect her because she was afterwards reconciled to him, so that he received her again, and in her seisin died, the tenant may say in answer that notwithstanding this she ought not to have dower, for that he did not receive her of his own accord, but against his will by coercion of Holy Church and by sentence of court Christian. And if this be proved, the plaintiff shall take nothing.

33 English Customary Laws

Local, customary law often overrules the common law in later medieval England. It has been argued that customary law offers much greater control over property and enhanced legal status to married women, who under the common law were simply subject to their husbands where questions of law and property were concerned. Two points need to be made concerning this: first, customary law varied considerably from place to place, and where in some cases it is more liberal towards

35 'Gavelkind' is a sort of land tenure.

married women than the common law, in some cases it erodes the rights that the common law gives them. This can be seen in the first two extracts below concerning the sale of the marriage portion (forbidden under the common law) – some custumals allow the husband to sell the marriage portion, some do not. The second point is that often the supposedly liberal attitude towards the property rights of married women applied only to women who were traders, and were sometimes motivated to prevent creditors from access to the goods of a female trader's husband. The custumal from Fordwich quoted below makes it clear that her legal status is dependent on her status as a trader, not as a married woman. The final custumal quoted here, from Bristol, concerns the rights of women to make a final testament. Under the common law, married women held no property and so could not make a will. The Church, however, advocated freedom of testament for all (see the discussion in the Introduction, above). The Bristol custumal quoted here forbids women from making wills apart from 'reasonable funeral expenses'.

Text: Mary Bateson (ed.) (1904–1906) *Borough Customs*, 2 vols, London: Quaritch.

(I) NORTHAMPTON, 1190

If a man marries a wife with land for her marriage portion, by reason of their poverty they can sell that marriage portion, and it will hold good by the law of the town if they sell it by reason of poverty, but they cannot sell it as long as they have any other land which they can sell. And if, on the death of her husband, the woman should marry again, having had children by the first husband, she and her second husband cannot sell that marriage-portion (aforesaid), or give it in fee or gage it in any way.

(II) LICHFIELD, 1221

And the township of Lichfield says that the custom of their town is such that no one can sell his wife's marriage portion.

(III) FORDWICH, FIFTEENTH CENTURY

And whenever a woman is a professional trader in fish, fruit, cloth, or the like, and is impleaded concerning any loan made to her in such trade as she practices, she must answer either with or without her husband, according to the will of the plaintiff. And if she be not a professional trader she ought not to answer, for in that case she is treated as an ordinary married woman.

(IV) BRISTOL, 1240

And that the wives of burgesses cannot bequeath the goods of their husbands except by leave of their husbands, saving reasonable funeral expenses, for it often has happened that their husbands are burdened with debts which their own property does not suffice to discharge.

34 Cases from the Manorial Courts

The first of these cases from the thirteenth and fourteenth centuries involves merchet (fines paid by unfree tenants for permission to marry): the tenants are challenging the lord's right to exact merchet where a tenant holds some land by free service and some land as a villein, an unfree person. Interestingly, the lord exacting the fine is the local abbot – the canon law's insistence that even slaves have free consent in matrimony doesn't get in the way of collecting revenues on ecclesiastical manors. The second extract concerns fines paid by unfree tenants for permission *not* to marry specific persons. The final extract concerns leyrwite (fines for fornication).

Further reading: on the peasantry's freedom to marry, Searle 1979, Brand, Hyams, Faith and Searle 1983. For an account of manorial life and manorial court records, Razi 1980.

Text: L. R. Poos and Lloyd Bonfield (ed. and trans.) (1998) *Select Cases in Manorial Courts, 1250–1550: Property and Family Law*, London: Selden Society.

(I) MERCHET. WORLINGWORTH, SUFFOLK, 7 JULY 1319

Respite.
Olive Duck was questioned whether she wished to make fine for licence to marry herself. She says no, because she has lands and

tenements by hereditary succession.[36] And thereupon all the tenants in villeinage of Worlingworth came, and they say and claim by custom that all men of the homage, whether they have lands in villeinage or do not have lands in villeinage, can marry themselves without the lord's licence. And they say and claim by custom that all women who have lands or tenements by hereditary succession can marry themselves without the lord's licence, because they say that the said women, by heriot after the death of their ancestors, ought to have entry into their inheritance, and also ought to be quit of marriage and of licence to marry themselves by the aforesaid heriot. And they say that other women, to whom an inheritance has not descended or who do not have lands or tenements by hereditary descent, cannot marry themselves without licence, but ought to make a fine for licence to marry themselves at the lord's will. They also say that the said women heirs, if they give birth outside of marriage, ought to give childwite,[37] as do other women who do not have lands by hereditary succession.

Being questioned whether they wish to claim the said custom at their peril, they say yes, because they have used that custom from time out of mind, and they pray that that custom be allowed to them. Being questioned whether that custom was allowed to them at any time, they say yes, etc. And it was said to them that they should show the court at what time and before whom that custom was allowed to them. They pray respite until the next [*court*] etc. And they have a day until the next [*court*] to show whether they know etc.

Afterwards they came into open court, and all say that always hitherto the aforesaid women having lands and tenements by inheritance have married themselves at their will without the lord's licence. But they say that it was never challenged therein, nor was it ever allowed to them by judgment of the court. And the rolls[38] being inspected, it clearly appears that such women have made fine for licence to marry themselves, namely in the court held on the Tuesday [23 October 1313] next before the feast of Apostles Simon and Jude in the seventh year of the present lord abbot. From Alice the daughter of Philip Stanhard etc. Therefore the aforesaid villeins are in mercy for false claim against the lord, and it is entered in the following court.

36 i.e. she holds some of her tenancy as a free person, not as a villein, an unfree person, and so claims that she need not pay merchet, a fine for permission to marry paid by the unfree.

37 A fine for giving birth outside of marriage.

38 Court records.

(II) HORSHAM ST FAITH, NORFOLK, 30 JANUARY 1285

12d.

Hubert Colberd gives the prior 12d. for this, that he should not espouse Maud Jolle and that he should be without a wife for an entire year if he should wish.

12d.

Robert the son of Walter Shepherd is in mercy, 12d., pledge, R. the beadle, that he should not espouse Amice Smith within the year. William Turkeby took Amice the daughter of Emma Colberd as his wife, that he should espouse her by the next court. Pledge, Walter Hering.

6d.

Roger Roust for this, that he refused Margaret the daughter of N. Yve. Pledges, W. at Mill and S. Ramay.

12d.

Henry King gives the prior 12d. that he should not espouse Mabel the daughter of Robert Cook within the year. Pledge, Hubert at Gate.

12d.

Walter Holcoc, because he refused Gunild Wydune, pledges N. Gotelyn and Simon Ramay, for this, that he should not take her within the year, 12d.

(III) CROWLE, LINCOLNSHIRE, 21 MAY 1319

They present that Alice Pacok was violated by Walter Serjaunt. Therefore she gives the lord leyrwite.

And Agnes the daughter of William the lord of Nalcok was violated by William le Fisher. Therefore she gives the lord leyrwite.

And Alice de Aland was violated by Adam de Picton. Therefore she gives the lord leyrwite.

The vill of Crowle is in mercy because it concealed Ellen the daughter of Thomas Sterting and Joan Norman, who were violated and were attainted thereof in chapter[39] before the official.

39 i.e. The ecclesiastical court.

35 The Case of John/Eleanor Rykener

This is the case of a transvestite prostitute, John / Eleanor Rykener, who appears in the secular courts in London in 1394: interestingly, because it was the ecclesiastical courts that normally had jurisdiction over sexual offences (on the response of the various English jurisdictions, ecclesiastical and secular, to prostitution, see Karras 1996: ch. 1). Although prostitution was accepted in legitimate brothels in three English towns (Sandwich, Southampton and Southwark) it was not so in London. The case is interesting both because it is a unique record of the sort of sexual practices that it describes, and also because the court seems to have all sorts of difficulties in categorizing John/Eleanor, and the offences committed.

Further reading: Karras and Boyd 1996, Dinshaw 1999. On transvestism, Bullough 1996. On prostitution in medieval England generally, Karras 1996.

Text: English translation printed as an appendix to Ruth Mazo Karras and David Lorenzo Boyd (1996) ' "Ut cum muliere": A Male Transvestite Prostitute in Fourteenth-Century London', in Louise Fradenburg and Carla Freccero (eds) (1996) *Premodern Sexualities*, London: Routledge: 101–116.

On 11 December, 18 Richard II, were brought in the presence of John Fressh, Mayor, and the Aldermen of the City of London John Britby of the county of York and John Rykener, calling [himself] Eleanor, having been detected in women's clothing, who were found last Sunday night between the hours of 8 and 9 by certain officials of the city lying by a certain stall in Soper's Lane, committing that detestable, unmentionable, and ignominious vice. In a separate examination held before the Mayor and Aldermen about the occurrence, John Britby confessed that he was passing through the high road of Cheap on Sunday between the above-mentioned hours and accosted John Rykener, dressed up as a woman, thinking he was a woman, asking him as he would a woman if he could commit a libidinous act with her. Requesting money for [his] labor, Rykener consented, and they went together to the aforesaid stall to complete the act, and were captured there during these detestable wrongdoings by the officials and taken to prison. And John Rykener, brought here in woman's clothing and questioned about this matter, acknowledged [himself] to have done everything just as John Britby had confessed. Rykener was also asked who had taught him to exercise this vice, and for how long and in what places and with what persons, masculine or feminine, [he] had committed that libidinous and unspeakable act. [He] swore willingly on [his] soul that a certain Anna, the whore of a former servant of Sir Thomas Blount, first taught him to practice this detestable vice in the manner of a woman. [He] further said that a certain Elizabeth Brouderer first dressed him in women's clothing; she also brought her daughter Alice to diverse men for the sake of lust, placing her with those men in their beds at night without light, making her leave early in the morning and showing them the said John Rykener dressed up in women's clothing, calling him Eleanor and saying that they had misbehaved with her. [He] further said that a certain Philip, rector of Theydon Garnon, had sex with him as a woman in Elizabeth Brouderer's house outside Bishopsgate, at which time Rykener took away two gowns of Philip's, and when Philip requested them from Rykener he said that [he] was the wife of a certain man and that if Philip wished to ask for them back [he] would make [his] husband bring suit against him. Rykener further confessed that for five weeks before the feast of St Michael's last [he] was staying at Oxford and there, in women's clothing and calling himself Eleanor, worked as an embroidress; and there in the marsh three unsuspecting scholars – one of whom was named Sir William Foxlee, another Sir John, and the third Sir Walter – practiced the abominable vice with him often. John Rykener further confessed that on Friday before the feast of St Michael [he] came to Burford in Oxfordshire and there dwelt with a certain John Clerk at the Swan in the capacity of tapster for the next six weeks,[40] during which time two Franciscans, one named Brother Michael and the other Brother John, who gave [him] a gold ring, and one Carmelite friar and six foreign men committed the above-said vice with him, of whom one gave Rykener twelve pence, one twenty pence, and one two shillings. Rykener further confessed that [he] went to Beaconsfield and there, as a man, had sex with a certain Joan, daughter of John Matthew, and there also two foreign Franciscans had sex with him as a woman. John Rykener also confessed that after [his] last return to London a certain Sir John, once chaplain at the Church of St Margaret Pattens, and two other chaplains committed with him the aforementioned vice in the lanes behind St Katherine's Church by the Tower of London. Rykener further said that he often had sex as a man with many nuns and also had sex as a man with

40 On the association of the profession of tapster with that of prostitute, see Karras 1996: 71–73.

many women both married and otherwise, how many [he] did not know. Rykener further confessed that many priests had committed that vice with him as with a woman, how many [he] did not know, and said that [he] accommodated priests more readily than other people because they wished to give [him] more than others.

Part III

LETTERS, CHRONICLES, BIOGRAPHY, CONDUCT BOOKS

INTRODUCTION

After Parts I and II, where the texts speak from a legal or theological standpoint, the texts in Part III are far more biographical in their focus, and real people and real lives are very much to the fore. The texts are divided here by genre. The first selection comes from saints' lives and female religious writings, and the extracts provided here are largely concerned with the role of female sanctity in relation to marriage. Important here is the idea of 'spiritual marriage', the taking of vows of chastity within marriage (on which see Elliott 1993). Importantly, neither partner could take vows of chastity without the other's consent, for, as Paul says in 1 Cor. 7, each partner has power over the other's body (cf. the Penitential of Theodore XIV. 7 – extract 7 and n.). These texts take the two paths in life usually available to medieval women – marriage and religion – and examine the difficulties that arise when they are juxtaposed.

While all of the texts in this opening selection are concerned with the lives of women, it should be noted that the women do not all speak entirely on their own behalf. Rather, their words are mediated through male clerical amanuenses. That authors should not themselves put pen to paper was not an uncommon thing in the Middle Ages, for writing was a form of manual labour, and the *scriptor*, the person who actually copied down the words, was usually understood to contribute nothing at all of their own to the text (Minnis 1988: 94–95). Rather, it was the *auctor* of the book who was the source of what it had to say. However, women's relationship to literary authority was problematic in the Middle Ages, given St Paul's injunction against the teaching of women in 1 Tim. 2. 12, where he says 'But I suffer not a woman to teach, nor to use authority over the man: but to be in silence.' And so the male amanuenses of female-authored texts, such as that of Margery Kempe, play a different role from that of the male *scriptor* of male-authored texts (see Johnson 1991).

It is possible to trace a line of influence between these texts. Mary of Oignies's *Vita* exercises an influence on Margery Kempe (Stargardt 1985) despite Jacques de Vitry's concern to discourage imitators. Bridget of Sweden does likewise. And we can see the influence of the story of St Cecilia upon both Christina of Markyate and Margery Kempe. Commenting on this tendency of pious women to adopt influences, Dyan Elliott writes:

> Pious behaviour is inevitably realized within a larger discourse of sanctity with which the confessor would attempt to align his holy charge. Clerical advisers would be inclined to recast their subject's marriage into an exemplary mold, constructed around a veritable handbook of marital usage. But the confessor was hardly alone in these efforts. Action and the narrative recital of action could not and did not exist independent of appropriate hagiographical structures. Female piety operated within this set of constraints.
>
> (Elliott 1993: 106–107)

Again, this is partly about authority. Pointing to the examples of St Bridget, St Mary of Oignies, St Cecilia and her contemporary Julian of Norwich, allows Margery Kempe to justify her own position in terms of orthodox models of Christian piety, when to some contemporaries her position seemed dangerously close to that of the heretical Lollards.

The second set of texts presented here are extracts from correspondence. Two come from very well-known collections – one from the letters that tell the tragic love story of the philosopher Peter Abelard and his pupil Heloise, and another from the enormous collection of correspondence relating to the fifteenth-century Paston family. The extract here from Abelard's *Historia Calamitatum* is a narrative account of his relationship with Heloise, the details of which are confirmed by her subsequent letters. The account is in some ways a literary one, for letters are a form of literature in the Middle Ages in a sense which is no longer current nowadays, when our definition of what constitutes 'literature' is far narrower (on which see Burrow 1982). So we should not be surprised to find, in this factual narrative account, an echo of Ovid, just as we find them in Andreas Capellanus, Guillaume de Lorris, Geoffrey Chaucer and John Gower. Abelard's account of being discovered with Heloise is phrased in part in terms of a comparison with Ovid's story of Venus caught in the act (Radice 1974: 69, n. 1). And Heloise herself goes on to have a literary career as a narrative *exemplum*, making an appearance in Chaucer's Wife of Bath's Prologue (extract 71). The other well-known extract here, from the Paston letters, is an account of a clandestine marriage. This is a real example of the sort of problematic unions that so troubled ecclesiastical legislators through the thirteenth and fourteenth centuries, as we have already seen (extracts 14, 15).

The third group of extracts are a selection of passages from chronicles, contemporary works of narrative history. Chronicles are rarely unbiased, factual accounts, and two here in particular – accounts of bestiality and hermaphrodism (extracts 43 and 44) – demonstrate the medieval chronicler's love of reporting 'wonders'. Richard of Devizes's chronicle, as John Scattergood argues, is deliberately 'misrepresenting' London here in literary terms derived from Horace (Scattergood 1996: 20), and Froissart's unreliability is notorious. Furthermore, hostility towards sexual activities can sometimes be matched to a political agenda in some of these chronicle accounts. Froissart's account of the execution of Hugh Despenser combines charges of sodomy, heresy and treachery (extract 45) – sexual, religious and political deviance are all part of the accusation here. Likewise Giraldus Cambrensis's account of the bestial practices of the Irish (extract 43) has a transparent association with a Norman political agenda. We cannot, then, take chronicle accounts of sexual behaviour at anything like face value. But they can, nonetheless, tell us a great deal about mindsets.

The fourth and final group of texts included in Part III are not descriptive but explicitly prescriptive: conduct books concerning virginity and marriage respectively. Each provides examples of what is to be emulated and what avoided: *Holy Virginity* is particularly interesting for the ferocity of its attack upon marriage. The texts also paint vivid descriptions of physical pain in women's lives, discussing as they do the pains of labour (extract 46, cf. extract 77) and domestic violence (extract 47), although in each case perhaps more for rhetorical effect than descriptive accuracy.

SAINTS' LIVES AND FEMALE RELIGIOUS WRITINGS

36 *The Life of Christina of Markyate*

Christina was born with the name Theodora into the Anglo-Saxon nobility, later becoming prioress of Markyate. Her *Life* was composed by a monk of St Albans who knew her personally. The *Life* describes how, having taken a vow of virginity, she rejects an attempt by Ralph Flambard (later bishop of Durham) to seduce her. Ralph then persuades her parents to marry her to a young man named Burthred. Christina exchanges consent to marry, but will not consummate the union. This is the episode described in this extract.

Further reading: Talbot 1959, Head 1990, Cartlidge 1997: ch. 3, Saunders 2001: ch. 3.

Text: C. H. Talbot (ed. and trans.) (1959) *The Life of St Christina of Markyate: A Twelfth-Century Recluse*, Oxford: Oxford University Press.

All I know is that by God's will, with so many exerting pressure on her from all sides, she yielded (at least in word) and on that very day Burthred was betrothed to her.

After the espousal the maiden returned once more to her parents' home while her husband, though he had houses elsewhere, built her a new and larger dwelling-place near his father-in-law. But although she was engaged,[1] her former intentions were not changed, and she

1 Talbot translates 'But although she was married'. The Latin reads 'Ipsi tamen etsi desponsata', which might be taken to mean that she was engaged rather than married. But see Head (1990: 89 and n. 53) on the lack of linguistic precision in distinguishing between betrothal and marriage in Christina's *Life*. On the distinction generally, Dauviller (1933: 18, 56) notes that Huguccio of Pisa reserves the terms *desponsatio* and *sponsalia* for future consent only, but earlier legislation refers to *desponsatio* simply as matrimonial consent, without distinguishing

freely expressed her determination not to submit to the physical embraces of any man. The more her parents became aware of her persistence in this frame of mind, the more they tried to break down her resistance, first by flattery, then by reproaches, sometimes by presents and grand promises, and even by threats and punishment. [. . .]

{Christina's parents try various means to outwit their daughter}

And at night they let her husband secretly into her bedroom in order that, if he found the maiden asleep, he might suddenly take her by surprise and overcome her. But even through that providence to which she had commended herself, she was found dressed and awake, and she welcomed the young man as if he had been her brother. And sitting on the bed with him, she strongly encouraged him to live a chaste life, putting forward the saints as examples. She recounted to him in detail the story of St. Cecilia and her husband Valerian, telling him how, at their death they were accounted worthy to receive crowns of unsullied chastity from the hands of an angel.[2] Not only this: but both they and many others after them had followed the path of martyrdom and thus, being crowned twice by the Lord, were honoured both in heaven and on earth. 'Let us, therefore,' she exhorted him, 'follow their example, so that we may become their companions in eternal glory. Because if we suffer with them, we shall also reign with them. Do not take it amiss that I have declined your embraces. In order that your friends may not reproach you with being rejected by me, I will go home with you: and let us live together there for some time, ostensibly as husband and wife, but in reality living chastely in the sight of the Lord. But first let us join hands in a compact that neither meanwhile will touch the other unchastely, neither will look upon the other except with a pure and angelic gaze, making a promise that in three or four years' time we will receive the religious habit and offer ourselves . . . to some monastery which providence shall appoint.' When the greater part of the night had

between present and future. Helmholz (1974: 31) argues for a difference between formal law and popular attitudes regarding the distinction of present and future consent in later medieval England.

2 On the popularity of the story of St Cecilia in Anglo-Saxon times, see Head 1990: 84. The story is subsequently told by Chaucer in his *Second Nun's Tale*. Cf. the echo of St Cecilia's life in *The Book of Margery Kempe* (extract 39).

passed with talk such as this, the young man eventually left the maiden. When those who had got him into the room heard what had happened, they joined together in calling him a spineless and useless fellow. And with many reproaches they goaded him on again, and thrust him into her bedroom another night, having warned him not to be misled by her deceitful tricks and naive words nor to lose his manliness. Either by force or entreaty he was to gain his end. And if neither of these sufficed, he was to know that they were at hand to help him: all he had to mind was to act the man.

When Christina sensed this, she hastily sprang out of bed and clinging with both hands to a nail which was fixed in the wall, she hung trembling between the wall and the hangings. Burthred meanwhile approached the bed and, not finding what he expected, he immediately gave a sign to those waiting outside the door. They crowded into the room forthwith and with lights in their hands ran from place to place looking for her, the more intent on their quest as they knew she was in the room when he entered it, and could not have escaped without their seeing her. What, I ask you, were her feelings at that moment? How she kept trembling as they noisily sought after her. Was she not faint with fear? She saw herself already dragged out in their midst, all surrounding her, looking upon her, threatening her, given up to the sport of her destroyer. At last one of them touched and held her foot as she hung there, but since the curtain in between deadened his sense of touch, he let it go, not knowing what it was. Then the maiden of Christ, taking courage, prayed to God, saying: 'Let them be turned backward, that desire my hurt':[3] and straightaway they departed in confusion and from that moment she was safe.

Nevertheless, Burthred entered her room a third time on a similar state of agitated fury. But as he came in one door, she fled through another. In front of her was a kind of fence which, because of its height and the sharp spikes on top of it, was calculated to prevent anyone from climbing over it: behind her almost on her heels was the young man, who at any moment would catch hold of her. With amazing ease she jumped over the fence and, looking back from her place of safety, saw her pursuer on the other side, standing there unable to follow. Then she said: 'Truly in escaping him, I have escaped from the devil I saw last night.' For, in her sleep, she had seen as it were a devil of horrible appearance with blackened teeth who was unavailingly trying to seize her, because in her flight she

3 Psalm 69.4.

had sprung at one leap over a high fence. Whilst her parents were setting these and other traps for her they fixed the day for the marriage with their son-in-law several times. For they hoped that some occasion would arise when they could take advantage of her. For what woman could hope to escape so many snares? And yet, with Christ guarding the vow which his spouse had made, the celebration of the wedding could nohow be brought about. Indeed, when the day which they had fixed approached and all the necessary preparations for the marriage had been arranged, it happened first of all that all the things prepared were burned with an unexpected fire, and then that the bride was taken with fever. In order to drive away the fever, sometimes they thrust her into cold water, at other times they blistered her excessively.

37 Jacques de Vitry, *The Life of Mary of Oignies*

This is an extract from the Middle English translation of Jacques de Vitry's 1215 Latin *Life of St Mary of Oignies*. Jacques takes great pains to stress that Mary's life is not to be imitated by the laity, and that she remains under her husband's authority. Nonetheless, Mary's *Life* is referred to by women in similar situations such as Margery Kempe.

Further reading: on Mary's influence on Margery Kempe, Stargardt 1985. On 'spiritual marriage' generally, Elliott 1993.

Text: C. Horstmann (1885) 'Prosalegenden: Die Legenden des ms. Douce 114', *Anglia* 8; Modern English: my translation.

CHAPTER 2. OF HER MATRIMONY

And therefore they [her parents] having envy of her gracious deeds, when she was fourteen years old, married her to a young man. So then she, removed from father and mother, was kindled into such overpowering fervour and with such great struggle chastised her body and brought it under control, that often, when she had worked with her own hands a great part of the night, after labour she was a very long time in her prayers; and that other portion of the night, as often as it was permissible for her, she slept very little, and that upon a lattice, which she had secretly hidden at the foot of her bed. And because she did not have power over her own body openly, she wore secretly under her smock a very sharp cord, with which she was tightly bound. I do not say this, praising the excess, but recounting the fervour. In this and in many other things that she did by privilege of grace, let the discreet reader take heed that the privilege of a few does not make a common law. We follow her virtues; [the works of her virtues] without special privilege we may not follow. Truly, though the body is to be constrained to serve the spirit; though we ought to bear in our body the wounds of our Lord Jesus Christ, nevertheless we know that the king's worship loves law and right, and that sacrifice of violence does not please our Lord. Certainly, necessities are not to be withdrawn from the poor flesh, but vices are to be refrained from. And therefore those things that we read some saints have done through familiar and homely counsel of the Holy Ghost, we shall rather marvel at them than follow them.

CHAPTER 3. OF THE CONVERSION OF HER SPOUSE AND THAT THEY FORSOOK THE WORLD AND LIVED CHASTELY

And when she so a good while had lived with John, her spouse, in matrimony, our Lord beheld the meekness of his maiden and graciously heard her prayers: for John was inspired to have Mary as a guardian, whom he had first to wife. He made the chaste man guardian of his maiden, that she should have solace of her keeper, and left to her a true overseer, that she might more freely serve Our Lord.

38 St Bridget (Birgitta) of Sweden, *Liber Celestis*

This extract from the fourteenth-century Middle English version of St Bridget's account of her revelations are God's words to Bridget (*c.*1303–1373) describing her spiritual marriage to him.

Further reading: on the influence of Bridget in fifteenth century England, Ellis 1982.

Text: Roger Ellis (ed.) (1987) *The Liber Celestis of St Bridget of Sweden*, Oxford: Oxford University Press.

'I have chosen you and taken you as my spouse, for it pleases me and likes me to do so, and for I wish to show to you my privy secrets. For you are mine by right in a way, for as much as you assigned your will into my hands at the time of your husband's dying, after whose burying you had great thought and prayed how you might be poor for me: and you had it in your will and desire to forsake all things for me. And then when you had by right made yourself mine in that way, it belonged to me to purvey and ordain for you; wherefore I take you to me as my spouse to my own personal delight, as it is according and fitting that God have his delight with a chaste soul. As you know, it belongs to a spouse to be honestly and seemingly arrayed and to be ready when the husband will make the wedding. Then you are made clean when, with regret that you have sinned, you call to mind how, in baptism, I cleansed you from Adam's sin, and how often afterwards, when you had fallen in sin, I tolerated it and supported you. Also, the spouse ought to have tokens of the husband upon her breast. So shall you ever carry freshly in the knowledge of your mind the kindness and the works which I have done for you: how nobly I made you, how generously I gave my gifts to you, how sweetly I redeemed you, and how goodly I restored you to your inheritance, if you will have it. The spouse ought to do also the husband's will. My will is that you love me above all other and that you will desire nothing but to please me.'

39 *The Book of Margery Kempe*

Margery Kempe (born *c.*1373, died after 1439) was a middle-class woman from King's Lynn in Norfolk who controversially abandoned her married life on being urged to do so by religious visions. Her Book, early fifteenth century, written with the aid of two amanuenses, records her life, and the extracts given below deal with her marriage, her desire to abandon her married life for a life of chastity, and her subsequent spiritual marriage to God.

Further reading: Stargardt 1985, Aers 1988, Lochrie 1991, Dinshaw 1999.

Text: B. A. Windeatt (trans.) (1985) *The Book of Margery Kempe*, Harmondsworth: Penguin.

(I)

One night, as this creature lay in bed with her husband, she heard a melodious sound so sweet and delectable that she thought she had been in paradise. And immediately she jumped out of bed and said,

'Alas that ever I sinned! It is full merry in heaven.' This melody was so sweet that it surpassed all the melody that might be heard in this world, without any comparison, and it caused this creature when she afterwards heard any mirth or melody to shed very plentiful and abundant tears of high devotion, with great sobbings and sighings for the bliss of heaven, not fearing the shames and contempt of this wretched world. And ever after her being drawn towards God in this way, she kept in mind the joy and the melody that there was in heaven, so much so that she could not very well restrain herself from speaking of it. For when she was in company with any people she would often say, 'It is full merry in heaven!'

And those who knew of her behaviour previously and now heard her talk so much of the bliss of heaven said to her, 'Why do you talk so of the joy that is in heaven? You don't know it, and you haven't been there any more than we have.' And they were angry with her because she would not hear or talk of worldly things as they did, and as she did previously.

And after this time she never had any desire to have sexual intercourse with her husband, for paying the debt of matrimony was so abominable to her that she would rather, she thought, have eaten and drunk the ooze and muck in the gutter than consent to intercourse, except out of obedience.

And so she said to her husband, 'I may not deny you my body, but all the love and affection of my heart is withdrawn from all earthly creatures and set on God alone.' But he would have his will with her, and she obeyed with much weeping and sorrowing because she could not live in chastity. And often this creature desired to live chaste and said that they had often (she well knew) displeased God by their inordinate love, and the great delight that each of them had in using the other's body, and now it would be a good thing if by mutual consent they punished and chastised themselves by abstaining from the lust of their bodies. Her husband said it was good to do so, but he might not yet – he would do so when God willed. And so he used her as he had done before, he would not desist. And all that time she prayed to God that she might live chaste, and three or four years afterwards, when it pleased our Lord, her husband made a vow of chastity, as shall be written afterwards, by Jesus' leave.

And also, after this creature heard this heavenly melody, she did great bodily penance. She was sometimes shriven two or three times on the same day, especially of that sin which she had so long concealed and covered up, as is written at the beginning of this book. She gave herself up to much fasting and keeping of vigils; she rose at two or three of the clock and went to church, and was there at her prayers until midday and also the whole afternoon. And then she was slandered and reproved by many people because she led so strict a life. She got herself a hair-cloth from a kiln – the sort that malt is dried on – and put it on inside her gown as discreetly and secretly as she could, so that her husband should not notice it. And nor did he, although she lay beside him every night in bed and wore the hair-shirt every day, and bore him children during that time.

(II)

It happened one Friday, Midsummer Eve, in very hot weather – as this creature was coming from York carrying a bottle of beer in her hand, and her husband a cake tucked inside his clothes against his chest – that her husband asked his wife this question: 'Margery, if there came a man with a sword who would strike off my head unless I made love with you as I used to do before, tell me on your conscience – for you say you will not lie – whether you would allow my head to be cut off, or else allow me to make love with you again, as I did at one time?'

'Alas, sir,' she said, 'why are you raising this matter, when we have been chaste for these past eight weeks?'

'Because I want to know the truth of your heart.'

And then she said with great sorrow, 'Truly, I would rather see you being killed, than that we should turn back to our uncleanness.'

And he replied, 'You are no good wife.'

And then she asked her husband what was the reason that he had not made love to her for the past eight weeks, since she lay with him every night in his bed. And he said that he was made so afraid when he would have touched her, that he dared do no more.

'Now sir, mend your ways and ask God's mercy, for I told you nearly three years ago that you[r desire for sex][4] would suddenly be slain – and this is now the third year, and I hope yet that I shall have my wish. Good sir, I pray you to grant what I shall ask, and I shall pray for you to be saved through the mercy of our Lord Jesus Christ, and you shall have more reward in heaven than if you wore a hair-shirt or wore a coat of mail as a penance. I pray you, allow me to make a vow of chastity at whichever bishop's hand that God wills.'

4 The addition in brackets was added by another hand to the manuscript. David Aers (1988: 93) argues for a parallel here with the life of St Cecilia whose husband will be slain by an angel if he attempts to have sex with her.

'No,' he said, 'I won't allow you to do that, because now I can make love to you without mortal sin, and then I wouldn't be able to.'

Then she replied, 'If it be the will of the Holy Ghost to fulfil what I have said, I pray God that you may consent to this; and if it be not the will of the Holy Ghost, I pray God that you never consent.'

Then they went on towards Bridlington and the weather was extremely hot, this creature all the time having great sorrow and great fear for her chastity. As they came by a cross her husband sat down under the cross, calling his wife to him and saying these words to her: 'Margery, grant me my desire, and I shall grant you your desire. My first desire is that we shall still lie together in one bed as we have done before; the second, that you shall pay my debts before you go to Jerusalem; and the third, that you shall eat and drink with me on Fridays as you used to do.'

'No sir,' she said, 'I will never agree to break my Friday fast as long as I live.'

'Well,' he said, 'then I'm going to have sex with you again.'

She begged him to allow her to say her prayers, and he kindly allowed it. Then she knelt down beside a cross in the field and prayed in this way, with a great abundance of tears: 'Lord God, you know all things. You know what sorrow I have had to be chaste for you in my body all these three years, and now I might have my will and I dare not, for love of you. For if I were to break that custom of fasting from meat and drink on Fridays which you commanded me, I should now have my desire. But, blessed God, you know I will not go against your will, and great is my sorrow now unless I find comfort in you. Now, blessed Jesus, make your will known to my unworthy self, so that I may afterwards follow and fulfil it with all my might.'

And then our Lord Jesus Christ with great sweetness spoke to this creature, commanding her to go again to her husband and pray him to grant her what she desired: 'And he shall have what he desires. For, my beloved daughter, this was the reason why I ordered you to fast, so that you should the sooner obtain your desire, and now it is granted to you. I no longer wish you to fast, and therefore I command you in the name of Jesus to eat and drink as your husband does.'

Then this creature thanked our Lord Jesus Christ for his grace and his goodness, and afterwards got up and went to her husband, saying to him, 'Sir, if you please, you shall grant me my desire, and you shall have your desire. Grant me that you will not come into my bed, and I grant you that I will pay your debts before I go to Jerusalem. And make my body free to God, so that you never make any claim on me regarding any conjugal debt after this day as long as you live – and I shall eat and drink on Fridays at your bidding.'

Then her husband replied to her, 'May your body be as freely available to God as it has been to me.'

This creature thanked God greatly, rejoicing that she had her desire, praying her husband that they should say three paternosters in worship of the Trinity for the great grace that had been granted them. And so they did, kneeling under a cross, and afterwards they ate and drank together in great gladness of spirit. This was on a Friday, on Midsummer's Eve.

Then they went on to Bridlington and also to many other places, and spoke with God's servants, both anchorites and recluses, and many other of our Lord's lovers, with many worthy clerics, doctors, and bachelors of divinity as well, in many different places. And to various people amongst them this creature revealed her feelings and her contemplations, as she was commanded to do, to find out if there were any deception in her feelings.

(III)

As this creature was in the church of the Holy Apostles at Rome on St Lateran's Day, the Father of Heaven said to her, 'Daughter, I am well pleased with you, inasmuch as you believe in all the sacraments of Holy Church and in all faith involved in that, and especially because you believe in the manhood of my son, and because of the great compassion that you have for his bitter Passion.'

The Father also said to this creature, 'Daughter, I will have you wedded to my Godhead, because I shall show you my secrets and my counsels, for you shall live with me without end.'

Then this creature kept silence in her soul and did not answer to this, because she was very much afraid of the Godhead; and she had no knowledge of the conversation of the Godhead, for all her love and affection were fixed on the manhood of Christ, and of that she did have knowledge and would not be parted from that for anything.

She had so much feeling for the manhood of Christ, that when she saw women in Rome carrying children in their arms, if she could discover that any were boys, she would cry, roar and weep as if she had seen Christ in his childhood. And if she could have had her way, she would often have taken the children out of their mothers' arms and kissed them instead of Christ. And if she saw a handsome man, she had a great pain to look at him, lest she might see him who was both God and man. And therefore she cried many times and often when she met a handsome man, and wept and sobbed bitterly for the manhood of Christ as she went about the streets of Rome, so that those who saw her were greatly astonished at her, because they did not know the reason.

Therefore it was not surprising if she was still and did not answer the Father of Heaven, when he told her that she should be wedded to his Godhead. Then the Second Person, Christ Jesus, whose manhood she loved so much, said to her, 'What do you say to my Father, Margery, daughter, about these words that he speaks to you? Are you well pleased that it should be so?'

And then she would not answer the Second Person, but wept amazingly much, desiring to have himself still, and in no way to be parted from him. Then the Second Person in Trinity answered his Father for her, and said, 'Father, excuse her, for she is still only young, and has not completely learned how she should answer.'

And then the Father took her by the hand [spiritually] in her soul, before the Son and the Holy Ghost, and the Mother of Jesus, and all the twelve apostles, and St Katharine and St Margaret and many other saints and holy virgins, with a great multitude of angels, saying to her soul, 'I take you, Margery, for my wedded wife, for fairer, for fouler, for richer, for poorer, provided that you are humble and meek in doing what I command you to do. For, daughter, there was never a child so kind to its mother as I shall be to you, both in joy and sorrow, to help you and comfort you. And that I pledge to you.'

(IV) [GOD SPEAKS TO HER]

'For it is appropriate for the wife to be on homely terms with her husband. Be he ever so great a lord and she ever so poor a woman when he weds her, yet they must lie together and rest together in joy and peace. Just so it must be between you and me, for I take no heed of what you have been but what you would be, and I have often told you that I have clean forgiven you all your sins.

'Therefore I must be intimate with you, and lie in your bed with you. Daughter, you greatly desire to see me, and you may boldly, when you are in bed, take me to you as your wedded husband, as your dear darling, and as your sweet son, for I want to be loved as a son should be loved by the mother, and I want you to love me, daughter, as a good wife ought to love her husband. Therefore you can boldly take me in the arms of your soul and kiss my mouth, my head, and my feet as sweetly as you want. And as often as you think of me or would do any good deed to me, you shall have the same reward in heaven as if you did it to my own precious body which is in heaven, for I ask no more of you but your heart, to love me who loves you, for my love is always ready for you.'

LETTERS

40 Letters of Abelard and Heloise

Peter Abelard (*c.*1079–*c.*1142) was a theologian and philosopher, Heloise (d. 1164) his pupil, his lover and then his wife, and, following their separation and entry into religion, eventually abbess of the Paraclete, near Troyes. These extracts are from Abelard's *Historia Calamitatum* (*c.*1132), a piece of autobiographical writing which seems to provoke the subsequent correspondence with Heloise. The extracts describe their affair and its disastrous consequences.

Further reading: as well as the letters in Radice 1974, see also the recently discovered additional correspondence in Mews 1999.

Text: Betty Radice (trans.) (1974) *The Letters of Abelard and Heloise*, Harmondsworth: Penguin.

There was in Paris at the time a young girl named Heloise, the niece of Fulbert, one of the canons, and so much loved by him that he had done everything in his power to advance her education in letters. In looks she did not rank lowest, while in the extent of her learning she stood supreme. A gift for letters is so rare in women that it added greatly to her charm and had won her renown throughout the realm. I considered all the usual attractions for a lover and decided she was the one to bring to my bed, confident that I should have an easy success; for at that time I had youth and exceptional good looks as well as my great reputation to recommend me, and feared no rebuff from any woman I might choose to honour with my love. Knowing the girl's knowledge and love of letters I thought she would be all the more ready to consent, and that even when separated we could enjoy each other's presence by exchange of written messages in which we could speak more openly than in person, and so need never lack the pleasures of conversation.

All on fire with desire for this girl I sought an opportunity of getting to know her through private daily meetings and so more easily winning her over; and with this end in view I came to an arrangement with her uncle, with the help of some of his friends, whereby he should take me into his house, which was very near my school, for whatever sum he liked to ask. As a pretext I said that my household cares were hindering my studies and the expense was more than I could afford. Fulbert dearly loved money, and was moreover always ambitious to further his niece's education in letters, two weaknesses which made it easy for me to gain his consent and obtain my desire: he was all eagerness for my money and confident that his niece would profit from my teaching. This led him to make an urgent request which furthered my love and fell in with my wishes more than I had dared to hope; he gave me complete charge over the girl, so that I could devote all the leisure time left me by my school to teaching her by day and night, and if I found her idle I was to punish her severely. I was amazed by his simplicity – if he had entrusted a tender lamb to a ravening wolf it would not have surprised me more. In handing her over to me to punish as well as to teach, what else was he doing but giving me complete freedom to realize my desires, and providing an opportunity, even if I did not make use of it, for me to bend her to my will by threats and blows if persuasion failed? But there were two special reasons for his freedom from base suspicion: his love for his niece and my previous reputation for continence.

Need I say more? We were united, first under one roof, then in heart; and so with our lessons as a pretext we abandoned ourselves entirely to love. Her studies allowed us to withdraw in private, as love desired, and then with our books open before us, more words of love than of our reading passed between us, and more kissing than teaching. My hands strayed oftener to her bosom than to the pages; love drew our eyes to look on each other more than reading kept them on our texts. To avert suspicion I sometimes struck her, but these blows were prompted by love and tender feeling rather than anger and irritation, and were sweeter than any balm could be. In short, our desires left no stage of love-making untried, and if love could devise something new, we welcomed it. We entered on each joy the more eagerly for our previous inexperience, and were the less easily sated.

[. . .]

But what is last to be learned is somehow learned eventually, and common knowledge cannot easily be hidden from one individual. Several months passed and then this happened in our case. Imagine the uncle's grief at the discovery, and the lovers' grief too at being separated! How I blushed with shame and contrition for the girl's plight, and what sorrow she suffered at the thought of my disgrace! All our laments were for one another's troubles, and our distress was for each other, not for ourselves. Separation drew our hearts still closer while frustration inflamed our passion even more; then we became more abandoned as we lost all sense of shame and, indeed, shame diminished as we found more opportunities for love-making. And so we were caught in the act as the poet says happened to Mars and Venus. Soon afterwards the girl found that she was pregnant, and immediately wrote me a letter full of rejoicing to ask what I thought she should do. One night then, when her uncle was away from home, I removed her secretly from his house, as we had planned, and sent her straight to my own country. There she stayed with my sister until she gave birth to a boy, whom she called Astralabe.

On his return her uncle went almost out of his mind – one could appreciate only by experience his transports of grief and mortification. What action could he take against me? What traps could he set? He did not know. If he killed me or did me personal injury, there was the danger that his beloved niece might suffer from it in my country. It was useless to try to seize me or to confine me anywhere against my will, especially as I was very much on guard against this very thing, knowing that he would not hesitate to assault me if he had the courage or the means.

In the end I took pity on his boundless misery and went to him, accusing myself of the deceit love had made me commit as if it were the basest treachery. I begged his forgiveness and promised to make any amends he might think fit. I protested that I had done nothing unusual in the eyes of anyone who had known the power of love, and recalled how since the beginning of the human race women had brought the noblest men to ruin. Moreover, to conciliate him further, I offered him satisfaction in a form he could never have hoped for: I would marry the girl I had wronged. All I stipulated was that the marriage should be kept secret so as not to damage my reputation.[5] He agreed, pledged his word and that of his supporters, and sealed the reconciliation I desired with a kiss. But his intention was to make it easier to betray me.

[. . .]

5 Abelard is proposing a clandestine union, which will be a valid marriage in canon law, making their child legitimate, and preventing either partner from marrying someone else. Being secret, however, it will not impede his career within the Church.

[Heloise objects to the proposed marriage]
[. . .]
And so when our baby son was born we entrusted him to my sister's care and returned secretly to Paris. A few days later, after a night's private vigil of prayer in a certain church, at dawn we were joined in matrimony in the presence of Fulbert and some of his, and our, friends. Afterwards we parted secretly and went our ways unobserved. Subsequently our meetings were few and furtive, in order to conceal as far as possible what we had done. But Fulbert and his servants, seeking satisfaction for the dishonour done to him, began to spread the news of the marriage and break the promise of secrecy they had given me. Heloise cursed them and swore that there was no truth in this, and in his exasperation Fulbert heaped abuse on her on several occasions. As soon as I discovered this I removed her to a convent of nuns in the town near Paris near Argenteuil, where she had been brought up and educated as a small girl, and I also had made for her a religious habit of the type worn by novices, with the exception of the veil, and made her put it on.

At this news her uncle and his friends and relatives imagined that I had tricked them, and had found an easy way of ridding myself of Heloise by making her a nun. Wild with indignation they plotted against me, and one night as I slept peacefully in an inner room in my lodgings, they bribed one of my servants to admit them and there took cruel vengeance on me of such appalling barbarity as to shock the whole world; they cut off the parts of my body whereby I had committed the wrong of which they complained. Then they fled, but the two who could be caught were blinded and mutilated as I had been, one of them being the servant who had been led by greed while in my service to betray his master.

41 The Paston Letters

This letter (September 1469) from Margaret Paston (d. 1484) to her son John Paston II describes the proceedings taken by the bishop of Norwich in attempting to determine whether or not Margery Paston, Margaret's daughter, had contracted a clandestine marriage with the family's bailiff, Richard Calle, as she claimed to have done.

Further reading: Haskell 1973, Richmond 1985.

Text: Middle English: Norman Davis (ed.) (1971–1976) *Paston Letters and Papers of the Fifteenth Century*, Oxford: Oxford University Press. Modern English: my translation.

I greet you and send you God's blessing and mine, letting you know that on Thursday last my mother and I were with my lord of Norwich, and asked him that he would do no more in the matter touching your sister until you and your brother, and others that were executors to your father, might be here together, for they had the rule of her as well as I. And he said plainly that he had been asked so often before to examine her that he might not, nor desired, to delay any longer, and charged me on pain of cursing that she should not be deferred but that she should appear before him the next day. And I said plainly that I would neither bring her nor send her; and then he said that he would send for her himself, and charged that she should be at her liberty to come when he sent for her. And he said by his faith that he would be as sorry for her if she did not do well as he would be if she were right near of his kin, for both my mother's sake and mine and others of her friends; for he knew well that her conduct had struck sorely at our hearts.

My mother and I informed him that we never could understand by what she said, nor by any language that she ever spoke to him, that neither of them were bound to the other, but that they might both choose. Then he said that he would say to her as well as he could before that he examined her; and so it was told me by diverse persons that he did as well and as plainly as she had been right close to him, which would be too long to write at this time. Hereafter you shall know, and who were labourers therein. The chancellor was not so guilty therein as I thought he had been.

On Friday the bishop sent for her by Asschefeld and others that are very sorry of their conduct. And the bishop said to her very plainly, and put her in remembrance of how she was born, what kin and friends that she had, and should still have if she was ruled and guided by them; and if she did not, what rebuke and shame and loss it should be to her if she were not guided by them, and cause of forsaking of her for any good or help or comfort that she should have of them; and said that he had heard say that she loved such a one that her friends were not pleased with that she should have, and therefore he bid her be very well advised how she acted, and said that he would understand the words that she had said to him, whether it made matrimony or not. And she rehearsed what she had said, and said if those words did not make it sure, she said boldly that she would make it sure before she went thence; for she said she thought in her conscience she was bound, whatsoever the words were. These lewd words grieve me and her grandmother as much as all the remnant. And then the bishop and the chancellor both said that there was neither I nor no friend of hers that would receive her. And then

Calle was examined apart by himself, that her words and his accorded, and the time and where it should have been done. And then the bishop said that he supposed that there should be found other things against him that might cause the hindrance thereof, and therefore he said he would not be too hasty to give sentence thereupon, and said that he would give over the day until the Wednesday or Thursday after Michaelmas, and so it is delayed. They would have had their will performed in haste, but the bishop said he wished no other way than he had said. I was with my mother at her place when she was examined, and when I heard her say what her conduct was I charged my servants that she should not be received in my house. I had given her warning, she might have been careful before if she had been gracious. And I sent to one or two more that they should not receive her if she came. She was brought again to my place for to be received, and Sir Jamys [Gloys, a servant] told them that brought her that I had charged them all, and she should not be received; and so my lord of Norwich has set her at Roger Bestys to be there until the day before said, God knows fully against his will and his wife's, if they dared do otherwise. I am sorry that they are encumbered with her, but yet I am better paid that she is there for the while than she had been in another place, because of the seriousness and good disposition of himself and his wife, for she shall not be suffered there to play the good-for-nothing.

I pray you and require you that you take it not sadly, for I know well it goes right near your heart, and so it does to mine and to others; but remember you, and so do I, that we have lost of her but a good-for-nothing, and take it less to heart; for if she had been good, whatsoever she had been it should not have been as it is, for if he were dead at this hour she would never be at my heart as she was. As for the divorce that you wrote to me of, I guess what you meant, but I charge you upon my blessing that you do not, nor cause any other to do, anything that should offend God and your conscience; for if you do, or cause it to be done, God will take vengeance upon you and you should put yourself and others in great jeopardy. For know it well, she shall very sorely repent her lewdness hereafter, and I pray God she may so. I pray you, for my heart's ease, be you of a good comfort in all things. I trust God shall help right well, and I pray God to do so in all your matters.

I would you took heed if there were any labour made in the court of Canterbury for the lewd matter aforesaid.

Unless the duke is provided for, he and his wise counsel shall lose this country. I'm told that he said that he will not spare to do what he is intending for any duke in England. God help at need.

CHRONICLES

42 *Chronicle of Richard of Devizes*

This is a (late twelfth-century) account of the sexual activities of Londoners, composed as a warning for a new arrival in the city. John Scattergood notes that part of this passage is based on Horace's *Satires* I.ii: 1–3. Richard's point in making the allusion is that what Horace says about first-century Rome is equally true of twelfth-century London (Scattergood 1996: 20).

Text: J. T. Appleby (ed. and trans.) (1963) *The Chronicle of Richard of Devizes*, London: Thomas Nelson.

When you reach England, if you come to London, pass through it quickly, for I do not at all like that city. All sorts of men crowd together there from every country under the heavens. Each race brings its own vices and its own customs to the city. No-one lives in it without falling into some sort of crime. Every quarter of it abounds in grave obscenities. The greater a rascal a man is, the better a man he is accounted. I know whom I am instructing. You have a warmth of character beyond your years, and a coolness of memory; and from these contrary qualities arises a temperateness of reasoning. I fear nothing from you, unless you live with evil companions, for manners are formed by association. Well, be that as it may! You will arrive in London. Behold, I prophesy to you: whatever evil or malicious thing that can be found in any part of the world, you will find in that one city. Do not associate with the crowds of pimps; do not mingle with the throngs in eating-houses; avoid dice and gambling, the theatre and the tavern. You will meet with more braggarts there than in all France; the number of parasites is infinite. Actors, jesters, smooth-skinned lads, Moors, flatterers, pretty boys, effeminates, pederasts, singing and dancing girls, quacks, belly-dancers, sorceresses, extortioners, night-wanderers, magicians, mimes, beggars, buffoons: all this tribe fill all the houses. Therefore, if you do not want to dwell with evildoers, do not live in London.

43 Giraldus Cambrensis, *The History and Topography of Ireland*

Giraldus Cambrensis (Gerald de Barry or Gerald of Wales, *c.*1146–*c.*1223) wrote two books about Ireland: one an account of the Anglo-Norman 'invasion' of 1169, in which his relatives the de Barrys played a prominent role, and the second a historical and topographical account (1188). The following extracts from the latter detail the supposedly bestial sexual practices of the Irish.

Text: Giraldus Cambrensis (1982) *The History and Topography of Ireland*, trans. John J. O'Meara, Harmondsworth: Penguin.

A MAN THAT WAS HALF AN OX AND AN OX THAT WAS HALF A MAN

In the neighbourhood of Wicklow at the time when Maurice fitzGerald[6] got possession of that country and the castle, an extraordinary man was seen – if indeed it be right to call him a man. He had all the parts of the human body except the extremities which were those of an ox. From the joinings of the hands with the arms and the feet with the legs, he had hooves the same as an ox. He had no hair on his head, but was disfigured with baldness both in front and behind. Here and there he had a little down instead of hair. His eyes were huge and were like those of an ox both in colour, and in being round. His face was flat as far as his mouth. Instead of a nose he had two holes to act as nostrils, but no protruberance. He could not speak at all; he could only low. He attended the court of Maurice for a long time. He came to dinner every day and, using his cleft hooves as his hands, placed in his mouth whatever was given him to eat. The Irish natives of the place, because the youths of the castle often taunted them with begetting such beings on cows,

6 Maurice Fitzgerald led the Anglo-Norman 'invasion' of Ireland in 1169 and was progenitor of the Geraldines, the leading Anglo-Norman dynasty in Ireland during the Middle Ages.

secretly killed him in the end in envy and malice – a fate which he did not deserve.

Shortly before the coming of the English into the island a cow from a man's intercourse with her – a particular vice of that people – gave birth to a man-calf in the mountains around Glendalough. From this you may believe that once again a man that was half an ox, and an ox that was half a man was produced. It spent nearly a year with the other calves following its mother and feeding on her milk, and then, because it had more of the man than the beast, was transferred to the society of men.

[. . .]

A GOAT THAT HAD INTERCOURSE WITH A WOMAN

Rothericus, king of Connacht,[7] had a tame white goat that was remarkable of its kind for the length of its coat and height of its horns. This goat had bestial intercourse with a certain woman to whom he was entrusted. The wretched woman, proving herself more a beast in accepting him than he did in acting, even submitted herself to his abuse.

How unworthy and unspeakable! How reason succumbs so outrageously to sensuality! That the lord of the brutes, losing the privileges of his high estate, should descend to the level of the brutes, when the rational submits itself to such shameful commerce with a brute animal! Although the matter was detestable on both sides and abominable, yet was it less so by far on the side of the brute who is subject to rational beings in all things, and because he was a brute and prepared to obey by very nature. He was, nevertheless, created not for abuse but for proper use. Perhaps we might say that nature makes known her indignation and repudiation of the act in verse:

> Only novelty pleases now: new pleasure is welcome;
> Natural love is outworn
> Nature pleases less than art; reason, no longer reasoning,
> Sinks in shame.

7 Ruadhrí Ó Conchubhair (or Rory O'Connor), king of Connacht and Ard Rí (high king) of Ireland, d. 1198.

A LION THAT LOVED A WOMAN

I saw in Paris a lion which a cardinal had given when it was a whelp to Philip the son of Louis,[8] then a boy. This lion used to make beastly love to a foolish woman called Johanna. Sometimes when he escaped from his cage and was in such fierce anger that no one would dare to go near him, they would send for Johanna who would calm his anger and great rage immediately. Soothing him with a woman's tricks, she led him wherever he wanted and changed all his fury immediately into love.

O Beasts! Both! Worthy of a shameful death! But such crimes have been attempted not only in modern times but also in antiquity, which is praised for its greater innocence and simplicity. The ancients also were stained with such unspeakable deeds. And so it is written in Leviticus: 'If a woman approaches any beast to have intercourse with him, ye shall kill the woman, and let the beast die the death.' The beast is ordered to be killed, not for the guilt, from which he is excused as being a beast, but to make the remembrance of the act as a deterrent, calling to mind the terrible deed.

44 *Annals of the Friars Minor of Colmar*

This is a chronicle's account (1308–1314) of an hermaphrodite. Interestingly, the idea of women as men turned inside out is a medieval medical commonplace, indebted to the authority of Galen (Bullough 1973: 492, Jacquart and Thomasset 1988: 17–18).

Further reading: Rubin 1994.

Text: Miri Rubin (1994), 'The Person in the Form: Medieval Challenges to Bodily "Order"', in *Framing Medieval Bodies*, ed. Sarah Kay and Miri Rubin, Manchester: Manchester University Press.

In a town near Bern . . . a woman lived for ten years with a man. Since she could not have sex with a man she was separated [from her partner] by the spiritual court. In Bologna (on her way to Rome), her vagina was cut open by a surgeon, and a penis and testicles came out. She returned home, married a wife, did hard [physical] labour, and had proper and adequate sexual congress with her wife.

8 Philip II (1165–1223), king of France (1180–1223), son of Louis VII.

45 Jean Froissart, *Chronicles*

Froissart (*c.*1337–*c.*1404), a French poet, chronicler and traveller, describes here the execution of Sir Hugh Despenser, accused among other things of being King Edward II's lover. John Boswell argues that the reported deaths of Hugh and Edward show the origin of the animosity against them. Despite the controversy surrounding the varying accounts of Edward's death, and the fact that Froissart is, as Boswell puts it, 'hardly the last word in accuracy', he notes that the penalty described here was the common French punishment for sodomy (Boswell 1980: 300 and nn. 92, 93).

Text: Froissart (1968) *Chronicles*, ed. and trans. Geoffrey Brereton, Harmondsworth: Penguin.

He was condemned by the unanimous verdict of the barons and knights to suffer the following punishment. First, he was dragged on a hurdle through all the streets of Hereford, to the sound of horns and trumpets, until he reached the main square of the town, where all the people were assembled. There he was tied to a long ladder, so that everyone could see him. A big fire had been lit in the square. When he had been tied up, his member and his testicles were first cut off, because he was a heretic and a sodomite, even, it was said, with the King, and this was why the King had driven away the Queen on his suggestion. When his private parts had been cut off they were thrown into the fire to burn, and afterwards his heart was torn from his body and thrown into the fire, because he was a false-hearted traitor, who by his treasonable advice and promptings had led the King to bring shame and misfortune upon his kingdom and to behead the greatest lords of England, by whom the kingdom ought to have been upheld and depended; and besides that, he had so worked upon the King that he, who should have been their consort and sire, had refused to see the Queen and his eldest son, but rather had expelled them from the realm of England, at the hazard of their lives.

CONDUCT BOOKS

46 *Holy Virginity* (*Hali Meiðhad*)

In the first extract from this early thirteenth-century text, the author discusses the evils of sex, through commenting on Psalm 44: 11: 'Listen daughter, and behold, and incline your ear; and forget your people and your father's house.' The second compares the merits of the virgin to those of the angels; the third describes the steps on the path to ruin for virgins; the fourth describes the physical pain involved in pregnancy and childbirth as a disincentive from sex. It's perhaps worth contrasting the tone here with that taken by Augustine in his discussion of the burdens of marriage in his *Holy Virginity*, quoted above.

Further reading: Cartlidge 1997: ch. 4.

Text: Bella Millet and Jocelyn Wogan-Browne (ed. and trans.) (1990) *Medieval English Prose for Women*, Oxford: Oxford University Press.

(I)

And forget your father's house too, as David advises next. 'Your father' he calls that sinful act through which your mother conceived you – that indecent heat of the flesh, that burning itch of physical desire, that animal union, that shameless coupling, that stinking and wanton deed, full of filthiness. (It is, nevertheless, to be tolerated to some extent within marriage, as you will hear later.) If you ask why God created such a thing, this is my answer: God never created it to be like this, but Adam and Eve perverted it through their sin and corrupted our nature, which is the house of this vice, which has – unfortunately – far too much dominance and mastery there.

(II)

Our flesh is our foe, and oppresses us and harms us as often as it defiles us; but if it keeps itself pure and intact, it is a very good friend to us and gives us help as a faithful servant. For in it and through it, maiden, you earn the right to be the equal of angels in the eternal bliss of heaven – and with good reason, when you lead their life in your frail flesh without unchastity. Angel and maiden are equal in virtue through the power of virginity, though as yet their degrees of blessedness divide them; and though their virginity is more blessed now, yours is more difficult to keep intact, and will be recompensed by a greater reward.

(III)

Lechery, with the help of physical desire, makes war on Virginity in this way. Her first help is sight: if you look often and intently at any man, Lechery at once prepares herself with that to make war on your virginity, and first advances on her face to face. Speech is her second help: if you then go on to talk together in a light way and speak of frivolous matters, Lechery slanders the honour of your virginity and abuses her outrageously, and threatens to do her shame and harm her later – and keeps her promise. For as soon as it comes to a kiss, which is her third help, then Lechery spits, as a sign of dishonour, in Virginity's face. The fourth help towards shame and the ruin of Virginity is indecent touching. Keep guard over her then; because if you then touch one another improperly in any place, then Lechery strikes at the virtue of Virginity and wounds her severely. The shameful act itself finally gives the death-blow. Oh, the pity of it! Virginity never revives after that wound. Oh, whoever saw then how the angels are distressed to see their sister so dreadfully overthrown, and the devils capering and clapping their hands together, laughing raucously, his heart would be stony if it did not melt in tears!

(IV)

Let us now go further, and see what happiness comes to you afterwards during pregnancy, when the child inside you quickens and grows, and how many miseries come into being at the same time, which cause you much unhappiness, assail your own flesh, and attack your own nature with many afflictions. Your rosy face will grow thin, and turn green as grass; your eyes will grow dull, and shadowed underneath, and because of your dizziness your head will ache cruelly. Inside, in your belly, a swelling in your womb which bulges you out like a water-skin, discomfort in your bowels and stitches in your side, and often painful backache; heaviness in every limb; the dragging weight of your two breasts, and the streams of milk that run from them. Your beauty is all destroyed by pallor; there is a bitter taste in your mouth, and everything that you eat makes you feel sick; and whatever food your stomach disdainfully receives – that is, with distaste – it throws up again. In the midst of all your happiness and your husband's delight, you are reduced to a wretch. Worry about your labour pains keeps you awake at night. Then when it comes to it, that cruel distressing anguish, that fierce and stabbing pain, that incessant misery, that torment upon torment, that wailing outcry; while you are suffering from this, and from your fear of death, shame added to that suffering with the shameful craft of the old wives who know about that painful ordeal, whose help is necessary to you, however indecent it may be; and there you must put up with whatever happens to you. You should not see this as morally wrong, for we do not blame women for their labour pains, which all our mothers suffered for ourselves; but we describe them as a warning to virgins, so that they should be the less inclined towards such things, and understand the better through this what they ought to do.[9]

47 *Book of the Knight of La Tour Landry*

This is a conduct book written by the Knight for the instruction of his daughters. The extract here concerns wifely obedience. The French text is from the 1370s, Caxton's English version from 1484.

Text: M. Y. Offord (ed.) (1971) *Caxton's Book of the Knight of the Tower*, Oxford: Oxford University Press. Modern English: my translation.

Accordingly, a woman in no way ought to strive against her husband, nor answer him so that he take displeasure thereby, as did the wife of a burgess who answered her husband so injuriously and shamefully before the public that he became angry to see himself treated

9 Cf. Trotula (extract 77) on childbirth.

so before the public, that he had shame thereof. And he said to her, and told her once or twice, that she should stop and be quiet, but she would not, and her husband who was angry struck her to the ground with his fist. And he hit her in the face with his foot so that he broke her nose, by which she was disfigured ever after. And so by her arguing and annoying she got herself a crooked nose, a great evil. It would have been much better for her if she had kept herself quiet and had endured, for it is reasonable and right that the husband have the loud words, and it is only honourable for a good woman to endure and keep herself quiet, and leave the violent language to her husband and lord. And also it is on the contrary a great shame and villainy for a woman to strive against her husband, be it wrong or right, and especially in public. I'm not saying that when she finds him alone at the right time, that she may not well reprehend him and advise him in showing courteously that he was wrong, and if a man is reasonable, he will feel thankful to her, and if he is otherwise, yet she has not done anything but her duty. For a wise woman should act just like this, as in the example of the wise Queen Esther, wife of the king Ahasuerus, who was very melancholic and short-tempered. But the good lady did not answer to his anger, but afterwards when she saw him better-tempered, at the right place and time, then she did what she wished to do. And this was great wisdom of a woman, and this is what women ought to do.

48 The Ménagier[10] of Paris, *Manual for his Wife*

This is a late fourteenth-century manual written by a husband for his young wife on her duties and responsibilities. The first extract here is a husband's imaginative portrait of domestic bliss, but the second is somewhat less blissful.

Text: Emilie Amt (1993) *Women's Lives in Medieval Europe: A Sourcebook,* London: Routledge; Amt's text adapted from Eileen Power (1928), *The Goodman of Paris,* London: Routledge.

(I)

The seventh article of the first section shows how you should be careful and thoughtful of your husband's person. So, fair sister, if you

10 'Householder' or 'Goodman'.

have another husband after me, know that you should think much of his person, for after a woman has lost her first husband and marriage, she commonly finds it hard to find a second to her liking, according to her rank, and she remains lonely and disconsolate for a long time, and the more so if she loses the second. So love your husband's person carefully, and I pray you keep him in clean linen, for that is your business, and because the trouble and care of outside affairs lies with men, so must husbands take heed, and go and come, and journey hither and thither, in rain and wind, in snow and hail, now drenched, now dry, now sweating, now shivering, ill-fed, ill-lodged, ill-warmed and ill-bedded. And nothing harms him, because he is upheld by the hope which he has of the care which his wife will take of him on his return, and of the ease, the joys and the pleasures which she will do to him, or cause to be done to him in her presence; to be unshod before a good fire, to have his feet washed and fresh shoes and hose, to be given good food and drink, to be well served and well looked after, well bedded in white sheets and nightcaps, well covered with good furs, and assuaged with joys and amusements, intimacies, loves and secrets whereof I am silent. And the next day fresh shirts and garments.

(II)

But there are certain old hags, who are sly and play the wise woman and pretend great love by way of showing their heart's great service, and nothing else; and be sure, fair sister, that the husbands are fools if they do not notice it. And when they do notice it, and the husband and wife grow silent, and pretend with each other, it is an ill beginning and will lead to a worse end. And there are some women who serve their husbands very well in the beginning, and then they find that their husbands are so loving to them and so good-tempered, that they think those husbands will scarcely dare to be angry with them, if they do less, so they slacken and little by little they try to show less respect and service and obedience, but – what is more – they take upon themselves authority, command and lordship, first in a small thing, then in a larger, and a little more every day. Thus they attempt and advance and rise, they think, and they think that their husbands, who say nothing about this because they are so good-tempered or perhaps because they are setting a trap, do not notice it, because they permit it thus. And certainly, it is an ill thought and deed, for when the husbands see that they cease their service, and climb to domination, and that they do it too much, and that by enduring ill, good may come, then those women are all at once, by their husband's rightful will, cast down even as Lucifer was . . . Wherefore you should be obedient in the beginning and ever persevere therein, according to this example.

Part IV

LITERARY SOURCES

INTRODUCTION

This part includes extracts from some of the best-known works of medieval literature – *Beowulf*, the *Romance of the Rose*, the *Canterbury Tales* – as well as many others that are less well known. The texts are subdivided into four sections. The first group of extracts are from Old English Literature. The others are from works written after 1100, and are grouped according to the language of composition: Latin, Old French and Middle English. These three languages are represented here because, while not all the texts here are composed in England, literate people in the multilingual culture of later medieval England would have had access to texts in all three, and most of the texts presented here would have been available to English readers.

Love, sex, and marriage are prominent themes in later medieval literature in particular (they are a less obvious concern in Old English literature). Love, sex, and marriage are thematically important in later medieval literary genres such as romance and *fabliau*. Furthermore, poems such as the *Canterbury Tales* and *Piers Plowman* are serious discussions of contemporary society, and so are concerned with major social issues like marriage. We might ask, however, whether imaginative texts can tell us anything about social realities in the medieval period? Reading literature for evidence about social practice is, of course, a risky business. I argued in the Introduction that in discussing the Middle Ages we might draw distinctions between acts and ideologies. If literary texts cannot offer us what we might regard as unproblematic empirical evidence about the actions of people in medieval society, they can tell us a great deal about ideologies. Like the chronicle accounts of Part III, even where factually dubious, literature can offer us evidence about mindsets.

Furthermore, we can trace overlaps between fictional and non-fictional texts, where each can help us to construct contexts for reading the other. Andreas Capellanus's *De Amore* (extract 55) is a good example of a text that is difficult to classify and which changes significantly depending upon the context in which it is read. C. S. Lewis (1936) read it as a manual of adultery. John T. Noonan (1986) and Jacquart and Thomasset (1988) read it as (among other things) a manual for contraception. Neil Cartlidge (1997) reads it as engaging with the canon law's formulation of what it is to be married. And so on. There are texts here that invite certain readings. *In the Ecclesiastical Court* (extract 66) for example, asks to be read alongside legal texts discussing the forcing of fornicators into marriage (or abjuration *sub pena nubendi* as it is called), and accounts of court cases where fornication occurs (see extract 15 above).

There are also some well-traced lines of influence in evidence. The opening lines of the *Wife of Bath's Prologue* (extract 71), perhaps the most richly allusive text here, declare a debt to the *Romance of the Rose* (extract 63). The names of the characters in the Wife's text imply a debt to the little lyric about Alison and Jankyn (extract 65): these are type names – note that Alison of Bath has a friend who is also called Alison, and there may or may not be more than one Jankyn in the Wife's prologue. The poem quotes exhaustively from Jerome, and from Theophrastus as he appears in Jerome (extract 6), and responds vigorously to Paul's 1 Corinthians 7. Whether deliberately or not, it covers some of the same territory as Augustine on widows (extract 4), and also the English statutes concerning bigamy (extract 15, on which see McCarthy 1999). And if the Wife's prologue is itself the subject of so many influences, it also goes on in turn to influence Chaucer's little poem of advice against marriage, *Envoy a Bukton* (extract 72) and Dunbar's poem *Upon the Midsummer's Eve, Merriest of Nights* (extract 76). In a broader view, the *Romance of the Rose* not only influences Chaucer's poem, but provokes the Debate of the Rose (extract 63) and the 'Letter of Cupid' (extract 75). And the classical Roman poet Ovid influences not just many of these texts, but also Andreas Capellanus, Peter Abelard and John Gower. Other suggestions for overlaps between the literary and non-literary: Angela Lucas (1983: 79–80) reads *The Wife's Lament* (extract 50) alongside a prescriptive text for the betrothal of a woman (extract 24). Jocelyn Wogan-Browne (2001: 128–131) draws a comparison between events in *Yonec* (extract 59) and the *Life* of Christine of Markyate (extract 36). Overall, then, literary texts have a great deal to say about love, sex and marriage, and what they have to say overlaps with non-literary texts in ways that can provide the modern reader with a broader sense of the thinking about these subjects in medieval culture.

OLD ENGLISH LITERATURE

49 *Beowulf*

The date of *Beowulf* is the subject of much controversy – the sole manuscript is from the early eleventh century.

This brief extract shows the use of marriages as peace treaties. Beowulf is speaking, describing his reception in the hall of Hrothgar, the Danish king. Hrothgar's daughter, Freawaru, is to be given in marriage to cement a peace agreement, but Beowulf is unconvinced that peace will be achieved, and allusions elsewhere in the poem confirm his suspicions to be correct.

Text: Michael Swanton (ed. and trans.) (1997) *Beowulf*, revised edn, Manchester: Manchester University Press.

At times the famous queen, peace-pledge of the nations,[1] passed through the entire building, encouraged the young warriors; often she presented a twisted circlet to a man before she went to her seat; at times Hrothgar's daughter carried an ale-cup before the tried men, to each of the warriors in turn. I heard those sitting in the hall call her Freawaru, as she presented the studded treasure to heroes.

Young, adorned with gold, she is promised to the gracious son of Froda.[2] That has been agreed upon by the Scyldings' friend, the guardian of the kingdom,[3] and he considers it good advice that, by means of this woman, he should settle their share of slaughterous feuds, of conflicts. It seldom happens after the fall of a prince that the deadly spear rests for even a little while – worthy though the bride may be!

1 The Danish queen, Wealhtheow. Wealhtheow's name means 'foreign slave'. For the implications of this meaning for marriage practices, see Hill 1990.

2 Ingeld, one of the Heathobards, who are feuding with the Danes.

3 Hrothgar, the Danish king.

50 *The Wife' s Lament*

Elegiac themes are common in Anglo-Saxon poetry, often emphasizing loss, absence, regret, and the transience of worldly things (Fell 1991). This poem (from the tenth-century manuscript the *Exeter Book*) and the two that follow it seem to apply these common motifs to love and marriage. All three poems, and the riddles of extract 53, are from the same manuscript, the *Exeter Book*, which contains a number of other 'elegiac' poems. Interpretation of *The Wife's Lament* depends on the view of the speaker's identity. Most take the speaker to be a wife lamenting her husband's absence (hence the title assigned to the poem), but others offer a supernatural interpretation.

Further reading: Leslie 1988, Fell 1991, Luyster 1998.

Text: Richard Hamer (ed. and trans.) (1970) *A Choice of Anglo-Saxon Verse*, London: Faber.

I sing this song about myself, full sad,
My own distress, and tell what hardships I
Have had to suffer since I first grew up,
Present and past, but never more than now;
I ever suffered grief through banishment.
For since my lord departed from this people
Over the sea, each dawn have I had care
Wondering where my lord may be on land.
When I set off to join and serve my lord,
A friendless exile in my sorry plight,
My husband's kinsmen plotted secretly
How they might separate us from each other
That we might live in wretchedness apart
Most widely in the world: and my heart longed.
In the first place my lord had ordered me
To take up my abode here, though I had
Among these people few dear loyal friends;
Therefore my heart is sad. Then had I found
A fitting man, but one ill-starred, distressed,
Whose hiding heart was contemplating crime,
Though cheerful his demeanour. We had vowed
Full many a time that nought should come between us
But death alone, and nothing else at all.
All that has changed, and it is now as though
Our marriage and our love had never been,

And far or near forever I must suffer
The feud of my beloved husband dear.
So in this forest grove they made me dwell,
Under the oak-tree, in this earthy barrow.
Old is this earth-cave, all I do is yearn.
The dales are dark with high hills up above,
Sharp hedge surrounds it, overgrown with briars,
And joyless is the place. Full often here
The absence of my lord comes sharply to me.
Dear lovers in this world lie in their beds,
While I alone at crack of dawn must walk
Under the oak-tree round this earthy cave,
Where I must stay the length of summer days,
Where I may weep my banishment and all
My many hardships, for I never can
Contrive to set at rest my careworn heart,
Nor all the longing that this life has brought me.
A young man always must be serious,
And tough his character; likewise he should
Seem cheerful, even though his heart is sad
With multitude of cares. All earthly joy
Must come from his own self. Since my dear lord
Is outcast, far off in a distant land,
Frozen by storms beneath a stormy cliff
And dwelling in some desolate abode
Beside the sea, my weary-hearted lord
Must suffer pitiless anxiety.
And all too often he will call to mind
A happier dwelling. Grief must always be
For him who yearning longs for his beloved.

51 *The Husband's Message*

Another elegiac poem from the tenth-century *Exeter Book*: the speaker here seems to be the rune-staff on which the message is carved.

Further reading: Leslie 1988, Fell 1991.

Text: Richard Hamer (ed. and trans.) (1970) *A Choice of Anglo-Saxon Verse*, London: Faber.

Now will I tell to you who live apart
How I grew up in youth among the trees.

On me must sons of men write messages,
Send me from foreign lands across the waves,
Thus guide their thoughts across the salty streams.
Often by boat have I sought out some land
Where my lord sent me forth to take some message
Over the deep wide sea; now have I come
On shipboard here, and now must I find out
How you feel in your heart about your love
Towards my lord. For I dare promise you
That you will find great loyalty in him.
He bids me tell you, then, who carved this wood,
That you, bejewelled, should yourself recall
In your own secret heart the vows and oaths
That you both made in former times together,
When you might still together live among
The festive cities, both dwell in one land,
And love each other. Feud drove him away
From this great people. Now he orders me
Himself to urge you joyfully to cross
The sea when at the hill-side's edge you hear
The cuckoo singing sad amid the grove.
Do not let any living man deter you
From travelling or stay you from the journey.
Go to the sea, the country of the gull,
And board a ship, that you may southwards thence
Rejoin your man across the water's ways,
There where your lord is waiting for your coming.
For in the world no stronger wish could come
Into his heart, he told me so himself,
Than that almighty God should grant you both
That you may distribute together treasures
And well-made rings to comrades and retainers.
He has in his possession burnished gold
Enough for him to hold a fine estate
Among the foreign people noble land
And loyal warriors, though here my lord
Compelled by need pushed out his boat and left,
And had to cross the rolling waves alone,
Sail on the sea, and, anxious to depart,
Stir up the water ways. Now has this man
Conquered his woes; he lacks not what he wants,
Horses or treasure or the joys of hall,

Or any noble treasure in this world,
O prince's daughter, if he may have you.[4]
About the former vows between you both,
I understand he coupled in his oath
Heaven and earth, and joined thereto himself
That he would keep, as long as he has life,
Truly with you the bond and pledge of faith
Which you made frequently in former days.

52 *Wulf and Eadwacer*

This is a poem (again from the tenth-century *Exeter Book*) which poses great difficulties of interpretation, and critics are divided even on the question of who the persons in the poem are. The speaker is female. 'Wulf' is sometimes taken to be an outlaw (the wolf being a symbol of outlawry), perhaps the speaker's lover, perhaps her husband. 'Eadwacer' (sometimes taken to mean 'property-watcher') may be a detested husband, or a gaoler. Some interpretations take Wulf and Eadwacer to be the same person. There is a summary of these interpretations and others in Aertsen 1994. In a recent interpretation, Tasoulias (1996) has argued that 'Wulf' is also the 'whelp' – i.e. the child of the speaker that she conceived with 'Eadwacer', her lover. Tasoulias suggests that the poem refers to the practice of exposing illegitimate children to the elements.

Further reading: Fell 1991, Aertsen 1994, Tasoulias 1996.

Text: Richard Hamer (ed. and trans.) (1970) *A Choice of Anglo-Saxon Verse*, London: Faber.

It is as though my people had been given
A present. They will wish to capture him
If he comes with a troop. We are apart.
Wulf is on one isle, I am on another.
Fast is that island set among the fens.
Murderous are the people who inhabit
That island. They will wish to capture him
If he comes with a troop. We are apart.

4 Fell comments on this line that although it offers an apparently happy ending, our background knowledge of the importance of transience in the Anglo-Saxon world-view means that we are more likely to take it as a warning signal (1991: 185–186).

Grieved have I for my Wulf with distant longings.
Then it was rainy weather, and I sad,
When the bold warrior laid his arms about me.
I took delight in that and also pain.
O Wulf, my Wulf, my longing for your coming
Has made me ill, the rareness of your visits,
My grieving spirit, not the lack of food.
Eadwacer, do you hear me? For a wolf
Shall carry to the woods our wretched whelp.
Men very easily may put asunder
That which was never joined, our song together.[5]

53 Riddles 25, 44, 45

Some Old English riddles dealing with sexual themes (again these are from the tenth century *Exeter Book*). Riddle 25 can mean 'onion', Riddle 44 'key', but both can also mean 'penis'. Riddle 45 means 'dough' or 'sexual intercourse'.

Text: W.S. Mackie (ed.) (1934) T*he Exeter Book. Part II: poems IX–XXXII*, Early English Text Society, original series no. 194, London: Oxford University Press..

RIDDLE 25

I'm a wonderful creature, bringing joy to women,
and useful to those who dwell near me. I harm
no citizen except only my destroyer.
My site is lofty; I stand in a bed;
beneath, somewhere, I am shaggy. Sometimes
the very beautiful daughter of a peasant,
a courageous woman, ventures to lay hold on me,
assaults my red skin, despoils my head,
clamps me in a fastness. She who thus confines me,
this curly-haired woman, soon feels
my meeting with her – her eye becomes wet.

5 These final lines are generally agreed to echo Christ's teaching about marriage in the Gospels of Matthew 19.6 and Mark 10.9.

RIDDLE 44

A strange thing hangs by a man's thigh,
under its master's clothes. It is pierced in front,
is stiff and hard, has a good fixed place.
When the man lifts his own garment
up above his knee, he wishes to visit
with the head of this hanging instrument the familiar hole
which it, when of equal length, has often filled before.

RIDDLE 45

I have heard of something growing in a corner,
swelling and standing up, raising its covering.
At that boneless thing a proud-hearted bride
grasped with her hands; a prince's daughter
covered that swelling thing with her robe.

54 *Judith*

Judith (from the same early eleventh-century manuscript as *Beowulf*) is an Old English poem that retells the events of the apocryphal Old Testament Book of Judith. The extract here describes Judith's killing of Holofernes, who has had Judith brought to his bed with the intention of raping her. A. H. Olsen (1982) has argued that this description of Judith's slaying of Holofernes, where she handles him 'shamefully', wields his passive body, and pierces him twice with a sword, decapitating him, is intended to be read as an inversion of the rape that Holofernes intended.

Further reading: Olsen 1982, Griffith 1997, Saunders 2001.

Text: Mark Griffith (ed.) (1997) *Judith*, Exeter: University of Exeter Press; my modern English translation.

Then was her heart relieved, hope renewed for the holy woman; she took the heathen man fast by his hair, pulled him by hand towards her shamefully, and skilfully positioned the evil one, the evil, hated man, so she could best manage him properly. The curly-haired woman then struck the hated foe with a decorated sword, so that she cut halfway through his neck, so that he lay in a swoon, drunken and wounded. He was not dead yet, utterly lifeless; then the brave woman earnestly struck the heathen hound a second time, so that his head rolled forth on the floor.

LATIN LITERATURE

55 Andreas Capellanus, *De Amore*

Andreas's Latin treatise (1180s?) on the subject of love, supposedly a guide to the subject addressed to a young friend called Walter, owes much to Ovid. Its first two books offer a discussion of the winning and maintaining of love, but the third produces an about turn, condemning love entirely. The interpretation of Andreas's text and its importance for the interpretation of love in medieval literature has been controversial, and indeed, Andreas's arguments often seems self-contradicting. The extracts below give Andreas's definition of love which opens the discussion, a discussion of the relationship between love and marriage taken from one of the dialogues of Book One, and the 'rules of love' given at the end of Book Two.

Further reading: for different readings of Andreas within the 'courtly love' tradition, see Lewis 1936, Jaeger 1985 and Bloch 1991. A feminist reading is Moi 1986. Noonan 1986, Jacquart and Thomasset 1988 and Wack 1990 read Andreas in terms of medical writings on love and sexuality. Cartlidge 1997 reads Andreas in the context of canon law on marriage. For the problem of the work's tone, see Monson 1988.

Text: P. G. Walsh (1982) (ed. and trans.) *Andreas Capellanus: On Love*, London: Duckworth.

(I) WHAT LOVE IS

Love (amor) is an inborn suffering which results from the sight of, and uncontrolled thinking about, the beauty of the other sex. This feeling makes a man desire before all else the embraces of the other sex, and to achieve the utter fulfilment of the commands of love in the other's embrace by their common desire.

(II) (DEBATE ON LOVE AND MARRIAGE BETWEEN A MARRIED WOMAN AND A MAN SEEKING HER LOVE)

The man says: 'I admit the truth that your husband rejoices in a character universally worthy, and is endowed with blessed joys more than all men alive, since he has deserved to savour in his embraces the joys of your exalted person. But I am mightily surprised that you consent to allow marital affection, which any couple is allowed to have after being joined in matrimony, to appropriate the name of love, for it is clearly known that love cannot claim a place between husband and wife. Although they may be united in great and boundless affection, their feelings cannot be gathered under the heading of any true definition of love.

Love is nothing other than an uncontrolled desire to obtain the sensual gratification of a stealthy and secret embrace. Now I ask you: what stealthy embrace could take place between a married couple, since they are acknowledged to possess each other, and can fulfil all the desires that they will from each other without fear of opposition? The most outstanding teaching of princes shows that no one can obtain the use of his own possessions by secret enjoyment of them.

Do not think absurd my statement that the relationship of a married couple, though joined in universal feelings of affection, cannot obtain the title of love, for we see the same outcome in the matter of friendship. A father and son can have regard for each other in all matters, but true friendship does not exist between them; for as the teaching of Cicero attests, it is merely blood-descent which preserves the affectionate regard between them.

So there is obviously as much difference between the all-embracing affection of a married couple and the obligation between lovers as there is between the mutual regard of a father and son and the most constant friendship between two men. In the first case, love is not considered to exist, and likewise in the second there is said to be no friendship. You see clearly, therefore, that Love can in no sense play his role between married people, but has desired his privileges to be wholly withdrawn.

Then there is a further argument opposing mutual love between husband and wife. Jealousy, which is of the nature of love itself and without which true love cannot exist, is wholly rejected between husband and wife, and must always be expelled by them as a harmful bane. But lovers must embrace it always as the mother, so to say, and nurse of love.

Hence it is clear to you that love can in no way flourish between your husband and yourself. So since it is appropriate for any honest woman to be a prudent lover, you can accept a suitor's prayers without harm to yourself, and enrich with your love him that asks for it.'

(The woman disagrees. The question is sent for arbitration to Marie, Countess of Champagne,[6] who upholds the argument offered here by the man.)

(III) (THE RULES OF LOVE)

Marriage does not constitute a proper excuse for not loving.
The person who is not jealous cannot love.
No one can be bound by two loves.
Love is known to be always waxing or waning.
A lover exacts from an unwilling partner bitter love.
A male usually loves only on reaching manhood.
When a lover dies, two years' solitary life is enjoined on the survivor.
No man should be deprived of his love save for a most compelling reason.
No man can fall in love unless impelled by Love's prompting.
Love is always prone to vacate a miserly house.
One should not seek love with ladies with whom it is disgraceful to seek marriage.
A true lover in his affection desires the embraces of none other than his partner.
Love does not usually survive being noised abroad.
An easy conquest makes love cheaply regarded; a difficult one causes it to be held dear.
Every lover tends to grow pale when his partner looks at him.
The heart of a lover beats fast at the sudden sight of his beloved.
A new love forces the old to give place.
Honesty of character alone makes a man worthy of love.
If love diminishes, it soon fades and hardly ever gains strength.
A person in love is always fearful.
True jealousy makes the feeling of love grow.
Once suspicion about a lover is entertained, jealousy and the feeling of love grow.

6 Marie, Countess of Champagne (d. 1198), daughter of Eleanor of Aquitaine, and patron of Chrétien de Troyes.

He who is troubled by the thought of love finds it harder to sleep and eat.
Every act of a lover is bounded by thoughts of his beloved.
The true lover regards nothing as good except what he thinks pleasing to his beloved.
Love could deny nothing to love.
A lover can never have enough of the consolations granted by his beloved.
The slightest suspicion forces a lover to entertain dark thoughts about his beloved.
The man affected by excessive sensuality is usually not in love.
The true lover is preoccupied by a constant and unbroken picture of his beloved.
There is nothing to prevent one woman being loved by two men, or one man by two women.

56 Alan of Lille, *The Plaint of Nature*

This is the opening of Alan's homophobic treatise (composed before 1203) which complains that Venus has turned aside from her role of ensuring reproduction to encourage humankind to enter into unnatural forms of intercourse. Alan's text goes on to exercise an influence upon Jean de Meun's *Romance of the Rose*, John Gower's *Confessio Amantis*, and is mentioned by Chaucer in his *Parliament of Fowls*.

Further reading: Boswell 1980: 310–312, Pittenger 1996, Jordan 1997: ch. 4.

Text: James J. Sheridan (trans.) (1980) *The Plaint of Nature*, Toronto: Pontifical Institute of Mediaeval Studies.

I turn from laughter to tears, from joy to grief, from merriment to lament, from jests to wailing, when I see that the essential decrees of Nature are denied a hearing, while large numbers are shipwrecked and lost because of a Venus turned monster, when Venus wars with Venus and changes 'hes' into 'shes' and with her witchcraft unmans man. It is not a case of pretence begetting a show of grief or faked tears giving birth to deceit: it is not an act, but rather an ache, that is in labour or, rather, actually giving birth. The Muse implores, grief itself orders, Nature begs that with tears I give them the gift of a mournful ditty.

Alas! Where has Nature with her fair form betaken herself? Where have the pattern of morals, the norm of chastity, the love of modesty gone? Nature weeps, moral laws get no hearing, modesty, totally dispossessed of her ancient high estate, is sent into exile. The active sex shudders in disgrace as it sees itself degenerate into the passive sex. A man turned woman blackens the fair name of his sex. The witchcraft of Venus turns him into a hermaphrodite. He is subject and predicate: one and the same term is given a double application.[7] Man here extends too far the laws of grammar. Becoming a barbarian in grammar, he disclaims the manhood given him by nature. Grammar does not find favour with him but rather a trope. This transposition, however, cannot be called a trope. The figure here more correctly falls into the category of defects.

That man, in whose case a simple conversion in an Art causes Nature's laws to come to naught, is pushing logic too far. He hammers on an anvil which issues no seeds.[8] The very hammer itself shudders in horror of its anvil. He imprints on no matter the stamp of a parent-stem: rather his ploughshare scores a barren strand. The one who has used the dactylic measure of Venus fares ill in iambics where a long syllable cannot be followed by a short.

However much all man's good looks bow humbly down to woman's beauty, being ever inferior to it in fair grace, however much beauty of countenance serves the daughter of Tyndareus,[9] and comely Adonis and Narcissus are overcome and worship her, she is herself despised, though that fair face may carry the day and her godlike form maintain that she is a goddess for whose sake the thunderbolt would lie idle in Jupiter's right hand, every string of Phoebus' harp would grow slack and inactive, a freeman would become a slave, and Hippolytus would sell his personal chastity to enjoy her love.

Why do so many kisses lie fallow on maidens' lips while no one wishes to harvest a crop from them? If these kisses were but once planted on me, they would grow honey-sweet with moisture, and grown honey-sweet, they would form a honeycomb in my mouth. My life breath, concentrating entirely on my mouth, would go out to meet the kisses and would disport itself entirely on my lips so that I might thus expire and that, when dead myself, my other self might enjoy in her a fruitful life.

7 Alan is using a grammatical metaphor here.

8 The hammer is an image of the male genitals, and so the anvil should be the female genitals (but here are not). 'Seeds' here is literally 'sparks'.

9 Helen of Troy.

No longer does the Phrygian adulterer[10] chase the daughter of Tyndareus but Paris with Paris performs unmentionable and monstrous deeds. No longer does Pyramus cleave to Thisbe through a cleft in the wall: the little cleft of Venus has no charm for him. No longer does the son of Peleus[11] belie the actions of a maiden and so prove to maidens that he is a man.

Yet the man who sells his sex for love of gain makes a miserable return to Nature for her gift to him. Men like these, who refuse Genius[12] his tithes and rites, deserve to be excommunicated from the temple of Genius.

57 *De Coniuge Non Ducenda*

De Coniuge Non Ducenda ('Against Marrying') is a short antimatrimonial poem, anonymously authored, where a number of 'angelic' speakers appear to the protagonist (sometimes called 'Gawain') to dissuade him from marrying. This is the final speaker, John, whose condemnation of marriage is a string of antifeminist commonplaces.

Text: A. G. Rigg (ed. and trans.) (1986) *Gawain on Marriage: The 'De Coniuge Non Ducenda'*, Toronto: Pontifical Institute of Mediaeval Studies.

John next, in whom God's grace abounds,
Inspired, a longer case propounds.
With eagle eye that penetrates
On marriage he expiates.

'A married man's a slave for sure,
His flesh and spirit pain endure –
Like ox from market homeward led
To work the plough until he's dead.

Who takes a wife accepts a yoke:
Not knowing pain, with pain he'll choke.
Who takes a wife, himself is caught
And to eternal serfdom brought.

10 Paris.
11 Achilles.
12 The god of reproduction.

To help their mates were wives designed,
To help the seed of humankind.
Apart from this a wife's a pain
But rules the roost in his domain.

By nature woman's quick to chide,
Deceitful, jealous, full of pride;
But donkey-like, the patient spouse
Accepts his burden like a mouse.

"Whose wife is good is blest," it's said,
But "good-wife" tales are rarely read.
She'll either nag or fornicate –
His lordship she'll not tolerate.

Of good wives there's a scarcity –
From thousands there's not one to see.
A man's injustice does less harm
Than woman's well-intentioned charm.

A woman will receive all males:
No prick against her lust prevails.
For who could fill his spouse's spout?
Alone she wears the district out.

Her lustful loins are never stilled:
By just one man she's unfulfilled.
She'll spread her legs to all the men
But, ever hungry, won't say "When."

Her appetite no man fulfils,
For too much copulation kills.
No man, as often as she'd choose,
Could pay to her his carnal dues.

Thus married women love to stray
And wish their husband's wives away.
Since none a woman's lust can sate
I don't commend the married state.

Her tongue's a sword: its cutting blow
Like lightning brings her husband low.

Her tongue dispels her husband's joy;
Like wind her words his home destroy.

Of trust there's little left to show
When horns of pride begin to grow.
Her wicked spiteful tongue rains down
A thunderstorm upon his crown.

In anger she'll his trust betray,
To murder open up the way.
With "love-sick" men she'll copulate
To pass the pox on to her mate.

If she's of noble family born
She treats her lowly spouse with scorn.
To make a stand if he should think,
She'll poison him with bitter drink.

The wife's demands are always met:
If not, she'll quarrel, rage, and fret.
The noise defeats the patient spouse;
He yields to her and quits the house.

A drip, a smoke, a wife – these three
Compel a man his house to flee.
The man speaks words of peace; the wife
Piles on the quarrels and the strife.

In cunning none outwits a snake;
For mischief women prizes take.
It's safer in a lion's cage
Than up against a woman's rage.

Than death there's no worse penalty,
Yet wives are worse for cruelty.
For death takes but an hour or so,
But marriage pains are long and slow.

Who takes a wife, to death is bound;
His mind decays that once was sound.
He starts to ail when he is wed,
But soon recovers once she's dead.

A husband's never free from pain;
He longs to die but must remain.
This woe exceeds the worst of woes,
The bush must burn without repose.

In brief, to sum up marriage well,
It's either purgatory or hell.
In hell there's neither rest nor peace -
A husband's pains have no release.

Hell's Mouth portrays the married state.
The wife's the Fury at the gate;
By Beasts his greedy brood is meant,
His many pains, his discontent.

Now who could stand the long misuse,
The many labours and abuse?
From marriage comes both wear and tear.
If wise, then marriage you'll forbear!'

The angels having said their bit,
Their hands upon the Holy Writ,
From fire they tried to pull me free.
I answered briefly: 'I agree.'

OLD FRENCH LITERATURE

58 Etienne de Fougères, *Livre de Manières*

This is an extract from a misogynistic poem describing sexual relations between women, written at the court of the English king Henry II, between 1173 and 1178.

Text: translated by Robert L. A. Clark, 'Jousting without a Lance: The Condemnation of Female Homoeroticism in the *Livre des Manières*', in Francesca Canadé Sautman and Pamela Sheingorn (eds) (2001) *Same Sex Love and Desire among Women in the Middle Ages*, New York, St Martin's Press.

There's nothing surprising about the 'beautiful sin'
when nature prompts it,
but whosoever is awakened by the vile sin
is going against nature.

One must pursue [him] with dogs,
throw[ing] stones and sticks;
one should smite him with blows
and kill him like any other cur.

These ladies have made up a game:
with two bits of nonsense they make nothing;
they bang coffin against coffin,
without a poker stir up their fire.

They don't play at 'poke in the paunch'
but join shield to shield without a lance.
They have no concern for a beam in their scales,
nor a handle in their mold.

Out of water they fish for turbot
and they have no need for a rod.
They don't bother with a pestle in their mortar
nor a fulcrum for their see-saw.

In twos they do their lowlife jousting
and they ride to it with all their might;
at the game of thigh-fencing
they pay most basely each other's share.

They're not all from the same mold:
one lies still and the other grinds away,
one plays the cock and the other the hen,
and each one plays her role.

59 Marie de France, *Yonec*

Marie's *lai* (a sort of short romance) deals with the common theme of the *malmariée*. In this poem, from the second half of the twelfth century, the unpleasantness of a real marriage is shown up and remedied by supernatural romance. Bloch (1991: 170–173) draws a parallel with Marie's lai of *Lanval*, arguing that the fantasy of escape through a fiction that remains intact so long as no one reveals its fictionality is a paradigm for understanding courtly literature, generally understood as the expression of a collective literary fantasy of escape from the harsh realities of medieval marriage. In an interesting recent reading, Wogan-Browne (2001: 128–131) argues for parallels between the narrative in *Yonec* and religious narrative, drawing a parallel with Christina of Markyate's attempt to escape *her* wedding chamber (extract 36). For Wogan-Browne, critical focus on the hawk-lover has distracted attention from the real focus of the tale, the child, Yonec. In her reading, the point of the story is not the fantasy of the lover, but that the woman's desire is to have a beloved child which replaces the husband.

Further reading: Bloch 1991, Wogan-Browne 2001.

Text: G. S. Burgess and K. Busby (trans.) (1986) *The Lais of Marie de France*, Harmondsworth: Penguin.

Now that I have begun to compose lays, I shall not cease my effort but shall relate fully in rhyme the adventures that I know. It is my intention and desire henceforth to tell you about Yonec, under what circumstances he was born and how his father, whose name was Muldumarec, first met his mother.

In Britain there once lived a rich old man who held the fief of Caerwent and was acknowledged lord of the land. The city lay on the river Duelas and formerly ships could reach it. This man was very old and, because his inheritance would be large, he took a wife in order to have children, who would be his heirs. The maiden who was given to the rich man was from a noble family, wise, courtly, and extremely beautiful. He loved her greatly on account of her beauty, but because she was so fair and noble, he took good care to watch over her and locked her in his tower in a large paved chamber. He had a sister, old and widowed, without a husband, and he placed her with the lady to keep her from going astray. There were other women, I believe, in a separate room, but the lady would never have spoken to them without the old woman's permission.

Thus he held her for seven years – they never had any children – and she did not leave the tower either for family or friend. When the lord went to bed, there was neither chamberlain nor doorkeeper who would have dared enter the chamber to light a candle before him. The lady was in great distress, and she wept and sighed so much that she lost her beauty, as happens to any woman who fails to take care of herself. She would herself have preferred death to take her quickly.

It was the beginning of the month of April, when the birds sing their songs, that the lord arose in the early morning and prepared to set out for the woods. He had made the old woman get up and lock the doors after him. When she had done his bidding, he left with his men. The old woman carried her psalter from which she intended to recite psalms. The lady lay awake weeping and looking at the sunlight. She noticed that the old woman had left the room and grieved, sighed and lamented tearfully: 'Alas,' she said, 'that ever I was born! My destiny is hard indeed. I am a prisoner in this tower and death alone will free me. What is this jealous old man afraid of, to keep me so securely imprisoned? He is extremely stupid and foolish, always fearing that he will be betrayed. I can neither go to church nor hear God's service. I could put on a friendly mien for him, even without any desire to do so, if I could talk to people and join them in amusement. Cursed be my parents and all those who gave me to this jealous man and married me to his person! I pull and tug on a strong rope! He will never die. When he should have been baptized, he was plunged into the river of Hell, for his sinews are hard, and so are his veins which are full of living blood. I have often heard tell that in this country one used to encounter adventures which relieved those afflicted by care: knights discovered maidens to their liking, noble and fair, and ladies found handsome and courtly lovers, worthy and valiant men. There was no fear of reproach and they alone could see them. If this can be and ever was, if it ever did happen to anyone, may almighty God grant my wish!'

Having lamented thus, she noticed the shadow of a large bird through a narrow window, but did not know what it could be. The bird flew into the room: it had straps on its feet and looked like a hawk of five or six moultings. It landed before the lady, and after it had been there for a while for her to see, it turned into a fair and noble knight. The lady was astounded by this. Her face became flushed, and she trembled and covered her head, being very afraid. The knight was extremely courtly and spoke to her first: 'Lady, do not be afraid! The hawk is a noble bird. Even if its secrets remain a mystery to you, be assured that you are safe, and make me your beloved! This is the reason I came here. I have loved you for a long time and desired you greatly in my heart. I never loved any woman but you, nor shall I ever love another. Yet I could not come to you, nor leave my country, unless you had wished for me; but now I can be your beloved!' The lady, now assured, uncovered her head and spoke. She answered the knight, saying that she would make him her lover, provided he believed in God, which would make their love possible. He was very handsome and never in her life had she seen such a handsome knight, nor would she ever again.

'Lady,' he said, 'you are right. I would not on any account want guilt, distrust or suspicion to attach to me. I do believe in the Creator who set us free from the sorrow in which our ancestor Adam put us by biting the bitter apple. He is, will be and always has been life and light to sinners. If you do not believe this of me, send for your chaplain. Tell him that an illness has come upon you and that you want to hear the service that God has established in this world for the redemption of sinners. I shall assume your appearance, receive the body of Christ, and recite all of my credo for you. Never doubt me on this count.' She replied that he had spoken well. He lay down next to her on the bed, but did not intend to touch, embrace or kiss her. Then the old woman returned, and when she found the lady she told her it was time to get up and that she would bring her clothes. The lady said that she was ill and she must ensure that the chaplain came quickly to her, for she was very much afraid of dying. The old woman said: 'Be patient now! My lord has gone to the woods. No one but me may enter here.' The lady was very afraid and pretended to faint, and when the old woman saw her she was greatly alarmed. She opened the door of the chamber and sent for the priest, who came as quickly as possible, bringing the corpus domini. The knight received it and drank the wine from the chalice, whereupon the chaplain left and the old woman closed the doors.

The lady lay next to her beloved: I never saw so fair a couple. When they had laughed and sported and exchanged confidences, the knight took his leave, for he wanted to return to his own country. She begged him gently to come back and to see her often. 'Lady,' he said, 'whenever it pleases you, I shall be with you within the hour, but observe moderation so that we are not discomfited. This old woman will betray us and keep watch over us night and day. When she notices our love, she will tell her lord about it. If this should happen as I say and we are betrayed in this way, I shall have no way of preventing my death.'

Thereupon the knight departed and left his beloved in great joy. The next day she arose quite recovered and was very happy that week. She looked after herself well and her beauty was quite restored. Now she was more content just to remain where she was than to amuse herself in any other way, for she wanted to see her beloved often and to take her pleasure with him as soon as her lord left. Night and day, early or late, he was hers whenever she wanted. Now may she, with God's grace, long enjoy her love! The great joy she often experienced on seeing her lover caused her appearance to alter. Her husband was very cunning and noticed that she was different from her usual self. He was suspicious of his sister, but spoke to her one day and said that he was astonished that the lady attired herself thus, asking what this might mean. The old woman replied that she did not know, for no one could speak to her nor did she have a friend or beloved, except that she had noticed that she remained alone more willingly than before. The lord then replied: 'In faith, that I believe! Now you must do something: In the morning, when I have got up and you have locked the doors, pretend to go outside and leave her to lie alone. Stay in a secret place and watch to see what it can be that keeps her so joyful.' With this plan they parted. Alas! how ill-served were they on whom he wanted to spy in order to betray and trap them.

Three days later, I heard tell, the lord pretended to leave, telling his wife that the king had summoned him by letter, but that he would soon be back. He then left the chamber and closed the door. The old woman arose and hid behind a curtain from where it was easy for her to hear and satisfy her curiosity. The lady lay there without sleeping, for she greatly desired her beloved who came without delay, in no time at all. They were full of joy to be with each other, to talk and exchange glances, until it was time to get up, for then the knight had to go. The old woman saw and took note of how he came and went, but was very much afraid because she saw him one moment a man and another a hawk. When the lord, who had not been far away, returned, she explained the truth about the knight. He was most distressed by this and quickly made traps to kill the knight. He had large iron spikes forged and the tips more sharply pointed than any razor. When he had prepared and cut barbs in them, he set them on the window, close together and well-positioned, in the place through which the knight passed whenever he came to see the lady. Oh God! if only he had known of the treachery that the villain was preparing.

The next morning the lord arose before daybreak and said that he intended to go hunting. The old woman went to see him off and then returned to bed, for dawn was not yet visible. The lady was awake, waiting for the man she loved faithfully, and said that he could now come and be with her quite at leisure. When she summoned him, he left without delay and flew through the window, but the spikes were in front of it. One of them pierced his body and the red blood flowed out. When he realized that he was mortally wounded, he freed himself from the prongs and entered. He sat down on the bed beside the lady, covering all the sheets in blood, and when she saw the blood and the wound she was grievously alarmed. He said to her: 'My sweet beloved, for love of you I am losing my life. I told you what would come of it: your appearance would slay us.' When she heard this, she fell into a swoon, and for a while seemed dead. He comforted her tenderly, saying that grief was of no avail, and telling her she was with child by him and would have a worthy and valiant son to comfort her. She was to call him Yonec, and he would avenge both of them and kill his enemy.

He could remain no longer, for his wound was bleeding continuously, and he left in great pain, with her following him with loud cries. She escaped through a window, but it was a wonder she did not kill herself, for she had to jump a good twenty feet. Naked but for her shift, she followed the trail of blood which flowed from the knight on to the path she was taking and to which she kept until she came to a hill. In this hill there was an opening, all covered in his blood, but she could see nothing beyond and therefore assumed that her beloved had entered there. She hurriedly went in, but finding no light, followed the straight path until she emerged on the other side of the hill, in a beautiful meadow. She found the grass wet with blood, which alarmed her greatly, and followed the trail through the meadow. There was a city nearby, completely enclosed by a wall, where there was not a house, hall or tower which did not seem to be made of solid silver. The state rooms were especially rich. Over towards the town were the marshes, the forests and the enclosures, and in the other direction, towards the keep, a stream flowed all around, where the ships used to arrive, and there were more than three hundred sails. Downstream the gate was unlocked, and so the lady entered the town, still following the fresh blood through the centre of the town up to the castle. No one at all spoke to her, for she encountered neither man nor woman. She came to the paved entrance of the palace and found it covered in blood, and when she went into a beautiful chamber she found a knight sleeping, but did not recognize him and continued into another, larger, room. There, finding nothing but a bed with a knight sleeping on it, she passed through. She entered the third room and found her beloved's bed. The bedposts were of pure gold, and I cannot estimate the worth of the bedclothes. The candles in the candelabra, lit by both night and day, were worth all the gold in an entire city. As soon as she saw the knight she recognized him, and approached in alarm, falling over him in a swoon. He who loved her deeply took her in his arms and lamented his misfortune repeatedly. When she had recovered, he comforted her gently: 'Fair beloved, in God's name, have mercy! Go away! Flee from here! I shall die soon, before daybreak. There would be such grief here if you were found, and you would be tormented, for my people would know that they had lost me because of my love for you. I am sad and troubled for your sake.' The lady said to him: 'Beloved, I should rather die together with you than suffer with my husband. If I go back to him, he will kill me.' The knight reassured her, gave her a ring, and told her that as long as she kept it her husband would remember nothing that had happened and would not keep her in custody. He gave and commended to her his sword, then enjoined her to prevent any man from ever taking possession of it, but to keep it for the use of her son. When he had grown up and become a worthy and valiant knight, she should take him and her husband to a feast. They would come to an abbey and at a tomb they would visit, they would again hear about his death and how he was unjustly killed. There she would give the sword to his son who was to be told the story of his birth and who his father was. Then they would see what he would do. When he had explained everything to her, he gave her a costly tunic, and ordered her to put it on. Then he made her leave him, and she went away wearing the ring and carrying the sword that comforted her. She had not gone half a league from the city when she heard the bells ringing and the lamentation in the castle. She swooned four times with grief and, when she recovered, made her way towards the hill, which she passed through and arrived back in her own region. She remained afterwards a long time together with her husband, who made no accusations against her, and neither slandered nor mocked her.

Their son was born and well brought up, well protected and well loved. They called him Yonec and in the whole kingdom there was not a fairer, worthier, more valiant or more generous man to be found. When he had come of age, they had him dubbed a knight, but now listen to what happened that same year!

As was the custom of the country the lord had been summoned with his friends to the feast of St Aaron, which was celebrated in Caerleon and in several other cities. He took his wife and son and dressed himself richly; so it was that they set out, not knowing exactly where they were going. With them was a young lad who led them along the straight road until they came to a castle, fairer than any other in the whole world. Inside there was an abbey with very holy people, where the squire who was taking them to the feast found them lodgings. They were well served and honoured in the abbot's chamber, and next morning went to hear mass. Then they intended to leave, but the abbot came to talk to them and begged them to stay, for he wanted to show them his dormitory, his chapter-house and his refectory, and since they were well-lodged, the lord consented to stay.

That day after dinner they visited the various rooms. First they came to the chapter-house where they found a great tomb covered with a cloth of striped brocade with a band of rich gold material running through it. At the head, feet and sides, there were twenty lighted candles. The candelabra were of fine gold, and the censers which were used by day to honour the tomb with fragrance, of amethyst. They inquired of the inhabitants whose tomb it was and who lay there. At this, the inhabitants began to weep and said amidst their tears that it was the best knight, the strongest and the fiercest, the fairest and the most beloved, who had ever been born. He had been king of that land and none had ever been as courtly. He had been destroyed at Caerwent and killed for the love of a lady: 'We have never since had a lord, but, just as he said and commanded, we have waited long for a son he gave the lady.' When the lady heard this news, she called aloud to her son: 'Fair son, you have heard how God has brought us here! It is your father who lies here, whom this old man unjustly killed. Now I commend and hand over to you this sword, for I have kept it long enough.' For all to hear, she revealed to him that this was his father and he his son, how he used to come to her and how her husband had betrayed him. She told him the truth, fell into a faint on the tomb, and, while unconscious, died. She never spoke again, but when her son saw she was dead, he struck off his stepfather's head, and thus with his father's sword avenged his mother's grief. When what had happened became known throughout the city, they took the lady in great honour and laid her in the tomb. Before leaving this place they made Yonec their lord.

Those who heard this story long afterwards composed a lay from it, about the sorrow and the grief that they suffered for love.

60 Guillaume de Lorris and Jean de Meun, *The Romance of the Rose*

The Romance of the Rose (1225–1230 [part 1], 1269–1278 [part 2] was an enormously influential poem, an allegorical account of a dream vision on the subject of love begun by Guillaume de Lorris, but finished by Jean de Meun after his death, Jean's section being by far the longer of the two. At least a portion of the poem was translated into Middle English by Chaucer, and Jean de Meun's portion of the poem provokes a protofeminist backlash in the 'Debate of the Rose' led by Christine de Pizan in the fifteenth century (see extracts 63 and 75). The extract given here is from Guillaume's portion of the poem, and it describes the process of falling in love.

Further reading: most modern commentators are concerned with Jean de Meun's continuation of Guillaume's original. For a study of Guillaume's poem, see Hult 1986.

Text: Frances Horgan (trans.) (1994) *The Romance of the Rose*, Oxford: Oxford University Press.

This is the perilous mirror where proud Narcissus looked at his face and his bright eyes, and afterwards lay stretched out in death. Whoever looks at himself in this mirror can have no help or remedy against seeing something which promptly causes him to fall in love. This mirror has caused the deaths of many valiant men, for the wisest, the bravest, and the most experienced are all caught and ensnared here. Here new and violent feelings spring up in men, and their hearts are changed; here sense and moderation are of no use, and there is only the total will to love; here no one knows what to do, for Cupid, Venus' son, sowed here the seed of Love which covers the whole spring; here he set his nets and snares to trap young men and maidens, for Love wants no other birds. Because of the seed that was sown here, this spring was rightly called the Spring of Love, and many have spoken of it in other places, in books and romances. But you will never hear a better exposition of the truth of the matter, once I have explained the mystery.

I was happy then to linger, admiring the spring and the crystals which revealed to me a thousand things around me. But it was an evil hour when I looked at my reflection. Alas, how often I have since sighed about it! The mirror deceived me, and if I had known in advance what force and power it had, I would never have approached it, for at once I fell into the trap that has captured and betrayed many men.

I perceived in the mirror, among a thousand other things, rose-bushes completely laden with roses in a secluded place completely enclosed by a hedge. Immediately I was seized with such desire that not for Pavia or Paris would I have failed to go to the place where I saw the greatest number of them. Possessed by this madness, as many others have been, I at once approached the rose-bushes, and I assure you that when I drew near, the sweet scent of the roses penetrated my very entrails, and I was all but filled with their fragrance. If I had not imagined that I would be attacked or insulted, I would have plucked at least one and held it in my hand, savouring its scent. But I was afraid that I might repent my action, since it could easily have displeased the lord of the garden.

There were roses in profusion, the most beautiful in all the world. There were buds, some tiny and closed up and others slightly larger, and some much larger ones which were coming into flower, and were on the point of bursting. These buds are attractive, for wide-open roses have completely faded after a day, whereas buds stay fresh for at least two or three days. The buds pleased me greatly, for none finer grew anywhere. The man who could pluck one should cherish it greatly, and if I could have made a garland of them, there is nothing I would have loved so well. From among these buds I chose one so beautiful that when I had observed it carefully, all the others seemed worthless in comparison. It shone with colour, the purest vermilion that Nature could provide, and Nature's masterly hand had arranged its four pairs of leaves, one after the other. Its stem was as straight as a reed, and the bud was set on top in such a way that it neither bent nor drooped. The area around it was filled with its perfume, and the sweet scent that rose from it pervaded the whole place. When I became aware of this scent, I had no wish to depart, but drew nearer and would have plucked it had I dared stretch out my hands. But sharp, pointed thistles forced me to draw back, while barbed, keen-edged thorns and prickly nettles and brambles prevented me from advancing, for I was afraid of hurting myself.

The God of Love, whose constant endeavour had been to watch and follow me with drawn bow, had stopped beneath a fig-tree; and when he observed that I had chosen that bud, which pleased me better than any of the others, he at once took an arrow. When the string was in the nock, he drew the bow, which was wonderfully strong, back to his ear, and loosed his arrow at me in such a way and with such force that the point entered my eye and penetrated my heart. Then I was seized with a chill which has often made me shiver since, even when wearing a warm, fur-lined cloak. When I had been thus shot, I immediately fell backwards. My heart was false and failed me and I lay for a long time in a swoon. When I recovered consciousness and came to my senses I was very weak and therefore imagined that I had lost a lot of blood. But the point that pierced me drew no blood at all, and the wound was quite dry. Then I took hold of the arrow with both hands and began to pull hard, sighing a great deal as I pulled. I pulled so hard that I drew out the flighted shaft, but the barbed point, which was named Beauty was so fixed in my heart that it could not be torn out; it remains there still, and yet the wound has never bled.

I was in great trouble and torment, unable, on account of this double danger, to do or say anything or to find a physician for my wound, for no medicine could be expected from herb or root; instead my heart drew me towards the rose-bud, and desired nothing else. If I had it in my possession, it would have given me back my life; the mere sight and scent of it brought me considerable relief from pain.

Then, as I began to make my way towards the sweetly scented rose-bud, Love had already grasped another arrow, worked in gold. It was the second arrow, named Simplicity, and it has caused many men and women throughout the world to fall in love. When Love saw me approach, without warning he loosed the arrow, which was made without steel, so that it entered my eye and wounded my heart. No man living will ever cure me of it, for when I pulled, I drew out the shaft without much effort, but the point remains within. Now you may know for certain that if I had greatly desired the rose-bud before, my longing was now increased, and as the pain grew more intense, so also did my desire continually to approach the little rose that smelled sweeter than violets. It would have been better for me to draw back, but I could not refuse the bidding of my heart. I was always compelled to go where it longed to be. But the archer, who strove hard and mightily to wound me, would not allow me to pass that way unharmed and, the better to hurt me, loosed his third arrow, named Courtesy, at me. The wound was deep and wide, and I perforce fell swooning beneath a spreading olive-tree, where I lay for a long time without moving. When I recovered my strength, I took hold of the arrow and removed the shaft from my side, but, do what I might, I could not draw out the point.

Then I sat down, very anxious and pensive. The wound caused me great distress, and urged me to approach the rose-bud that I desired. But the archer rekindled my fear, and I was right to be afraid, for the man who has been scalded should fear water. However, necessity is a powerful force, and even if I had seen it raining crossbow bolts and stones, pelting down as thick as hail, I would still have had to approach, for Love, who is greater than anything, gave me courage and daring to obey his command. I got to my feet, weak and feeble as a wounded man, and, undaunted by the archer, made a great effort to walk towards the little rose to which my heart was drawn; but there were so many thorns and thistles and brambles that I was unable to get past them and reach the rose-bud. I had to stay near the hedge of very sharp thorns which was next to the roses. I was very happy to be so close to the rose-bud that I could smell the sweet scent that issued from it, and filled with delight to be able to look upon it freely. Thus I was well rewarded and forgot my troubles in my joy and delight. I was very glad and joyful, for nothing ever pleased me so greatly as being in that place, and I would never have wished to depart. But when I had been there for some time, the God of Love, tearing apart my body, which had become his target, launched a new assault. In order to hurt me, he loosed yet another arrow and wounded me once more in my heart, beneath my breast. The arrow's name was Company, and there is none that conquers ladies or maidens more quickly. At once the great pain of my wounds was reawakened, and I swooned away three times in succession.

On coming to my senses, I moaned and sighed, for my pain was growing worse and I had no hope of cure or relief. I would rather have been dead than alive, for in the end, I thought, I would become a martyr to Love, there was no other way out. Meanwhile he took another arrow, which he prized greatly and which I hold to be most wounding; it was Fair Seeming, which does not permit a lover to repent of serving Love, whatever he may feel. It is sharp and piercing and keen as a steel razor, but Love had thoroughly anointed its tip with precious ointment so that it would not hurt me too much, for Love did not want me to die, but rather to find relief through the application of the ointment, which was full of comfort. Love had made it with his own hands to comfort true lovers, and to soothe my hurts he shot this arrow at me, and made a great wound in my heart. The ointment spread through my wounds and gave me back my heart, which had failed me completely. I would have been dead and in a bad way had it not been for that sweet ointment. I quickly drew out the shaft, but the point, newly sharpened, remained within. Five arrowheads were thus embedded and it will scarcely be possible to remove them. The ointment was very good for my wounds, yet the wound hurt me so much that the pain made me change colour. It is the strange property of this arrow to be both sweet and bitter. I felt and realized that it helped me, but it also hurt me; the point was painful although the unction brought relief. On the one hand it soothed, on the other it made me smart, and thus it both helped and harmed. Straightaway Love came towards me with rapid steps, crying as he came: 'Vassal, you are captured, there is no way to escape or defend yourself. Yield, and do not resist. The more willingly you surrender, the sooner you will find mercy. It is foolish to behave arrogantly towards one whom you should flatter and beseech. You cannot struggle against me, and I wish you to learn that wickedness and pride will avail you nothing. Surrender, since I wish it, peacefully and with good grace.'

61 Jean Bodel, *The Peasant from Bailleul*

Fabliaux are humorous, bawdy stories, sexually explicit, often set among the peasantry or the bourgeoisie rather than the nobility, and sometimes parodic of romance conventions of love. The thirteenth-century French *fabliau* given here has a number of regular ingredients: the love-triangle, the deceitful wife and lecherous clerk, and the gullible husband who sees himself cuckolded but cannot do anything about it.

Further reading: Harrison 1974, Muscatine 1986.

Text: Robert Harrison (trans.) (1974) *Gallic Salt*, Berkeley: University of California Press.

If fabliaux are ever true,
then once there lived (according to
my master) near Bailleul a swain
who farmed both pasture land and grain;
no usurer nor changer he.
One day at noon he hurriedly
came homeward, ravenous for food,
a hulking brute, ill tempered, rude,
remarkably grotesque and grim.
His wife did not think much of him,
for he was dangerously cracked,
but loved the chaplain and in fact
had made a date to spend the day
together with the good curé.
By now she'd finished every task,
had poured some wine into a cask,
had put a capon in to bake,
and now I think of it, a cake
stood underneath a napkin, cooling.
Lo! Here came the peasant, drooling,
famished, and in a wretched state.
She ran up to open the gate
and meet him, though she didn't care
especially to see him there
– another she had rather greet –
then said to him with sly deceit,
like one who doubtlessly preferred
to see him decently interred:
'Milord, God bless my soul,' said she,
'How weak and pale you seem to me!
I swear you're only skin and bone.'
'I'm starved to death, Erme, that I own;
the custards – are they cooked?' he said.
'I know for sure you'll soon be dead;
a truer word you'll never hear.
Now go to bed; you're dying, dear.
Oh, woe is me! When you are gone,
I'll lack the will to carry on,
because you'll be away so far.
Oh sire, how very pale you are!
You've only got the briefest term.'
'You're kidding,' said he, 'aren't you, Erme?

I hear so well our milk cow lowing,
I really can't believe I'm going;
maybe I can still pull through.'
'Milord, Death has befuddled you,
and on your pallid spirit weighed,
you're no more solid than the shade
that shortly you shall come to be.'
'Then lay me down, my dear', said he.
'I really must be awfully sick.'
She needed to be very quick
and take him in by hook or crook.
Preparing in a distant nook
a little bed of straw and hay
with canvas sheets, she straightaway
undressed him, made him lie composed,
and got his mouth and eyelids closed,
then fell across him on the bed,
lamenting: 'Brother, you are dead!
May God have mercy on your soul!
Oh, how can a wretched wife console
herself, and keep from dying too?'
Beneath the sheet, the peasant knew
He certainly must be deceased.
She now went out to fetch the priest,
for she was wise and politic,
and told him all about the hick
and let him understand her ploy.
The two were overcome with joy
because of what had come to pass,
and headed back, as bold as brass,
en route discussing their affair.
On coming through the doorway there,
the priest began to read his psalms;
the woman, meanwhile, beat her palms.
Dame Erme dissembled very well,
though not a single teardrop fell.
It bored her, and she soon withdrew;
the priest cut short his reading too,
not wanting to commend the soul,
then off into a cubbyhole
he led her by her little paw,
undressed her, laid her on the straw,

which had but recently been threshed:
the two of them were soon enmeshed,
with him above and her below.
The peasant saw the whole tableau
while lying underneath the covers;
open eyed he watched the lovers,
clearly saw the strawsack jumping,
saw as well the chaplain humping,
knew it was the chaplain too,
and raised an awful hullaballoo.
'Ahi, Ahi!' the peasant said.
'You son of a bitch, if I weren't dead,
you certainly would catch all hell.
No man was ever beat as well
as you would be, Sir Priest, by me.'
'My friend', the priest said, 'that may be:
you'd know, however, were you living,
I'd come here only with misgiving
if your soul were in your body yet.
But now that you are dead, I'll bet
my luck improves with your demise.
Just lie back down and shut your eyes;
You mustn't leave them open thus.'
He closed his eyes and made no fuss,
but lay as still as he had done,
whereat the priest resumed his fun,
without anxiety or care;
and whether they interred him there
at dawn or not, I do not know;
the tale says in conclusion though:
he must be taken for a fool
who lets his wife's opinion rule.

62 Christine de Pizan, *The Tale of Griselda*

This is Christine's version of a story also told by Petrarch, Chaucer and Boccaccio, about an obedient wife and a tyrannical husband. Christine includes it in her *Book of the City of Ladies* (fifteenth century), a protofeminist defence of women, but it's hard to see how Griselda can be seen as being a straightforwardly admirable character – perhaps the point of the story is the tyranny of the husband more than the obedience of the wife?

Further reading: Chaucer's version of the story is in Benson (ed.) 1987, Petrarch's in Bryan and Dempster 1941, Boccaccio's in Boccaccio 1972. On Christine generally, see Willard 1984. Two essays that discuss this tale and its relationship to Boccaccio and Petrarch's versions are Richards 1992 and Phillipy 1997. On Christine as making the 'case for women' in the *Book of the City of Ladies*, see Blamires 1997.

Text: Christine de Pizan (1982) *The Book of the City of Ladies*, trans. E. J. Richards, New York: Persea.

It is written that there was a marquis of Saluces named Gualteri. He was a handsome and honest man but he behaved in an extraordinarily strange manner. His barons would frequently admonish him to marry in order to have a successor. After refusing for a long time, he finally agreed to marry on the condition that they promise to accept whatever woman he might choose, and his barons agreed and swore to this. The marquis often took pleasure in hunting birds and game. Near his fortress was a small country village where a weak, old, and impoverished peasant named Giannoculo lived among the poor labourers there. He had been a good and upright man all his life. This man had an eighteen-year-old daughter, named Griselda, who waited upon him with great diligence and supported him with her spinning. The marquis, who often passed by the village, had carefully noted this maiden's upright conduct and integrity, as well as the beauty of her body and face, and therefore he held her in great favour. It happened that the marquis, after having agreed with his barons to take a wife, told them to assemble on a particular day for the wedding, and he ordered all ladies to be present. He had magnificent preparations made, and on the appointed day, after everyone was assembled before him, he had the entire company mount on horseback to accompany him as he sought his bride. He went straight to Giannucolo's house and met Griselda, who was coming back from the fountain with a jug of water on her head. He asked her where her father was, and Griselda knelt down and told the marquis that her father was at home. 'Go fetch him,' he ordered. When the good man arrived, the marquis told him that he wished to marry his daughter. Giannucolo answered that he should do his will, whereupon the ladies entered the little cottage and dressed and adorned the bride in the noble fashion and befitting the position of the marquis – with the robes and jewels which he had readied. Then he brought her to the palace, where he married her. And to make the story short, this lady conducted herself so well towards everyone that the nobles – both the great and minor nobility – and the people greatly loved her and she handled herself to the satisfaction of all and served and cherished her lord as she should have. That year the marquise bore a daughter whose birth was received with great joy, but when the child was old enough to be weaned, the marquis, in order to test Griselda's constancy and patience, made her believe that the barons were unhappy that one of her descendants would reign over them and therefore wished the child killed. To this matter (which would be difficult for any mother) Griselda replied that the daughter was his and that the nobles should do as they pleased, and so she gave the child to one of the marquis' squires, who, all the while pretending to have come to fetch the child to kill her, brought her secretly to Bologna to the countess of Panico (a sister of the marquis) for her to shelter and nourish the child. At the end of the following year, the marquise was pregnant and bore a most beautiful son who was joyfully received. Once again the marquis wished to test his wife and told her that the boy would have to be killed to satisfy his barons and subjects. And the lady replied that if her son's death was not enough, she was ready to die if he wanted. So she gave her son to the squire, just as she had done with her daughter, without showing the slightest trace of sadness, nor did she say anything except to beg the squire to bury the child after killing him so that wild beasts and birds would not eat the infant's tender flesh. Faced with such overwhelming harshness, Griselda showed not the slightest change. The marquis, however, did not stop at this but wanted to test her once more. They had been together twelve years, during which time the good lady had acted so well that it should have been more than enough proof of her virtue, when one day the marquis summoned her to his chamber and told her that he was unpopular with his subjects and his people and in danger of losing his dominion because of her, for they felt too much of an aversion to his keeping Giannucolo's daughter as his lady and mistress. Therefore it was necessary, if he wanted to appease his subjects, for her to return to her father's house and for him to marry another, more noble woman. To this proposal, which must have been extremely harsh and severe for her, Griselda replied, 'I have always known very well and often thought there could never be any comparison between your nobility and magnificence and my poverty, nor have I ever reputed myself worthy enough to be either your wife or your maid. From this moment on, I am ready to return to my father's house, where I will spend my old age. As for the dowry which you commanded me to bring, I know, as you well realize, that when you received me at the door of my father's house, you had me stripped completely naked and dressed in the robes with which I came into your company, nor did I bring any other dowry except faith, maturity, love, reverence, and poverty. Therefore it is right that I restore your property to you. Here is the dress which I myself will strip off, and let me give you back the ring with which you married me, and I will return to you all the other jewels, rings, vestments, and ornaments with which I was adorned and enriched in your chamber. I left my father's house completely naked and I will return there completely naked, except that it does not appear fitting to me that this womb, wherein lay the children which you fathered, should appear totally naked before the people, and so for this reason, if it pleases you, and for no other, I beg you in compensation for my virginity (which I brought when I came into your palace and which I cannot take back with me when I leave it) that a single slip be granted to me, with which I shall cover the womb of your former wife and marquise.' The marquis could hardly keep himself from weeping out of compassion; yet he overcame his feelings, and leaving his chamber he ordered that a single slip be given to her.

Then Griselda stripped herself before all the knights and ladies, removing her shoes and all her jewelry, and she had on nothing except her slip. The rumour had spread everywhere that the marquis intended to divorce his wife, and all his subjects arrived at the palace much grieved at the news. And Griselda, completely naked except for her slip, bare-headed, and barefoot, mounted a horse and rode out, accompanied by the barons, knights, and ladies, who all wept, cursing the marquis and mourning the lady's goodness. But Griselda herself never shed a tear. She was conveyed to the house of her father, that old man who had always been in doubt about this whole affair, thinking that her lord would one day grow tired of his poor marriage. Hearing the uproar, he went out to meet his daughter and brought her an old worn tunic of hers which he had kept, and he covered her with it, showing not the least sign of grief. So Griselda remained with her father for some time, living in humility and poverty and serving her father as she had done before, without a single trace of sadness or regret; rather, she comforted her father in his grief at seeing his daughter fall from such a great height to such lowly poverty.

When it seemed to the marquis that he had sufficiently tested his loyal wife, he ordered his sister to come to him in the noble company of lords and ladies and to bring his two children without giving the least hint that they were his. He informed his barons and his subjects that he intended to take a new wife, to marry a most noble maiden whom his sister had in tutelage. He had a handsome company of knights and ladies assembled in his palace on the day when his sister was supposed to arrive. He also had a great celebration readied. He gave Griselda the following orders: 'Griselda, the maiden whom I will marry will be here tomorrow, and because I want my sister and her entire noble company to be magnificently received, and since you know my customs and are familiar with the chambers and the rooms, I want you to be in charge. All the servants shall obey you so that each member of the company can be received according to his rank, particularly my bride-to-be. Take care that everything is well arranged.' Griselda replied that she would gladly do this. The following day when the company had arrived, the celebration was magnificent. Even in spite of her shabby dress Griselda did not hesitate to go out with a glad face to meet the maiden who, she believed, would be the new bride. Humbly curtseying to her, Griselda said, 'My lady, you are most welcome.' She curtseyed to her son and to all the members of the company and she received each cordially, according to their rank. Even though she was dressed so poorly, it was perfectly clear from her bearing that she was a woman of the highest distinction and prudence so that the strangers wondered how such eloquence and honour could simultaneously be present with such poverty. Griselda had arranged everything so well that nothing was out of place. But she was drawn so strongly to the maiden and to her son that she could not leave and she carefully took note of their beauty which she greatly praised. The marquis himself had arranged everything to look as though he was going to marry the maiden. When the time came to celebrate the Mass, the marquis came forward, and in front of all, called to Griselda and said to her before everyone, 'What do you think, Griselda, of my new bride? Is she not beautiful and upright?' She answered loudly, 'Indeed, my lord, there is no woman more beautiful or more upright. I would however make a single request of you and give you only one bit of advice: that you neither trouble nor needle her with the torments which you inflicted upon your first wife. This woman is younger and has been raised more delicately so that she probably cannot bear as much as your other wife did.' The marquis, hearing Griselda's words, recalled her unsurpassed steadfastness, strength, and constancy and was filled with admiration for her virtue. Pity overwhelmed him because he had made and was making her suffer so much and for so long and so undeservedly. Thereupon, in the presence of all, he began to speak:

'Griselda, this is a sufficient test of your constancy and of the faith, loyalty and great love, obedience and proven humility which you feel for me. Rest assured that there is no man under the heavens who has come to know the love of the marriage bond through so many trials as I have with you.' Then the marquis approached her, embraced her warmly, kissed her, and said, 'You alone are my wife, I want no other and will have no other. This young girl, who you thought was to be my wife, is your daughter and mine, and this other child is your son. Let all who are here know that everything which I have done has been to test my loyal wife and not to condemn her. I have had my children raised in Bologna with my sister and I did not have them killed – they are right here.' Hearing the words of her lord, the marquise fainted with joy; when she came to, she took her children in her arms and they were soon wet with her tears. There is not the slightest doubt that her heart was filled with great joy. Everyone who saw this wept for joy and pity. Griselda was restored to greater authority than ever before and she was richly fitted out and bejeweled. The celebration was magnificent and joyful, and during it, all spoke in praise of this lady. They lived together another twenty years in joy and peace. The marquis also summoned to the palace Giannucolo, his wife's father, whom he had ignored in the past, and he held him in high esteem. He married his children in great honour. His son succeeded him following his death with the barons' assent.

63 The Debate on the Rose

The early fifteenth-century debate on the morality of Jean de Meun's *Romance of the Rose* featured some of the leading writers and thinkers of early fifteenth-century France: Jean de Montreuil, Gontier Col, Pierre Col, Christine de Pizan and Jean Gerson. This extract is from the *Treatise of Gerson*, the chancellor of the university of Paris, attacking the poem: the fictional speaker petitioning for justice here is Chastity; the Foolish Lover, the Old Woman, the Jealous Man, Venus, Cupid, Genius, and Reason are all characters from the *Romance of the Rose*.

Further reading: Willard 1984, Fenster and Erler 1990, Minnis 2001.

Text: Joseph L. Baird and John R. Kane (ed. and trans.) (1978) *La Querelle de la Rose: Letters and Documents*, Chapel Hill, North Carolina: University of North Carolina Department of Romance Languages.

ARTICLE ONE

This Foolish Lover seizes every chance to drive me, who am innocent, from the earth, and with me my good attendants: Modesty, Fear, and Dangier, the good door-keeper. None of them would either dare or deign to grant a single shameful kiss, a shameless look, a come-hither smile, or a frivolous word. And the Foolish Lover does this through an accursed Old Woman worse than the devil, who teaches, shows, and exhorts all young virgins to sell their bodies quickly and dearly without fear or shame. Nor should they, she holds, put a high premium on deceiving or forswearing, provided always that they gain something thereby. Neither need they hesitate at all before abandoning themselves, quickly while they are still beautiful, to every dishonour and to carnal filth, whether with clerics or laymen or priests, without any discrimination.

ARTICLE 2

He wishes to forbid and condemn marriage, without exception by means of a suspicious, hateful, and evil-minded Jealous Man, both through his own words and those of my adversaries. And he enjoins men to hang or drown themselves, or to commit sins which ought not to be named, rather than to marry. And he reviles all women, without any exception, and renders them so hateful to all men that none would wish to take them in the bonds of matrimony.

ARTICLE 3

He castigates young men who have given themselves to religion, because, as he says, they are striving to lay aside their nature, and this thing is a prejudice against me, for I am especially dedicated to religion.

ARTICLE 4

He throws everywhere a fire more burning and more foul than Greek Fire or sulphur. He throws, I say, the fire of lecherous words, impure and prohibited, sometimes in the name of Venus and Cupid or Genius, more often in his own name, through which burn and are consumed my beautiful home and habitations, my sacred temples of human souls; and I am most shamefully cast down.

ARTICLE 5

He slanders Lady Reason, my good Mistress, by imputing to her the madness and wicked blasphemy of encouraging people to speak bluntly, openly, and basely about everything, however abominable or shameful, even to people already dissolute and enemies of mine. Alas, if he did not wish to spare me, what wrong has Reason ever done against him? But that's the way it is. Indeed, he makes war against all the virtues.

ARTICLE 6

When he speaks of holy, divine, and spiritual things, he immediately mixes in the most dissolute words, in order to incite to every impurity. However, impurity shall not enter into that Paradise, which he himself describes.

ARTICLE 7

He promises Paradise, glory, and reward to all men and women who perform the works of the flesh, even outside marriage. For in his own person and by his own examples, hc counsels men to try out all kinds of women indiscriminately; and he slanders all those who would not do so, at least all those who cherish and revere me.

ARTICLE 8

In his own person, he uses holy and sacred words to name the dishonourable parts of the body and impure and shameful sins, as if such works were divine, sacred, and holy, even though they are done through frauds and violence and not within the married state. He was not content simply to utter the above-mentioned affronts everywhere publicly, but he also took care, to the limits of his power, to have them portrayed skilfully and lavishly in words and pictures, the more quickly to allure people into hearing, seeing, and holding fast to these things. But still worse remains: the more subtly to deceive, he mixed honey with poison and sweetness with venom, like poisonous serpents lying under the green grass of devotion. And he does this by drawing together diverse materials, which often are scarcely to his purpose, aside from such deception, so that, by seeming to have experienced and studied many things, he would be the better believed and have greater authority.

64 François Rabelais, *Garagantua and Pantagruel*

This is a brief extract from his gargantuan satire. François Rabelais (*c.*1490–1553) pokes fun at ecclesiastical control of marriage.

Text: François Rabelais (1955), *The Histories of Gargantua and Pantagruel*, trans. J. M. Cohen, Penguin: Harmondsworth.

For in my day there was found on the Continent a country in which lived certain image-bearing molecatchers, who were as hostile to marriage as the priests of Cybele in Phrygia – only they were not capons but the most lecherous and salacious of cocks – and they dictated laws to married folk on the subject of marriage. Really I don't know which is the more abominable, the tyrannical presumption of these dreaded molecatchers – who do not confine themselves within the bars of their mysterious temples but meddle with matters utterly foreign to their condition – or the superstitious stupidity of the married folk, who have sanctioned and obeyed such perfectly malicious and barbarous laws. For they do not see what is clearer than the morning star, that these connubial sanctions are entirely to the advantage of the Fraternity, and in no way for the good and profit of husbands and wives; which is sufficient reason to arouse suspicions of iniquity and fraud. It would be no more presumptuous if the married were to set up laws for the Fraternity to govern their ceremonies and sacrifices, seeing that these image-bearers take tithe of their goods, and nibble at the profit earned by their labours and by the sweat of their brows, to provide themselves with abundant food and ample leisure. Such laws would not, in my opinion, be as perverse and as presumptuous as those which the married folk have received from the Fraternity. For, as you very well said, there has never been a law in the world that gave children permission to marry without their fathers' knowledge, will, and consent. Yet by the laws of which I am speaking there is no scoundrel, criminal, rogue, or gallows-bird, no stinking, lousy, leprous ruffian, no brigand, robber, or villain in their country, who may not snatch any maiden he chooses – never mind how noble, lovely, rich, modest, and bashful she may be – out of her father's house, out of her mother's arms, and in spite of all her relations, so long as this ruffian has entered into an agreement with some image-bearer, for a future division of the spoils.

MIDDLE ENGLISH LITERATURE

65 Middle English Lyrics

Love – religious or secular – is an important theme in medieval lyric poetry. This is a small sample.

Text: Maxwell S. Luria and Richard L. Hoffman (eds) (1974) *Middle English Lyrics*, London: Norton; my translation.

(I)

'Kyrie,' so 'Kyrie,'
Jankin sings merrily
With 'aleison.'[13]

As I went on Yule Day in our procession
Knew I jolly Jankin by his merry tone.
Kyrieleison.

Jankin began the service on the Yule Day,
And yet I think it does me good, so merrily did he say
Kyrieleison.

Jankin read the Epistle full fair and full well,
And yet I think it does me good, as ever have I fortune.
Kyrieleison.

13 Jankin sings "Kyrie aleison," God have mercy on us, but there is a pun on 'Alison', the name of his lover. On these names, cf. Chaucer's Wife of Bath's prologue (extract 71) which also has characters called Alison and Jankyn.

Jankin at the *Sanctus* sang a merry note
And yet I think it does me good – I paid for his coat.
Kyrieleison.

Jankin sang notes a hundred at a time,
And yet he hacked them smaller than vegetables in the pot.
Kyrieleison.

Jankin at the *Agnus* carried the *pax-brede*;
He twinkled, but said nothing, and on my foot he trod.
Kyrieleison.

Let us bless the Lord, Christ shield me from shame.
Thanks be to God, also – alas, I am with child.
Kyrieleison.

(II)

Love is soft, love is sweet, love is good speech.
Love is much grief, love is much care.
Love is the greatest bliss, love is a fast cure.
Love is distress and woe, to fare with.

Love is luck, for who has it; love is good health.
Love is lecherous and false, and pleased to entrap.
Love is doughty in the world, to deal with.
Love makes many in the land unloyal.

Love is stalwart and strong to stride on a steed.
Love is a lovely thing to women's need.
Love is hardy and hot as a glowing ember.
Love makes many a maiden rage in tears.

Love has his steward by path and by street
Love makes many a maiden wet her cheeks.
Love is luck, for who has it, to inflame.
Love is wise, love is wary and wilful and proper.

Love is the softest thing that may sleep in heart.
Love is craft, love is good with cares to heed.
Love is false, love is dear, love is longing.

Love is foolish, love is secure, love is comfort.
Love is a marvellous thing, whoever shall sing about it truly.

Love is wealth, love is woe, love is gladness;
Love is life, love is death, love may feed us.

Were love as long-enduring as it's as first keen,
It would be the worthiest thing in the world, I think.
It's said in a song, the truth is seen,
Love comes with care and ends with grief,
For lady, for wife, for maiden, for queen.

(III)

I shall say what inordinate love is:
The furiousness and madness of mind,
An inextinguishable burning, lacking bliss,
A great hunger insatiate to find,
A dulcet ill, an evil sweetness blind,
A right wonderful sugared sweet error,
Without labour rest – contrary to nature –
Or without rest to have huge labour.

66 In the Ecclesiastical Court

This thirteenth-century poem, from the famous collection of alliterative poems in MS. Harley 2253, is an account of the practice of abjuration *sub pena nubendi*, whereby the ecclesiastical courts force recidivist fornicators into marriage (see extract 15).

Further reading: Turville-Petre 1989, 1997, Scattergood 2000. On the legal issues, Sheehan 1974, Helmholz 1987b.

Text: Thorlac Turville-Petre (ed.) (1989) *Alliterative Poetry of the Later Middle Ages*, London: Routledge; my translation.[14]

No unlearned man may live in land,
Be he never in court so skilful of hand,

14 The difficulty of some of the language in this poem means that the translation given here occasionally employs conjecture.

The learned harass us so.
If I have dealings anywhere with a maid
I shall fall before them and learn their law
And rue all their decrees;
Ah unless I be there before them on the earliest day,
I shall not so easily escape from their register,
So grimly he growls at me,
If I do not conduct myself there with my defence
With all manner of oaths that they will frighten me with,
As they open their book.
They turn over open books
And make men mad for a month,
I want to clear myself of harm,
And flee from my mistress,
He doesn't care what it was
As long as he had it.

First there sits an old churl in a black cap,
Of all that sit there he seems best master,
And lays his leg outstretched.
A hick in a cloak with hanging sleeves,
And more than forty before him to report my misdeeds,
If I sank in sin.
They stab with their pens on their parchment
And say I am reported and brought in
For all my proud goods;
They are all ready to describe my sorrows,
There I must for favour pay some reward
And thankfully them thank.
Shall I thank them before I go?
Yes, the master and his men both!
If I am written in their writing,
Then I am defamed,
For many a man they blame
For women's woe.

Yet there sit summoners six or seven,
Falsely accusing men all by their nature,
And read out all their roll.
Retainers hate them, and each man's servant,
For they cause suffering in every parish.
And shut us up with their trickery.

Now will each foul clerk that is delinquent
Go to the bishop and deceive the bailiff,
There is no wit in his head;
Come to county court, cowering in a cape,
And say he has privilege proud of the pope,
All dark and swollen.
Are those swollen men perjured?
Yes, the hatred of hell be theirs!
For there they swear on a book
To say that I lechery took.
They should in hell on a hook
Hang for that!

There stands up a crier, crying in the yard,
And shouts out on high that all the court heard,
And calls Maggie and Mary;
And she comes muddied as a moorhen
And shrieks for shame and is ashamed before men,
Uncomely under her cowl.
She begins to shriek and screams at once
And says by my gabbing it shall not go so,
And 'That shall be on you all,
That you shall wed me and take as a wife!'

Ah I would rather for law lose my life
Than fall to their feet so.
Shall I fall to the feet of my foe?
Yes, they persuade many so!
Of serfs I am there threatened
That sit dark and sweating,
That I must bind myself in a promise
Before I go home.

Such goods I bought at the chapterhouse
That makes many a vigorous man feeble
With thanks full thin,
And since I went to cower at the consistory
And fell to the foot of each delinquent,
Theirs is the world's joy.
Since I pleaded at the bishop's court,
Ah I would rather be sunk in the sea
In grief without sin.

At church and through the market as a dog I am driven
That I would rather be dead than to live so
For care of all my kin.
At the consistory they teach us care
And wish us evil and worse to fare.
A priest proud as a pea
Then wedded us both.
Far and wide they cause us woe
For women's wares![15]

67 *The Owl and the Nightingale*

The Owl and the Nightingale is an anonymously authored thirteenth-century poem describing a debate between the two birds of the title. Here, the Nightingale defends herself against the accusation that her singing encourages lechery. This extract is remarkable for its sympathetic attitude to extramarital love among the young.

Further reading: Coleman 1987, Cartlidge 1997: ch. 5, Holsinger 2002.

Text: E. G. Stanley (ed.) (1960) *The Owl and the Nightingale*, London: Nelson; my modern English translation.

Tell me truly, if you know it,
Which does worse, flesh or the spirit?
You might say, if you wish,
That less is the flesh's guilt:
Many a man is of his flesh clean
That is in spirit the devil's companion.
No man shall cry out against woman
And upbraid her for fleshly lusts;
Such he may blame for lechery
He that sins worse in pride.
Yet if I should to love bring
Wife or maid when I sing
I would with the maid hold,
If you can consider it correctly.
Listen now! I'll tell you wherefore
Up to the top from the root:
If a maid loves secretly

15 'Ware' means 'possessions' but also 'genitals'.

She stumbles & falls, naturally;
For though she some while plays
She is not far out of the way;
She may turn from her guilt,
To the right path through the church's bond,
And may afterwards have as husband
Her lover without blame,
And go to him by the day's light
That she sneaked to before by darkness at night.[16]
A youngling doesn't know what such a thing is,
Her young blood draws her astray,
And some foolish man entices her thereto
With all that which he may do:
He comes & goes, bids & begs,
And harasses and neglects her
And she sighs often & long.
What may that child do if it goes wrong?
She never knew what it was,
That is why she thought to try it,
And know indeed what is the game
That of such wild creatures makes tame ones.
Nor may I for pity refrain,
When I see the taut expression
That love brings on the youngling,
That I may not sing to her of mirth.
I teach them by my song
That such love doesn't last long;
For my song lasts a little while,
And love does nothing but [briefly] rest
On such children & soon goes,
And the hot passion falls away.[17]
I sing with them for a while,
Begin on high and end low,

16 Coleman (1987: 537–539) argues that these lines refer to a clandestine marriage, which can be legitimated through a public ceremony. But Holsinger (2002: 163) argues that there is perhaps a latent antimatrimonial argument here: he notes that the Middle English word *sake* in line 1430 (she has 'hire leofmon wiþute sake') can mean 'jurisdiction' – and so that the line can mean not that she has 'her lover without blame' but that she has her lover without surrendering her economic and legal authority to that of a husband.

17 Middle English 'breth' here and in the subsequent phrase 'nothing but a little breath', means both 'breath' and 'passion'.

And let my song fall away
After a little while altogether.
That maid knows, when I stop,
That love is like my song:
For it is nothing but a little breath
That soon comes & soon goes.
That child by me it understands,
And her naivete turns to wisdom,
And [she] sees well by my song
That foolish love does not last long.

(The Nightingale goes on to say that this attitude of tolerance and sympathy does not apply to adultery.)

68 *Cleanness*

Cleanness is a late fourteenth-century alliterative poem retelling some episodes from biblical history, generally supposed to be written by the same anonymous author as *Sir Gawain and the Green Knight*, which appears in the same manuscript. In this extract from the description of the destruction of Sodom and Gomorrah, God is speaking to his servant describing his intention to destroy the city. The passage is unusual in its unambiguous praise of heterosexual intercourse, but this may arise from the context of its attack on homosexuality.

Further reading: Frantzen 1996.

Text: J. J. Anderson (ed.) (1996) *Sir Gawain and the Green Knight, Pearl, Cleanness, Patience*, London: Dent; my modern English translation.

'The great sound of Sodom sinks in my ears,
And the guilt of Gomorrah causes me to become angry
I shall come down to that people and see for myself
If they have done as the din is raised above.
They have learned a trick that pleases me ill,
In that they have found in their flesh the worst of faults;
Each man makes a man like himself his mate,
And they join together lewdly in female fashion.
I devised for them a natural way, and taught it to them secretly,
And valued it most dearly in my plan of creation,
And set love therein, the sweetest sharing;
And the play of lovers I devised myself,

And made for that purpose a practice more merry than any other.
When two true people had fastened themselves together,
Between a man and his mate such mirth should come,
That Paradise itself might hardly prove any better.
As long as they might honestly use each other,
At a still, secret meeting, hidden from sight,
The fire of love would burn so hotly between them
That all the misfortunes in the world might not quench it.
Now they have disobeyed my will and scorned nature,
And they adopt in contempt an unclean usage.
I intend to smite them sharply for that smut
So that people shall beware because of them, world without end.'

69 John Gower, *Confessio Amantis*

Two extracts from Gower's lengthy late fourteenth-century poetical portrait 'The Lover's Confession'. The story of Iphis and Iante is about two girls who are married to each other because one is thought to be a boy; the story of Venus and Cupid is about the incestuous love of the God and Goddess of Love. Both stories are told by Genius, the priest of Venus, who is the lover's confessor.

Further reading: Bennett 1968, Collins 1981, Nicholson (ed.) 1991, McCarthy 2000b.

Text: G. C. Macaulay (ed.) (1900, 1957) *The English Works of John Gower*, London: Oxford University Press; my modern English translation.

(I)

The king Ligdus in an argument[18]
Spoke to Thelacuse his wife,
Who was then heavily pregnant;
He swore that it should not happen,
That if she bore a daughter,
That it should not be lost
And slain, at which she was distressed.
So it happened in this case,

18 The story of Iphis and Ianthe is from Ovid, *Metamorphoses*, Book IX, where Ligdus is not a king, but of humble ancestry although freeborn. His wife's name is Telethusa.

When she should be delivered,
Isis by night in secrecy,
Who is the goddess of childbirth,
Came forward to help in that distress,
Until that lady was all small,
and had had a daughter also;
Which the goddess in all ways
Bid her keep, and that she should say
It was a Son: and so Iphis
They named him, and upon this
The father was made so to believe.
And so in the bedroom with the queen
This Iphis was brought up,
And clothed and arrayed so
Just as a king's son should be.
Until afterwards, as fortune wished it,
When he was ten years old
He was given in marriage
To marry a duke's daughter,
Who was called Iante, and often in bed,
These children lay, she and she,
Which both were of the one age.
So that within time of years,
As they were playfellows together
Lying in bed at night
Nature, which causes every person
To muse upon her law,
Constrained them, so that they practiced
Something which to them was entirely unknown;
Whereof Cupid at this time
Took pity for the great love,
And placed nature above,
So that her law might be used,
And they upon their lust excused.
For love hates nothing more
Than something which stands against the lore
Of what nature has proclaimed as natural:
Therefore Cupid had so beset
His mercy upon these events,
That he accorded with nature,
When he saw the best time,
That each of them had kissed the other,

He transformed Iphis into a man,
Whereof the natural love he won
Of lusty young Iante his wife;
And then they led a merry life,
Which was to nature no offence.

(II)

My son, I have omitted it for shame,
Because I am their own priest;
But because they stand near the heart
Of the confession of your matter
You shall hear the truth about them:
And understand the case well now.
Venus was Saturn's daughter
Who disregarded all wariness
Of love, and found to lust a way;
So that of her in sundry places
Diverse men fell into grace,
And such a lusty life she led,
That she diverse children had,
Now one by this, now one by that.
Of her it was that Mars begat[19]
A child, which was called Harmony;
Of her also came Androgene,
To whom Mercury father was:[20]
Anchises begat Aeneas[21]
Of her also, and Ericon[22]
Biten begat, and thereupon,
When she saw there was no other,
By Jupiter her own brother
She lay, and he begat Cupid.
And this Son in time,
When he had grown up,
He had a wondrously fair appearance,
And found his Mother amorous,

19 Mars, the Roman god of war.

20 Mercury is the messenger of the gods, father of Androgene (or Hermaphroditus).

21 Aeneas, son of Venus and the Trojan Anchises, hero of Virgil's *Aeneid*.

22 Venus is also called 'Ericyna' by Ovid.

And he was also lecherous:
So when they were both alone
He who had no eyes
To see reason, his Mother kissed;
And she also, that nothing knew
Except that which belonged to lust,
To be her love he undertook.
So was he blind, and she unwise:
But nonetheless this is the reason
That Cupid is the god of love,
For he loves his mother.

70 Geoffrey Chaucer, *Portrait of the Pardoner*

This extract from Chaucer's late fourteenth-century portrait of the Pardoner in the General Prologue to the *Canterbury Tales* suggests a sexual relationship between the Pardoner and his fellow pilgrim, the Summoner.[23] The narrator is suspicious but unsure of the nature of the Pardoner's gender identity and sexual orientation. His lack of a beard, his squeaky voice, and the stuffed pouch in his lap are all suspicious signs.

Further reading: Dinshaw 1989, Frantzen 1994.

Text: John M. Manly and Edith Rickert (eds) (1940) *The Text of the Canterbury Tales Studied on the Basis of all Known Manuscripts*, Chicago: University of Chicago Press; my modern English translation.

With him there rode a noble Pardoner
Of Rouncivale, his friend and companion,
That had come straight from the court of Rome.
Very loudly he sang 'Come hither, love, to me.'
This Summoner carried to him a strong accompaniment[24]
There was never a trumpet of half so great a sound.
This Pardoner had hair as yellow as wax
But it hung smooth as does a clump of flax
By strands his locks hung that he had
And these he spread over his shoulders

23 A pardoner is a cleric who collects alms and distributes indulgences for the remission of sins. A summoner is an official of the ecclesiastical court who summons people to court (see also extract 66).

24 The Middle English, while meaning 'strong accompaniment', has a punning meaning of 'stiff pilgrim's stick' (Davis *et al.* 1979: 19).

But it lay thin, by strands one and one.
But hood, for ease, wore he none
For it was trussed up in his pouch.
He thought he rode in all the latest fashion;
Dishevelled, except for his cap, he rode all bareheaded.
Such glaring eyes had he as a hare.
  A Veronica had he sewn upon his cap[25]
His pouch before him in his lap
Brimful of pardons come from Rome all hot.
  A voice had he as small as has a goat.
No beard had he nor never should have
As smooth it was as if it had just been shaved.
I think that he was a gelding or a mare.[26]

71 Geoffrey Chaucer, *The Wife of Bath's Prologue*

The Wife of Bath's Prologue and her subsequent tale are the centrepiece of the marriage debate in the *Canterbury Tales*: almost all of the tales have something to say about marriage, but the Wife's contribution to the debate provokes explicit responses from the Clerk and the Merchant in particular, both of whom refer to her in their narratives. Chaucer's poem owes something to previous antifeminist writings, and modern commentators debate whether or not the Wife's text transcends its sources.

Further reading: for Chaucer on marriage, see Brewer 1954, Kittredge 1960, Kelly 1975. On the Wife, see Cooper 1989, Dinshaw 1989, Mann 1991, Carruthers 1994, Delany 1994.

Text: John M. Manly and Edith Rickert (eds) (1940) *The Text of the Canterbury Tales Studied on the Basis of all Known Manuscripts*, Chicago: University of Chicago Press; my modern English translation.

  'Experience, though no authority
Were in this world, is certainly enough for me
To speak of woe that is in marriage,[27]

25 A 'Veronica' is a token of pilgrimage to Rome (Benson 1987: 34 n.).
26 i.e. a eunuch or a homosexual, but the narrator's uncertainty is visible.
27 These opening lines that seem to privilege experience above authority are themselves a quotation from an authority, the *Romance of the Rose*. Manuscripts of the poem are heavily glossed with the authorities quoted by the Wife, largely St Jerome's *Against Jovinian* (extract 6).

For sirs, since I was twelve years of age
(Thanks be to God that lives eternally)
Husbands at church door I have had five
(If I might have been married so often)
And all were worthy men in their way.
But I was told certainly, not long ago,
That since Christ never went except once
To a wedding, in Cana of Galilee,
That by the same example he taught me
That I should not be wedded except once.
Listen also, oh, what a sharp word indeed
Beside a well, Jesus, God and man,
Spoke in reproof of the Samaritan.
"You have had five husbands," said he,
"And that same man that has you now
Is not your husband," this is certainly what he said.
But what he meant by that, I cannot say.
But I ask, why that the fifth man
Was not husband to the Samaritan?
How many might she have in marriage?
Yet I never heard tell in my time
A definition of this number.
Men may speculate and interpret, up and down,
But I know well, clearly, without lie,
God told us to increase and multiply.
That noble text I can well understand.
I also know well he said my husband
Should leave father and mother and give himself to me,
But he did not make mention of any number
Of bigamy, or octogamy.[28]
Why should men then speak shamefully of it?
Look here at the wise king, master Solomon,
I think he had more wives than one.
Would that God would grant that it were lawful for me
To be refreshed half so often as he.
What a gift from God he had because of all his wives,
No man has such that in this world is alive.
God knows this noble king, as I think,
The first night had many a merry episode
With each of them, so happy was he to be alive.

28 'Bigamy' here is the remarriage of widows and widowers.

Blessed be God that I have wedded five
[Of which I have picked out the best
Both of their nether purse and of their coffers.
A diversity of schools makes perfect students
And different practice in many sorts of work
Makes the workman perfect certainly
Of five husbands' schooling am I.][29]
Welcome the sixth whenever he arrives.
For truly I will not keep myself chaste forever,
When my husband is gone from the world
Some Christian man shall marry me quickly.
For then the Apostle says that I am free
To marry, for God's sake, where it pleases me.
He says that to be married is no sin,
It's better to be married than to burn.[30]
What do I care if folk speak shamefully
Of cursed Lamech and his bigamy?
I know well Abraham was a holy man,
And Jacob also, as far as I know,
And each of them had more than two wives,
And many another holy man also.
Where can you say, in any era,
That the high God forbade marriage
By explicit words – I ask you, tell me?[31]
Or where did he command virginity?
I know as well as you, there is no doubt.
The apostle, when he speaks of virginity,
He said that he had no command about that.[32]
Men may advise a woman to be one
But advice is no commandment
He put it in our own judgment,
For had God commanded virginity,
Then had he damned marriage with the deed.
And certainly, if there were no seeds sown,
Virginity then, where should it grow from?

29 These lines do not appear in some manuscripts.

30 St Paul, 1 Corinthians 7.

31 Blamires (1989) compares the Wife's methods of scriptural interpretation with those of the contemporary Lollards, who were later persecuted as heretics.

32 'The apostle' is St Paul.

Paul dared not command at least
Something concerning which his master gave no commandment.
The prize is set up for virginity,
Let whoever is able to catch it, let's see who runs best.
  But these words do not apply to everybody,
But to whoever God desires to give it of his greatness.
I know well that the apostle was a virgin,
But nonetheless, although he wrote and said
That he wished that everybody were such as he,
This is only advice to adopt virginity,
And he allowed me to be a wife
By permission, so it is no shame
To marry me if my mate dies,
Without objection of bigamy.
Although it is good to touch no woman
(He meant in his bed or in his couch,
For it is perilous to bring fire and flax together,
You know well what this example may resemble)
This is all, and some: he considered virginity
More perfect than marrying in frailty.
I call it frailty, unless he and she
Desire to lead their entire lives in chastity.
  I concede it, certainly, I have no envy
That virginity takes precedence over bigamy.
It pleases them to be clean in body and soul.
Of my position I will not make any boast.
For well you know, a lord in his household
Has not every vessel all of gold,
Some are of wood and do their lord service.
God calls people to him in different ways,
And each has of God an individual gift,
Some this, some that, as he wishes to provide.
  Virginity is great perfection,
And continence also with devotion.
But Christ, that is perfection's well,
Did not urge everyone that he should go sell
All that he had and give it to the poor,
And in such a way follow him and his footsteps.
He spoke to those who wished to live perfectly.
And masters, by your leave, that's not me.
I will give the flower of my years
In the acts and fruit of marriage.

Tell me also, to what end
Were bodily parts for generation made,
And of so perfectly wise a maker made?
Trust well indeed, they were not made for nothing.
Interpret whoever that will, and say both up and down
That they were made to purge
Urine, and that both our small things
Were also to know a female from a male
And for no other cause, say you no?
The experience shows well it is not so.
So that the learned are not angry with me
I say this, that they are made for both,
That is to say for bodily function, and for pleasure
In procreation where we do not displease God.
Why else should men in their books set
That man shall give to his wife her debt?[33]
Now with what should he make his payment
If he did not use his harmless instrument?
Then were they made in a creature
To purge urine, and also for reproduction.
But I do not say that every person is held to this
That has such harness as I told to you
To go and use them for reproduction.
Then men would not pay any attention to chastity.
Christ was a virgin and shaped as a man
And many a saint since the world began,
Yet they always lived in perfect chastity.
I will not envy any virginity.
Let them be bread of purified wheat-seed
And let us wives be called barley-bread,
Yet with barley-bread, as Mark can tell,
Our Lord Jesus refreshed many a man.
In such a role as God has called us to
I will persevere. I'm not fussy.
In wifehood I will use my instrument
As freely as my maker has sent it.
If I am stingy, God give me sorrow.
My husband shall have it both evening and morning,
When he wants to come forward and pay his debt.
A husband I want to have, I will not leave off,

33 1 Cor. 7. The 'marital debt' is sexual intercourse.

Who shall be both my debtor and my slave,
And have his suffering also
Upon his flesh, while I am his wife.
I have the power during all my life
Over his own body, and not he,
Just so the Apostle told it to me,
And instructed our husbands to love us well.
All of this judgment pleases me, each bit' –
   Up jumped the Pardoner, and that immediately,[34]
'Now, Madam,' he said, 'by God and by St John,
You are a noble preacher in this matter.
I was about to marry a wife, alas,
Why should I pay for it so dearly with my flesh?
Yet had I rather marry no wife this year.'
   'Wait,' she said, 'my tale has not begun,
No, you shall drink from another barrel
Before I go, that will taste worse than ale.
And when I have told you my tale
Of suffering in marriage
(Of which I am the greatest expert of my time,
That is to say, I myself have been the whip)
Then you may choose whether you will sip
Of this barrel that I shall breach.
Beware of it before you come too near,
For I shall tell examples more than ten.
Whoever will not be warned by [the example of] other men,
By his example shall other men be corrected.
Ptolemy writes these same words
Read his Almagest, and find it there.'
   'Madam, I would ask you, if it were your will,'
Said this Pardoner, 'as you began,
Tell your tale, hold back for no man,
And teach us young men of your practice.'
   'Gladly,' said she, 'since it may please you,
But yet I ask all of this company,
If I speak according to my fancy,
Don't be aggrieved with what I say,
For my intent is only for to play.
   Now then, Sir, I will tell you my tale.
As ever I might drink wine or ale,

34 This is the Pardoner of the previous extract.

I shall say truly, these husbands that I had,
Three of them were good, and two were bad.
The three men were good, and rich, and old,
They might hardly keep the statute
Through which they were bound to me.[35]
You know well what I mean by this, by God.
So help me God, I laugh when I think
How piteously at night I made them work,
And by my faith, I set no store by it.
They had given me their land and their treasure.
I didn't need to make any further effort
To win their love, or do them reverence.
They loved me so well, by God above,
That I didn't put any value on their love.
A wise woman will busy herself at all times
To get herself love, indeed, where she has none.
But since I had them wholly in my hand,
And since they had given me all their land,
Why should I take heed to please them
If it were not for my profit and my ease?
I set them to work so, by my faith,
That many a night they sang, "alas,"
The bacon was not fetched for them, I think,
That some men have in Essex, at Dunmowe.[36]
I governed them so well, according to my law,
That each of them was very blissful and eager
To bring me gay things from the fair.
They were so glad when I spoke to them nicely,
For, God knows it, I chided them spitefully.
Now listen how I conducted myself properly
You wise wives, that can understand.
This is how you should speak and accuse them wrongly,
For no man knows half so boldly how to
Swear and lie, as a woman can.
I say this not of wives that are wise,
But if it happens that they misconsider.
A wise wife, if she knows what's good for her,
Shall convince him that the chough is mad[37]

35 i.e. pay the marital debt.

36 A prize for couples who did not quarrel (Benson 1987: 108 n.).

37 A chough is a talking bird (Benson 1987: 108n.).

And bring her own maid as a witness
Who agrees. But listen how I spoke.[38]
"Mister old fogey, is this your splendour?
Why is my neighbour's wife so well-dressed?
She is honoured wherever she goes,
I sit at home, I have no decent clothes.
What do you do at my neighbour's house?
Is she so fair? Are you so amorous?
What do you whisper to our maid? Benedicite!
Mister old lecher, let your deceiving be.
And if I have a companion or a friend,
Without guilt, you chide like a fiend,
If I walk or amuse myself at his house.
You come home as drunk as a mouse
And preach on your bench, bad luck to you.
You say to me that it's a great mischief
To marry a poor woman because of the cost.
And if she is rich, of high birth,
Then you say that it's a torment
To endure her pride and her melancholy.
And if she is fair, you wretch,
You say that every lecher will have her.
She may not live in chastity long
That's assaulted from every side.
You say some folk desire us for riches,
Some for our shape, and some for our fairness,
And some for she can either sing or dance,
And some for graciousness and flirtatiousness,
Some for their hands and their slender arms,
That's how all go to the devil, the way you tell it.
You say that men cannot keep a castle wall,
It may be attacked for so long from all sides.
And if she is foul, you say that she
Covets every man that she may see.
For like a spaniel she will leap on him,
Until she finds some man to take her.
Nor no goose so grey goes there in the lake
As, you say, wants to be without a mate.
And you say it is a hard thing to wield
A thing that no man wishes willingly to hold.

38 For what follows, cf. extract 6 above, Jerome's quotation of Theophrastus, which is Chaucer's source here.

That's what you say, scoundrel, when you go to bed,
And that no wise man needs to wed,
Nor any man that intends to go to heaven.
With wild thunder-dent and fiery lightning
May your withered neck be broken!
   You say that leaking houses, and also smoke,
And chiding wives make men flee
Out of their own houses, ah, benedicitee!
What ails such an old man to complain?
   You say we wives will hide our vices
Till we are secure, and then we will show them.
Well may that be a proverb of a scoundrel.
   You say that oxen, asses, horses, and hounds,
They are assessed at different times,
Basins, washbowls, before men buy them,
Spoons and stools, and all such household goods.
And so are pots, cloths and clothes,
But men make no assessment of wives,
Until they are wedded (old doting scold)
And then, says you, we will show our vices.
   You say also that it displeases me
Unless you praise my beauty,
And unless you pore always on my face,
And call me 'fair lady' in every place.
And unless you make a feast on that day
That I was born, and make me fresh and gay,
And unless you do honour to my nurse,
And to my chambermaid within my bedroom,
And to my father's folk and all my kin . . .
This is what you say, old barrelful of lies!
   And also of our apprentice Jankyn,
Because of his curly hair, shining like gold so fine,
And because he escorts me both up and down,
All the same, you have a false suspicion.
I don't want him, though you were dead tomorrow!
   But tell me this, why do you hide (bad luck to you)
The keys of your chest away from me?
They are my goods as well as yours, by God.
What, do you think to make an idiot of the lady of the house?
Now, by that lord that is called St James,
You shall not both (though you were mad)
Be master of my body and my goods.

One of these you will forego, damn your eyes.
What does it help to ask about me, or spy?
I believe you would lock me in your chest!
You should say, 'Wife, go where you want.
Take your pleasure. I will not believe any tales.
I know you for a faithful wife, lady Alice.'
We love no man who takes heed or notice
Where we go to. We want to be free to go where we want.
Of all men blessed shall he be,
The wise astronomer master Ptolemy,
That gives this proverb in his Almagest.
'Of all men his wisdom is the highest
That never cares who controls the world'.
By this proverb you should understand:
'If you have enough, what do you care or worry
How merrily other folk fare?'
For, certainly, old fool, by your leave,
You shall have something quaint, right enough, in the evening.
He is too great a miser that would refuse
A man to light a candle at his lantern.
He shall not have any less light, by God.
If you have enough, you have no need to complain.
You say also that if we make ourselves splendid
With clothing, and with dressing richly,
That it is to the peril of our chastity.
And yet (with sorrow!) you must insist
And say these words, in the Apostle's name.
'In clothes made with chastity and shame
You women shall apparel yourselves', said he,
'And not in tressed hair and bright jewelery,
Like pearls, nor with gold, nor with rich clothes.'
After your text, nor after your rubric,
I will not work as much as a gnat.
You say this, as if I was like a cat.
For whoever would singe a cat's skin,
Then the cat would certainly stay in his house.
And if the cat's skin is sleek and bright,
She will not stay in her house half a day,
But out she'll want to go, before day has dawned at all,
To show her skin, and go caterwauling.
This is to say if I look well, mister scold,
I will run out to show my cheap clothes.

Old mister fool, what does it help you to spy?
Though you ask Argus with his hundred eyes
To be my bodyguard (as far as he's able),
In faith, he shall not keep me unless I want him to.
Yet could I trick him, as I may prosper!
You say also that there are three things
Which are things that trouble all this earth,
And that no-one may endure the fourth.
Oh dear mister nag, Jesus shorten your life!
Still you preach, and say a hateful wife
Is considered to be one of these misfortunes.
Are there no other sorts of resemblance
That you can compare your parables to
Unless an unfortunate wife is one of them?
You also compare women's love to hell,
To barren land, where water may not dwell.
You also compare it to Greek fire.
The more it burns, the more it has desire
To consume everything that can be burned.
You say, just as maggots destroy a tree,
Just so a wife destroys her husband.
Those who are bound to wives know this."
Sirs, just so, as you have understood,
I swore strongly to my old husbands
That they spoke like this in their drunkenness,
And all was false, except that I took witness
Of Jankyn, and of my niece also.
Oh, Lord! The pain I did to them, and the woe.
Totally guiltless, by God's sweet suffering!
For I could bite and whine like a horse.
I could complain when I was in the wrong,
Otherwise I would have been ruined many a time.
Whoever comes to the mill first, grinds first,
I complained first, and that's how our conflict was stopped.
They were very glad to excuse themselves quickly
Of something that they had never been guilty of in their lives.
I would accuse them about prostitutes,
When they might hardly stand up for sickness.
Yet I tickled his heart, for he
Thought that I had for him such great fondness.
I swore that all my walking out by night
Was to spot prostitutes that he had sex with.

Under that excuse I had many a laugh.
For all such cleverness is given to us at our birth,
Deceit, weeping, spinning, God has given
To women naturally, while they may live.
And so of one thing I'll boast:
In the end I had the better in all respects,
By sleight, or force, or by some sort of thing,
By continually complaining or grouching.
Particularly, they had misfortune in bed.
There I would chide and give them no pleasure,
I would no longer stay in the bed,
If I felt his arm over my side,
'Til he had paid his ransom over to me.
Then I would put up with him doing his foolishness.
And therefore I tell this tale to every man:
Let whoever is able to succeed, for everything is for sale,
Men may not lure hawks with an empty hand.
For profit I would endure all his lust,
And make myself a pretended appetite . . .
And yet I never took delight in bacon.[39]
That made me that I would always chide them,
For if the pope had sat beside them,
I would not spare them at their own table
For, by my faith, I paid them back word for word.
So help me, true God omnipotent,
If I should right now make my testament,
I don't owe them a word that it hasn't been repaid.
I brought it about by my wit
That they must give it up, for the best,
Or else we would never give it a rest.
For though he might look like a mad lion,
Yet he would fail to get what he wanted.
   Then I would say, "Sweetheart, take heed
How meekly Wilkyn, our sheep, looks.
Come here, husband, let me kiss your cheek!
You should be all patient and meek,
And have a sweet, spiced manner,
Since you preach so of Job's patience.
Always endure, since you can preach so well,
And unless you do so, certainly we shall teach you

39 i.e. in old, preserved meat.

That it is good to have a contented wife.
One of us two must give in, doubtless,
And since a man is more reasonable
Than a woman is, you must be willing to suffer.
What ails you to grouch and groan like that?
Is it because you would want my quaint thing alone?
Why, take it all, oh, have it, every bit!
By St Peter, curse you, but you love it well,
For if I wanted to sell my *bele chose*,
I could walk as fresh as a rose.
But I will keep it for your own taste.
You are to blame, by God. I'm telling you the truth."
These are the sort of words that we had between us.
Now I will speak of my fourth husband.
My fourth husband was a reveller,
That's to say he had a lover,
And I was young, and full of lechery,
Stubborn and strong, and jolly as a magpie.
How I could dance to a little harp,
And sing, indeed, like any nightingale,
When I had drunk a draught of sweet wine!
Metellius, the foul villain, the swine,
That with a club took his wife's life from her,
Because she drank wine, if I had been his wife,
He would not have frightened me from drink!
And after wine, of Venus mostly I think,
For just as sure as cold produces hail,
A liquorous mouth must have a lecherous tail.
In drunken women there's no defence,
Lechers know this from experience.
But, Lord Christ, when I think back to myself
On my youth, and on my happiness,
It tickles me about my heart's root.
To this day it does my heart good
That I have had my world in my time.
But age, alas, that will envenom all
Has taken from me my beauty and my energy.
Let go. Farewell. The devil go with it!
The flour is gone, there is no more to tell.
The bran, as best I can, now I must sell.
But still I will try to be very cheerful.
Now I will tell of my fourth husband.

I say, I had in my heart great spite
That he of any other had delight,
But he was repaid, by God and St Judocus!
I made him a cross from the same wood!
Not of my body, in any foul manner,
But certainly I gave folk such attention
That in his own grease I made him fry,
For anger, and for true jealousy.
By God, on earth I was his purgatory,
For which I hope his soul is in glory,
For, God knows it, he often sat and sang
When his shoe wrung him bitterly.
There was no-one, except God and he, that knew
In many ways, how sore I twisted him.
He died when I came back from Jerusalem,
And lies buried under the cross beam [of the church],
But his tomb is not so curious
As was the sepulchre of that Darius
Which Appelles crafted intricately.
It's nothing but waste to bury him expensively!
Let him fare well, God give his soul rest,
He is now in his grave and in his coffin.
Now of my fifth husband I will tell.
God let his soul never come to hell!
And yet he was to me the biggest scoundrel.
I can feel that on my ribs in a row,
And ever shall do to my ending day,
But in our bed he was so fresh and cheerful,
And therewithal he could flatter me so well
When he would have my *bele chose*,
That though he had beaten me on every bone,
He could win my love again, immediately.
I believe that I loved him best, because he
Was hard to get in his love for me.
We women have, if I shall not lie,
In this matter a strange inclination.
Watch whatever thing we may not easily have,
After that thing will we cry and crave all day.
Forbid us something, and we desire it,
Try hard to force us, and then we will flee.
Faced with disdain we produce all our merchandise.
A great crowd at the market makes expensive ware,

And something too cheap is considered of little value,
Every woman knows this that is wise.
My fifth husband, God bless his soul,
Who I took for love, and not riches,
He was at one time a student at Oxford,
And had left school, and went home to board
With my friend, living in our town,
God have her soul, her name was Alison.
She knew my heart and also my secrets
Better than our parish priest, so may I thrive,
To her I betrayed all my confidences.
For had my husband pissed against a wall,
Or done something that should have cost his life,
To her, and to another worthy wife,
And to my niece, who I loved well,
I would have told his secrets, every bit.
And so I very often did, God knows,
That made his face often red and hot
For certain shame, and he blamed himself for he
Had told to me so great a secret.
And it so happened that once during Lent
(For many times I went to my friend's,
For ever yet I loved to be happy,
And to walk in March, April, and May,
From house to house, to hear different tales)
That Jankyn the student, and my friend Mrs. Alice,[40]
And I myself, went into the fields.
My husband was in London all that Lent.
I had the better leisure to play,
And to see, and also to be seen
By gallant folk. What did I know how my fortune
Was destined to be, or in what place?
Therefore I made my visitations
To vigils and to processions,
To preaching also, and to these pilgrimages,
To miracle plays, and to marriages,
And wore my bright scarlet robes.
These worms, nor these moths, nor these mites,
On peril of my soul, don't chew on them a bit.
And do you know why? For they were well used.

40 i.e. Alison.

Now I will tell on about what happened to me.
As I say, we walked in the fields,
Until truly we had such intimacy,
This student and I, that in my foresight
I spoke to him, and said to him how that he,
If I were widowed, should marry me.
For certainly, I say this without boasting,
I was never yet without provision
In marriage, nor in other things either.
I think a mouse's heart not worth a leek
That has only one hole to scoot to,
And if that fails, then all is done.
I led him to believe he had enchanted me
(My mother taught me that subtlety)
And also I said I dreamed of him all night,
He would have slain me as I lay on my back,
And all my bed was full of blood.
"But yet I hope that you shall do me good,
For blood symbolizes gold, as I was taught."
And all was false, I did not dream of it at all,
But I always followed my mother's advice,
As well in this as in other, greater, things.
But now, sir, let me see what I shall say . . .
Aha! By God, I have my tale again!
When my fourth husband was on his bier,
I wept continuously, and made a sorry appearance,
As wives must, for it's the done thing,
And with my scarf covered my face.
But because I was provided with a husband,
I wept but a little, and that I declare.
To church was my husband taken the following morning
With neighbours that were sorry for him,
And Jankyn, our student, was one of those.
So help me God, when I saw him go
After the bier, I thought he had a pair
Of legs and of feet so neat and fair
That all my heart I gave into his grasp.
He was, I suppose, twenty winters old,
And I was forty, if I shall speak the truth,
But yet I always had a colt's tooth.
Gap-toothed I was, and that suited me well.

I had the print of Saint Venus's seal.[41]
So help me God, I was a lusty one,
And fair, and rich, and young, and happy,
And truly, as my husbands told me,
I had the best whatsit there might be.
For certainly, I am all Venerean
In feeling, and my heart is Martian.
Venus gave me my lust, my lecherousness,
And Mars gave me my sturdy hardiness,
My ascending sign was Taurus, and Mars therein.
Alas, alas! That ever love was sin!
I followed always my inclination,
Through the power of my horoscope.
That made me so I could not withhold
My chamber of Venus from a good fellow.
Yet have I Mars' mark upon my face
(And also in another secret place),
For God so wisely be my salvation,
I never loved through any moderation,
But always followed my appetite.
Whether he was short, or long, or black, or white;
I took no heed, as long as he liked me,
How poor he was, nor of what status neither.
What should I say, but at the month's end,
This lovely student, Jankyn, that was so gentle,
Had married me with great solemnity,
And to him I gave all the land and fiefs
That ever were given to me before that.
But afterwards I repented very sorely.
He wouldn't put up with any of my desires.
By God, he hit me once on the ear,
Because I ripped a leaf out of his book,
That from the blow my ear became entirely deaf.
I was as stubborn as a lionness,
And of my tongue, a true chatterbox,
And wished to walk, as I had done before,
From house to house, even if he had sworn against it,
For which he oftentimes would preach,
And teach me of old Roman deeds.
How one Simplicius Gallus left his wife,

41 i.e. a birthmark.

And forsook her for the length of all his life,
For nothing except that he saw her bareheaded
Looking out his door one day.
   Another Roman he told me about by name,
That, because his wife was at a summer game
Without his knowing, he left her also.
And then he would seek in his Bible
That same proverb of Ecclesiasticus
Where he commands, and firmly forbids,
Man shall not allow his wife to go wandering about.
Then he would say just like this, without doubt:
   "Whoever builds his house all from willow,
And spurs his blind horse over the fallow [ground],
And allows his wife to go seek shrines,
Is fit to be hanged on the gallows!"
But all for nothing. I did not give a hawthorn berry
For his proverbs nor for his old sayings,
Nor would I be corrected by him.
I hate anyone who tells me my weaknesses,
And so do more of us than I, God knows.
This made him absolutely furious with me!
I didn't want to put up with him in any case.
   Now I will tell you truly, by St Thomas,
Why it was that I ripped a leaf out of his book,
For which he thumped me so that I was deaf.
   He had a book that gladly, night and day,
For his amusement he would read, always.
He called it Valerius and Theophrastus,
At which book he always laughed very heartily.
   And also at some time there was a scholar at Rome,
A cardinal, that was called Saint Jerome,
That made a book, "Against Jovinian".[42]
In that book also there was Tertullian,
Crisippus, Trotula, and Heloise,[43]
That was abbess not far from Paris,
And also the Parables of Solomon,
Ovid's *Art*, and books many a one,
And all these were bound in one volume.

42 Extract 6, above.

43 *Trotula* is extract 77, the letters of Abelard and Heloise are extract 40.

And every night and day it was his custom,
When he had leisure and vacation
From other, worldly, occupations,
To read this book of wicked wives.
He knew of them more stories and biographies
Than there are of good wives in the Bible.
For trust well, it is an impossibility
That any scholar will speak well of women,
Unless it's of holy saints' lives,
Not of any other woman in any way.
"Who painted the lion, tell me, who?"
By God, if women had written histories,
As scholars have, within their oratories,
They would have written of men more wickedness
Than all the mark of Adam may redress.
The children of Mercury and Venus
Are in their workings entirely contrarious,
Mercury loves wisdom and knowledge,
And Venus loves disorder and extravagance,
And, because of their diverse dispositions,
Each falls in the other's exaltation,
And so, God knows, Mercury is desolate
In Pisces, where Venus is exalted,
And Venus falls where Mercury is raised.
Therefore no woman is praised by any scholar.
The scholar, when he is old, and may not carry out
Any of Venus's works worth his old shoe,
Then he sits down, and writes in his senility,
That women cannot maintain their marriages!

But now to the point, why I told you
That I was beaten for a book, by God!
One night, Jankyn, that was master of our house,
Read his book, as he sat by the fire,
Of Eve first, that because of her wickedness
All mankind was brought to wretchedness,
For which Jesus Christ himself was slain,
That bought us with his blood again.
Now, here you may find it clearly said of woman
That woman was the loss of all mankind.

Then he read to me how Samson lost his hair.
Sleeping, his lover cut it with her shears,
Through which treason he lost both his eyes.

Then he read to me, if I shall not lie,
Of Hercules and of his Deianeira,
That caused him to set himself on fire.
He did not forget any of the care and the woe
That Socrates had with his wives two,
How Xantippe threw piss upon his head,
This hapless man sat as still as if he was dead,
He wiped his head, nothing else he said,
Except, "Before thunder stops, rain comes!"
Of Pasiphae, that was the queen of Crete,
For sourness, he thought the tale sweet . . .
Ah! Don't say any more, it is a hideous thing,
Of her horrible lust and her liking.
Of Clytemnestra, for her lechery,
That treacherously made her husband die,
He read it with very close attention.
He told me also for what reason
Amphiaraus at Thebes lost his life.
My husband had a biography of his wife,
Eriphile, that for a brooch of gold
Had secretly to the Greeks told
Where her husband had hidden himself in a place,
For which he had poor fortune at Thebes.
Of Lyvia he told me, and of Lucy,[44]
They both caused their husbands to die,
The one for love, the other was for hate.
Lyvia her husband, on an evening late,
Had poisoned, for she was his foe.
Lucia, lecherous, loved her husband so
That, so he should always upon her think,
She gave him such a sort of love drink
That he was dead before it was the morning.
And so husbands always have sorrow.
Then he told me how one Latumius
Complained to his companion Arius
That in his garden there grew a tree
On which he said that his wives three
Had hanged themselves for their resentful hearts.
"Oh, dear brother," said this Arius,

44 Manly and Rickert (1940: III, 264) read 'Lyma' and give alternate readings 'Lyuia' and 'Lyna'. 'Lyvia' here is from Benson (1987: 115).

"Give me a clipping from this blessed tree
And in my garden it shall planted be."
Of later times, of wives he read
That some had slain their husbands in their beds,
And let their lovers have sex with them all night
When the corpse lay flat upon the floor.
And some had driven nails into their brains,
While they slept, and so they had them slain.
Some had given them poison in their drink,
He spoke more harm than the heart may think,
And along with that he knew more proverbs
Than in this world grows grass or herbs.
"It's better," says he, "that your habitation
Be with a lion or a foul dragon,
Than with a woman who likes to nag.
It's better," he says, "to live up on the roof,
Than with an angry wife down in the house,
They are so wicked and contrarious,
They hate everything that their husbands love."
He said, "A woman threw her shame away,
When she took off her underwear"; and furthermore,
"A beautiful woman, unless she's chaste also,
Is like a gold ring in a sow's nose."
Who would think, or who would suppose,
The woe that was in my heart, and pain?
And when I saw he would never cease
To read this cursed book all night,
All of a sudden three leaves had I plucked
Out of his book, while he was reading, and also
I caught him on the cheek with my fist so
That he fell down backwards into our fire.
And he jumped up as a mad lion does,
And with his fist he punched me in the head
So that on the floor I lay as if I was dead.
And when he saw how still I lay,
He was aghast, and would have run away,
Until at last I woke from my swoon.
"Oh! Have you killed me, false thief?" I said,
"And have you murdered me like this for my land?
Before I die, I still want to kiss you."
And he came near, and kneeled down gently,
And said, "Dear sister Alison,

So help me God, I shall never hit you,
That I have done, it's yourself that is to blame.
Forgive me for it, and that I beg you!"
And yet at once I hit him on the cheek,
And said, "Thief, this much I am avenged!
Now I will die, I may no longer speak."
But at last, with much care and woe,
We were reconciled by our two selves.
He gave me the bridle entirely in my hand,
To have the governance of house and land,
And of his tongue, and of his hand also,
And I made him burn his book right there, immediately.
And when I had gained for myself,
By mastery, all the sovereignty,
And that he said, "My own faithful wife,
Do as you wish the length of all your life,
Keep your honour, and keep also my property,"
After that day we never had an argument.
God help me so, I was to him as kind
As any wife from Denmark to India,
And also faithful, and so was he to me.
I pray to God, that sits in majesty,
To bless his soul for his dear mercy.
Now I will tell my tale, if you wish to hear it.'

72 Geoffrey Chaucer, 'Envoy a Bukton'

This brief fourteenth-century poem advising against marriage, given here in full, sees Chaucer referring back to his fictional creation, the Wife of Bath, as putting the case against matrimony.

Further reading: Scattergood 1987, McCarthy 1999.

Text: W. W. Skeat (ed.) (1899) *The Complete Works of Geoffrey Chaucer*, 2nd edition, Oxford; my modern English translation.

My master Bukton, when Christ our king[45]
Was asked, 'What is truth, or faithfulness?'
He answered not a word to that question,

45 Bukton might be either Sir Peter Bukton or Sir Robert Bukton, both courtiers (Benson 1987: 1087).

As he who says, 'No man is entirely faithful,' I guess.
And therefore, though I promised to express
The sorrow and woe that is in marriage,
I dare not write of it any wickedness,
For fear that I myself might fall again into such folly.

I will not say, how it is the chain
Of Satan, on which he is always gnawing,
But I daresay, if he was released from his punishment,
So by his will he would never wish to be bound.
But this senile fool that would rather
Be chained up again than creep out of prison,
God let him never be parted from his woe,
Nor any man lament for him, though he weeps.

But yet, for fear that you could do worse, take a wife;
It is better to marry, than to burn in a worse manner.
But you shall have sorrow on your flesh, your life,
And be your wife's slave, as these wise people say,
And if Holy Writ is not sufficient,
Experience may teach you, so it may happen,
That you would prefer to be taken prisoner in Frisia
Than to fall into the trap of marrying again.

This little piece of writing, proverbs, or metaphor
That I'm sending you, I advise you to take heed of it:
Unwise is he that can no joy endure.
If you are secure, don't put yourself in danger.
The Wife of Bath I pray you that you read
Concerning this matter that we are discussing.
God be generous and grant you your life to lead
In freedom; for it is very hard to be enslaved.

73 William Langland, *Piers Plowman*

Passus 2 of this fourteenth-century allegorical dream-vision describes the marriage ceremony between Mede ('Reward') and False. The description of the ceremony focuses entirely on the enfeoffment, the transfer of property to the married couple. In it, Langland seems to be satirizing the corrupting power of money in general, but also specifically the power of money to dominate marriage agreements to the exclusion of any spiritual aspect (cf. the legal texts in Part II which discuss the financial basis for marriage satirized here by Langland). The extract opens with the figure of Holy Church speaking to the Dreamer about Mede.

Further reading: Bloomfield 1958, Morgan 1987, 1988, Tavormina 1995, Fowler 1995, McCarthy 2000a.

Text: A. V. C. Schmidt (ed.) (1987) *The Vision of Piers Plowman*, London: Dent; my modern English translation.

'That is Mede the maid,' she said, 'who has often harmed me,
And disparaged my sweetheart that is called Justice
And told lies about him to lords that have laws to uphold.
In the Pope's palace she is as familiar as myself,
But truthfulness does not want it so – for she is a bastard,
For False was her father who has a fickle tongue
And never told the truth since he came to earth;
And Mede is mannered after him, just as nature demands:
Like father, like son. A good tree brings forth good fruit.
I ought to be (ranked) higher than her, I came from a better (parentage).
My father is the great God and source of all mercy,
One God without beginning, and I his good daughter,
And (he) has given me Mercy to marry myself with;[46]
And whatever man shall be merciful and loyally love me
Shall be my lord and I his love in the high heaven;
And whatever man takes Mede, I dare bet my head
That he shall lose for her love a portion of *Charity*.
How does David the king judge men that take Mede,
And men of this world that maintain truth,
And how shall you save yourself? The Psalter bears witness:
Lord, who shall dwell in your Tabernacle? &c.
And now shall this Mede be married to a cursed rascal,
To one False Fickle-tongue, a fiend's offspring.
Deceit through his false speech has enchanted these folk,
And it is all through Liar's leading that she is wedded so.
Tomorrow shall be made the maiden's bridal;
And there might you know if you will who they all are
That belong to that lordship, the lesser and the greater.
Know them there if you can, and keep yourself from them all,
And criticize them not but let them be, until Justice is judge

46 i.e. Mercy is Holy Church's dowry.

And has power to punish them – then put forward your reason.
Now I commit you to Christ,' she said, 'and his pure mother,
And let no guilty conscience encumber you for covetousness of
Mede.'
So that lady left me lying asleep,
And how Mede was married I thought in a dream –
(I dreamed) that all the rich retinue that reigns with the False
Were bidden to the bridal on both sides,
Of all manner of men, the poor and the rich.
To marry this maiden was many a man assembled,
As of knights, and clerks, and other common people,
As assizers and summoners, sheriffs and their clerks,
Beadles and bailiffs and brokers of trade,
Purveyors and victuallers and advocates of the Arches;
I cannot reckon the crowd that ran about Mede.
But Simony and Civil and jurors of courts
Were most familiar with Mede of any man, I thought.
But Desire was the first that fetched her out of her room
And as a matchmaker brought her to be joined with False.
When Simony and Civil saw the will of both,
They assented for silver to say as both wished
Then Liar ran forward and said, 'Lo! Here is a charter
That Guile with his great oaths grants them together.' –
And asked Civil and Simony to read it.
Then Simony and Civil both stepped forward
And unfolded the enfeoffment that False had made,
And so these men began to announce loudly:
'*Let all, present and future, know &c.*[47]
Know and witness, who live upon this earth,
That Mede is married more for her goods
Than for any virtue or fairness or any noble blood.
Falseness wants her because he knows she's rich;
And Desire with his deceptive speech grants her by this charter
To be Princess in Pride, and poverty to despise,
To slander and to boast and bear false witness,
To scorn and to scold and slander to make,
Disobedient and bold to break the ten commandments.
And the earldom of Envy and Wrath together
With the castlelet of quarelling and unreasonable chatter.
The county of Coveting and all the areas around it –

47 This is a Latin formula for the beginning of a charter.

That is usury and avarice – I grant them all to them
In bargains and in brokerage with all the borough of theft,
And all the lordship of Lechery in length and in breadth –
As in works and in words and in wanton looks with eyes,
And in clothes and in wishes and with idle thoughts
Where will would and performance fails.'
Gluttony he gave them too, and great oaths together,
And to drink all day at different taverns,
And to argue and joke and judge their fellow Christians,
And on fasting days to eat before it's appropriate.
And then to sit and sup until sleep assails them,
And breed like town pigs, and go to bed at ease
Until Sloth and sleep slick his sides;[48]
And then despair to wake up with no will to amend,
For he believes he is lost – this is his last end.
'And they to have and to hold and their heirs afterwards,
A dwelling with the devil, and be damned forever,
With all the appurtenances of Purgatory into the pain of Hell;
Yielding in exchange for this thing at one year's end
Their souls to Satan, to suffer pains with him,
And with him to live with woe while God is in heaven.'
In witness of which document Wrong was the first,
And Peter the Pardoner of Pauline doctrine,
Bette the Beadle of Buckinghamshire,
Reynald the Reeve of the Soke of Rutland,
Munde the Miller – and many others more.
'In the date of the devil I seal this deed
In sight of Sir Simony and by Civil's permission.'

74 *Ballad of the Tyrannical Husband*

This is a popular late medieval poem about the division of labour between husbands and wives. The text is a fragment – all that survives of the poem is given here – but the existing text seems to set the husband up for a series of comic disasters. Seeing that the wife has sabotaged the butter-churn, and pointed out that he is not to lose the geese or burn the malt in the oven, it seems likely that all his endeavours in these areas will be comically undone.

48 The poem has moved briefly away from Mede and False here to describe an archetypal sinner.

Text: Carolyne Larrington (ed.) (1995), *Women and Writing in Medieval Europe: A Sourcebook*, London: Routledge. The text given here has been slightly adapted to remove archaic words.

Jesus that is gentle, for joy of your mother
As you made all this wide world, in heaven is your home,
Save all this company and shield them from shame
That will listen to me and attend to this game.

God keep all women that to this town belong
Maidens, widows, and wives among;
For much are they blamed, and sometimes with wrong
I take witness of all folk that hear this song.

Listen, good sirs, both young and old
By a good husband this tale shall be told;
He wedded a woman that was fair and bold,
And good enough to do as they would.

She was a good housewife, courteous and skilled
And he was an angry man and soon would be stirred.
Chiding and brawling and fared like a fiend
As they that often will be wrathful with their best friend.

Till it befell upon a day, short tale to make,
The goodman would to the plough, his horse he did take.
He called forth his oxen, the white and the black,
And he said, 'Wife, make our dinner in good time, for God's sake.'

The goodman and his lad to the plough are gone
The goodwife had much to do, and servant had she none.
Many small children to keep beside herself alone,
She did more than she might within her own house.

Home came the goodman by the time of the day
To look that all things were as he would like them.
'Wife,' he said, 'is our dinner made?' 'Sir,' she said, 'No,
How would you have me do more than I may?'

Then he began to chide and said 'Bad luck to you,
I wish you would all day go to plough with me,
To walk in the clods that are wet and miry.
Then would you know what it was to be a ploughman.

Then the goodwife answered and this did she say,
'I have more to do than I may;
And if you should follow me fully one day
You would be weary of your part, my head I dare lay!'

'Weary! In the devil's name', said the goodman,
'What have you to do but sit here at home?
You go to your neighbour's house, by one and one,
And you sit there chattering with Jack and with John.

'Then,' said the goodwife, 'Fair may you befall!
I have more to do, whoever knows all.
When I lie in my bed, my sleep is but small.
Yet early in the morning you will up me call.

When I lie all night waking with our child
I rise up in the morning and find our house wild.
Then I milk our cows and turn them to field,
While you sleep full still, as Christ me shield.

Then I make butter further on in the day,
After I make cheese – these you consider good.
Then will our children weep and up must they,
Yet will you blame me for our goods, if any be away.

When I have so done yet there comes more even
I give our chickens food or else they will be lost.
Our hens, our capons and our ducks are seen to
Yet tend I to our goslings which go on the green.

I bake, I brew, it will not else be well,
I beat and swingle flax, as ever I have health.
I twist up the tow, I bind and I coil
I tease wool and card it and spin it on the wheel.'

'Wife,' said the goodman, 'the devil have your bones!
You need not bake and brew in a fortnight but once.
I see no good that you do within these wide rooms
But ever you excuse yourself with grunts and with groans.'

'If a piece of linen and woolen I make once a year
For to clothe ourselves and our children altogether,

Otherwise we should go to the market and buy it full dear.
I am as busy as I may be in every year.

When I have so done, I look at the sun,
I ordain food for our beasts for when you come home.
And food for ourselves before it be noon.
Yet I have not a fair word when I have done.

So I look to our goods without and within
That there be none away, neither more nor less.
Glad to please you to your liking, lest any fight begin
And for to chide thus with me, in faith you are in sin.'

Then said the goodman in a sorry time
'All this would a good housewife do before it was nine.
And since the goods that we have is half-deal yours
You shall labour for your part as I do for mine.

Therefore wife, make yourself ready, I warn you now,
Tomorrow with my lad to the plough you shall go,
And I will be housewife and keep our house at home
And take my ease, as you have done, by God and St John.'

'I agree,' said the goodwife, 'as I understand
Tomorrow in the morning I will be walking
Yet will I rise while you are sleeping
And see all things ready to be laid to your hand.'

So it passed all to the morning so that it was daylight.
The goodwife thought on her deeds, and she rose right.
'Wife,' said the goodman, 'I swear by God's might,
I will fetch home our beasts and help so that you are prepared.'

The goodman took himself eagerly to the field.
The goodwife made butter, her deeds were secret.
She took again the buttermilk and put it in the churn,
And said, 'Yet of one point our sire shall be to learn.'

Home came the goodman and took good notice
Of how wife had put the meat to soak.
She said, 'Sir, all this day you need not sleep.
Keep well our children, and let them not weep.

If you go to the oven, malt for to make
Put a small fire underneath, sir, for God's sake.
The oven is low and dry, take good care
For if it catches fire, it will be terribly blackened.

Here sit two geese abroad, keep them from woe,
If they may come to good, that ends sorrow enough.
'Wife,' said the goodman, 'take yourself to the plough,
Teach me not housewifery, for I know enough.'

Forth went the housewife, courteous and skilled,
She called to her lad and to the plough they went.
They were busy all day, a verse here I find,
If I had a drink once, you will hear the best behind.

75 Thomas Hoccleve, *Letter of Cupid*

This is the opening of Thomas Hoccleve's 1402 translation of Christine de Pizan's 'Letter of Cupid' in which he describes smooth-talking but deceptive masculine suitors. Christine's original is part of the debate on the *Romance of the Rose* (see extracts 60 and 63), in which she takes issue with Ovid and Jean de Meun. As Fenster and Erler observe in their edition (1990: 31), Hoccleve's translation is a loose one, an adaptation rather than a translation.

Further reading: Fenster and Erler 1990.

Text: F. J. Furnivall and I. Gollancz (eds), J. Mitchell and A. I. Doyle (rev.) (1970) *Hoccleve's Works: The Minor Poems*, Oxford: Oxford University Press; my modern English translation.

Cupid, to whose commandment
the noble kindred of gods on high,
and people infernal are obedient,
and mortal folk all serve busily,
The goddess Cythera's[49] son truly,
to all those that to our deity
are subjects, heartily we send greeting!

In general, we wish you to know
that ladies of honour and reverence,

49 Venus.

and other noble women have sown
such seed of complaint in our audience,
of men that do them outrage and offence,
that it grieves our ears for to hear it;
so piteous is the effect of this matter.

Surpassing all lands, of the little isle
that is called albion they most complain[50]
they say that here is the crop and root of guile:
so can those men dissemble and feign
with standing drops on both their eyes,
When that their hearts feel no distress,
to blind women with their deceitfulness.

Their words are spoken so sighingly,
with such pitiful appearance and expression,
that every person that means truly,
believes that they have such grief in their heart;
They say, so insufferable is their penance,
that unless their lady desires to show them mercy;
they must instantly die in the place.

'Ah, my lady,' they say, 'I assure you,
have mercy on me, and I shall ever be –
while my life may last and endure –
to you as humble and low in each degree
as is possible, and keep everything secret
just as you desire yourself that I do;
and otherwise my heart must break in two.'

76 William Dunbar, *Upon the Midsummer Eve, Merriest of Nights*

Dunbar's fifteenth-century bawdy and satirical poem, somewhat indebted to Chaucer's Wife of Bath, situates the poet in hiding in a garden, where he overhears a conversation between two married women and a widow about their marriages. This extract, lines 150 to 244 of the poem, is the second wife's account of her marriage.

Further reading: Ross 1981: ch. 4, Bawcutt 1992: ch. 8.

50 In Christine de Pizan's original it is France which is the source of complaint.

Text: Douglas Gray (ed.) (1998) *Selected Poems of Robert Henryson and William Dunbar*, Harmondsworth: Penguin; my modern English translation.

The widow to the other beautiful woman spoke these words:
'Now, fair sister, it falls to you without feigning to tell;
Since man first with matrimony honoured you in church,
How have you fared, by your faith, confess the truth to us,
That bond to bless or to curse, whichever you think best,
Or how you like leading life in lawful marriage?
And afterwards you examine me in the same way,
And I shall speak out the truth, dissembling no word.'
The pleasant lady said, 'I protest, if the truth I reveal,
That of your tongues you be trustworthy.' The other two agreed.
With that sprang up her spirit by a span higher.
'To speak,' said she, 'I shall not spare; there is no spy near.
I shall reveal a catalogue from the root of my heart,
A rancour that is so rankled until my stomach rises.
Now shall the boil all burst out that has festered so long.
For to bear it on my breast was an overheavy burden;
I shall cast out the venom with a great discharge,
And relieve myself of the swelling that had swelled so big.
My husband was a whoremaster, the hugest in earth;
Therefore I hate him with my heart, so help me our Lord.
He is a young man, very lively, but not in the flower of youth,
For he is faded very far and enfeebled of strength.
He was as flourishing fresh within these few years,
But he is very greatly weakened and exhausted in labour.
He has been a lecher so long until his potency is lost,
His tool has become impotent, and lies in a swoon.
There was never a rest worse set than on that tired slug,
For after seven weeks' rest it will not strike once.
He has been wasted upon women before he chose me as his wife,
And in adultery in my time I have caught him often.
And yet he is as prancing with his bonnet at an angle,
And staring at the prettiest that dwell in the town,
As courtly of his clothes and combing of his hair,
As he that is more valiant in Venus' chamber.
He seems to be worth something, that nothing in the bedroom,
He looks as though he wants to be loved, though he's worth little,
He does as a doted dog that pisses on all the bushes,
And lifts his leg up high though he doesn't want to piss.

He has a look without lust and life without desire;
He has a form without force and appearance without power,
And fair words without reality, all useless in deeds.
He is for ladies in love a very lustful shadow,
But in private, at the deed, he shall be found drooping.
He rails and makes uproar with riotous words,
Always boasting of his rides and passion in the bedroom;
But God knows what I think when he speaks so wildly –
And how little it suits him, to men of such matters –
But if he some evening might assay amongst them;
But he is not such a one, but none of nature's possessors.[51]
She that has an old man is not all beguiled;
He is at Venus' works no worse than he seems.
I thought I had a gem and I have gotten jet;
He had the gleaming of gold and was found only glass.
Though men be fierce, well I find – from the failing of their power –
There is only jealousy and anger within their hearts.
You speak of birds on the bough – of bliss may they sing,
That on St Valentine's day are free each year.
Had I that pleasant privilege, to depart when it pleased me,
To change and also to choose again – then goodbye chastity!
Then should I have a fresh companion to fold in my arms –
To keep a man while he grows weary may be called folly.
Upon such matters I often muse at midnight
And mourn so in my mind I murder myself.
Then I lie awake from woe and toss and turn,
Often cursing my wicked kin that cast me away,
That knit my bright beauty to such a craven without courage,
And so many keen knights within this kingdom.
Then I think on a similar, the truth for to tell,
Seven times more than my husband – with that I sigh often.
Then he very tenderly turns his feeble body to me,
And with an exhausted rod does yoke me in arms,
And says, "My sovereign sweet thing, why sleep you no better?
I think a fever grips you, as if you suffered some illness."
I say, "My honey, hold back, and don't handle me so painfully;
An ache has come hastily at my heart's root."
With that I seem to swoon, though I never faint –
And so I deceive that churl with my sweet words.

51 The meaning of these two lines is unclear.

I cast on him a crabbed eye when clear day is come
And pretend it's a love-look when he glances around;
I turn it to a tender look that I used in anger,
And look at him lovingly with heartfelt smiling.
I wish a tender girl that might endure no thrust,
That hated men with hard gear for hurting of the flesh
Had my goodman for her lover, for I dare swear to God,
She should not jump for his stroke a straw's breadth of earth.
And then I wish that same bond that you call so blessed
Had bound him to that bright girl while his back ached,
And I would be brought to bed with a man that I liked –
I think that girl should lack a share of my delight.'
And then when this amiable woman had ended her speech
Laughing loudly, the others praised her greatly.
These gay wives made games among the green leaves:
They drank and put away sadness under secluded boughs
They drank down the sweet wine, those swan-white of hue,
But all the pertlier, plainly, they made their speeches.

Part V

MEDICAL WRITINGS

INTRODUCTION

Medieval medical knowledge about sexuality and psychological thinking about the nature of love is not confined simply to medical texts, but has a very visible influence on the wider culture. According to Jacquart and Thomasset, 'medieval medical thought relating to sexuality was all-pervasive' (1988). Hence they (and Noonan) read passages in Andreas Capellanus as containing *double entendres* which make it a manual for *coitus interruptus* (Noonan 1986: 182, Jacquart and Thomasset 1988: 96–110). The discussions of love as a psychological phenomenon found in Avicenna and Constantine Africanus (extracts 79, 80) can be compared and contrasted with similar discussions in Andreas (extract 55), with the *Romance of the Rose* (extract 60), and with Chaucer, a portion of whose *Knight's Tale* is included here as a piece of medical evidence, but who also describes lovesickness in medical terms in *Troilus and Criseyde* and elsewhere. Pseudo Albertus Magnus's discussion of leprosy/venereal disease overlaps with that of the thirteenth-century Statutes of Coventry tract on confession and penance (extract 15).

Medieval medical knowledge was founded on authorities, classical and Arabic: Aristotle, Galen, Avicenna, Averroes. Vern L. Bullough argues that the ancient world's medical and scientific assumptions about sexuality make a significant contribution to medieval misogyny. Nonetheless, it is important not to caricature or oversimplify the state of medieval medical knowledge. He notes that even medieval Aristoteleans did not uphold the alleged reading of Aristotle whereby a woman was held to be a defective male (Bullough 1973). And the myth of the 'wandering womb', derived from Plato's *Timaeus*, was not undisputed in the Middle Ages, because of the contrary views of Galen (Bullough 1973: 494–495).

The texts below are divided into two subcategories: the first extracts are from medical texts on women's health. The texts here purport to be similar to one another, but are in fact very different. The first is by a female physician, Trota of Salerno, an eleventh-century female medical practitioner (it's notable, however, that 'Trotula' appears in Chaucer's Wife of Bath's prologue [extract 71] in a list of antifeminist writings). That is certainly where the second text, by Pseudo-Albertus Magnus, belongs: an example of misogynistic literature posing as a medical text. The second subcategory contains medieval writings about love from a medical viewpoint. The sort of love discussed here is what Arabic commentators called *'ishq*, 'passionate love', translated into Latin as amor, eros, or 'amor heros'.

MEDICAL WRITINGS ON WOMEN'S HEALTH

77 *Trotula*

'Trotula' is a compilation of three originally separate medical texts circulating under the name of one of the authors, Trota of Salerno, a female medical practitioner from the late eleventh- to the early twelfth-century Italy (Green 1996: 119–203).

Further reading: Lemay 1990, Green 1996, 2000.

Text: Trotula of Salerno (1940) *The Diseases of Women*, trans. Elizabeth Mason-Hohl, New York: The Ward-Ritchie Press.

CHAPTER XV. ON REGULATIONS FOR PREGNANT WOMEN

When a woman is first pregnant care must be taken that nothing be named in her presence which cannot be had because if she shall ask for it and it not be given to her she has occasion for miscarrying. But if she should seek to have potter's earth or chalk or coals, let beans cooked with sugar be given to her. When the time for parturition is imminent the woman should be bathed often; anoint her abdomen with olive oil or oil of violets and let her eat light and digestible foods. If her feet have swollen, let them be anointed with oil of roses and with vinegar. Instead of heavy foods let her eat quickly digested things like citrons and pomegranates. If her abdomen is distended with flatulence take three drams each of parsley seed, amoes, mint, mastic, garyophyllons, cardamon, roots of carrots, coffee, galangale, iris, and five drams of sugar; make a very fine powder and cook it all with honey; give three scruples[1] to her with wine for this substance removes flatulence and prevents abortion if properly taken.

1 One-third of a dram.

CHAPTER XVI. ON THE REGULATIONS FOR THE WOMAN ABOUT TO GIVE BIRTH

When the time for giving birth is imminent, let the woman prepare herself as the custom is, and the midwife also. Let sneezing be done with great caution, holding tightly the nostrils and the mouth, in order that the greater part of the strength and spirits may tend towards the womb [. . .] Above all things let her guard herself from cold. Let an aromatic fumigation be made below the nostrils; it can also safely be applied at the mouth of the womb because then a fragrant womb follows and an ill smelling one is avoided. For this purpose fragrant kinds of substances avail as musk, amber, wood of aloe and the like for rich patients, and fragrant herbs such as mint, pennyroyal, calamentum, wild marjoram and the like for the poor. It is to be noted that there are certain physical remedies whose virtues are obscure to us but are advanced as done by midwives. They let the patient hold a magnet in her right hand and find it helpful. Likewise they let her drink a powder of ivory or they find that coral suspended on the neck is helpful. In similar fashion that white substance which is found in the dung of an eagle, when given in drinks is advantageous. Likewise give the dung of baby birds which is found in the swallow's nest. Washings of this are serviceable for this and for many other purposes.

CHAPTER XVII. ON DIFFICULTY OF PARTURITION

There are, however, certain women so narrow in the function of childbearing that scarcely ever or never do they succeed. This is wont to happen for various reasons. Sometimes external heat comes up around the internal organs and they are straightened in the act of giving birth. Sometimes the exit from the womb is too small, the woman is too fat, or the foetus is dead, not helping nature by its own movements. This often happens to a woman giving birth in winter. If she has by nature a tight opening of the womb, the coldness of the season constricts the womb still more. Sometimes the heat all goes out of the woman herself and she is left without strength to help herself in childbearing.

In the first place and above all things when there is difficulty in childbirth one must have recourse to God. Descending then to lower means, it is helpful to the woman in difficult labour to be bathed in water in which has been cooked mallow, chick peas, flaxseed, and barley. Let her sides, abdomen, hips, and flanks be rubbed with oil of roses or oil of violets. Let her be rubbed vigorously and let vinegar and sugar be given her as a drink, and powdered mint and a dram of absinth. Let sneezing be provoked by placing dust of incense in the nostrils, or powder of candisium, or pepper or euphorbia. Let the woman be led with slow pace through the house. Do not let those who are present look her in the face because women are wont to be bashful in childbearing and after the birth. If the child does not come forth in the order in which it should, that is, if the legs or arms should come out first, let the midwife with her small and gentle hand moistened with a decoction of flaxseed and chick peas, put the child back in its place in the proper position. If the child be dead take rue, mugwort, absinth, and black pepper and give this pulverised in wine or in water in which lupins have been cooked. Or let savory be mashed and bound over the abdomen and the foetus, whether dead or alive, will come forth. [. . .] Also those who are in difficult labour must be aided in the following manner: Let a bath be prepared and the woman put in it; after she has come out let a fumigation be made of wheat and similar aromatics for comforting and relaxing. Let sneezes be produced with white hellebore well reduced to powder. Colphon says to let the limbs be shaken to break the bag of water and in this way the foetus will come forth. Thus also those may be aided who are labouring much to bring forth a dead foetus: Let the patient be placed in a linen cloth stretched by four men at the four corners with the patient's head somewhat elevated. Let the four corners be strongly drawn this way and that by the opposite corners and she will give birth immediately, God favouring her. If the afterbirth has remained within there is need of haste that it shall come out. Let sneezing be provoked with mouth and nostrils shut. Or take lye made from ash tree ashes and mix it with one dram of powdered mallow seed. Give this to the woman to drink and she will immediately vomit. Or give mallow seed powder alone in a drink of hot water and if she vomits it will be a good thing. Also let her be fumigated below with bones of salted fish or with horses hoofs, or with the dung of a cat or lamb. These things bring out the afterbirth. Also let those things be done which have been mentioned before for bringing forth menstruation. If difficulty in childbirth should result from tightness of the mouth of the womb, the cure of this is more difficult than anything else therefore we subjoin this advice: let the woman take care in the last three months in her diet that she so use light and digestible foods that through them the limbs may be opened. Such foods are egg yolks, the meat and juice of chickens and small birds – partridges and pheasants, and scaly fish of good flavour. Let her often take a bath in fresh water to which has been added herbs of softening character such as matura and the like. Let her avoid a bath tinctured with copper and calcium. When she comes out of the bath, let her be anointed with hot ointment such as oil of laurel, oil of flaxseed, or the grease of goose, duck, or hen. Let this anointing be done from the navel down.

78 Pseudo-Albertus Magnus, *De Secretis Mulierum*

Like *Trotula*, *De Secretis Mulierum* ('Women's Secrets') presents itself as a textbook on women's health, but it is in fact more of a manual of antifeminism: its primary purposes do not seem to be medical. The extracts below illustrate something of its sexual suspicion of women.

Further reading: Jacquart and Thomasset 1988, Lemay 1990, 1992, Lochrie 1996.

Text: H. R. Lemay (1992) *Women's Secrets*, Albany: State University of New York Press.

CHAPTER IX: ON THE SIGNS OF CORRUPTION OF VIRGINITY

Text

Now let us take note of the signs of corruption of chastity.

Sometimes virgins are gravely corrupted so that their vagina is greatly enlarged because the male member is exceedingly large and inept. When this happens the woman's vagina becomes so widened that the man can enter there without any pain to his member, and this is a sign that the woman was first corrupted.

This is the reason why when young women first lose their virginity they have pain in the vagina for a time, because it is being enlarged and disposed for coitus. Another reason for this pain is that there is a certain skin in the vagina and the bladder which is broken. But the more they have sex, the more they become accustomed to it.

Commentary A

Another sign that is not noted in the text is that the vagina of a virgin is always closed, but a woman's is always open, therefore a virgin voids her urine higher up than a woman does. If you want to determine if a virgin has been corrupted, grind up the flowers of a lily and the yellow particles that are in between the flowers, and give her this substance to eat. If she is corrupt, she will urinate immediately. Another way to tell is to have her urinate on a certain kind of grass which is commonly known as 'papel de mane'; if it becomes dry she is corrupt. You can also take the fruit of a lettuce and place it in front of her nose, and she will urinate immediately.

Commentary B

Note that in the text there are mentioned two causes relating to corruption in women, one of which is particular and the other common. The particular is that some young women suffer extreme pain when they are first corrupted because of the ineptitude of the male penis, and this is referred to as a particular because it is not found in all women, and is rather a sign than a cause. The second cause is universal, because all virgins, when they first consort with men, have a certain membrane broken, called the hymen, and this is the guardian of virginity. It is located near the bladder and the opening of the womb above the vulva. This is a universal cause because it is found in all women when they are first corrupted.

The more women have sexual intercourse, the stronger they become, because they are made hot by the motion that the man makes during coitus. Further, male sperm is hot because it is of the same nature as air and when it is received by the woman it warms her entire body, so women are strengthened by this heat. On the other hand, men who have sex frequently are weakened by this act because they become exceedingly dried out.

CHAPTER X: ON THE SIGNS OF CHASTITY

Text

The signs of chastity are as follows: shame, modesty, fear, a faultless gait and speech, casting eyes down before men and the acts of men. Some women are so clever, however, that they know how to resist detection by these signs, and in this case a man should turn to their urine. The urine of virgins is clear and lucid, sometimes white, sometimes sparkling. If the urine is of a golden colour, clear and heavy, this is the sign of a temperament with an appetite for pleasure, however this is found in women who are not corrupted. Corrupted women have a muddy urine because of the rupture of the aforementioned skin, and male sperm appear in the bottom of this urine.

In menstruating women the urine is bloody, and when a woman suffers menstrual pain she has watery eyes, the colour of her face is changed, and she has no taste for food. A man should beware of having sex with women in this condition, and prudent women know how to keep themselves apart, and remain separated from men during their monthly flow.

Commmentary A

Note that the urine of virgins is clear, because they are hot and digest well, and urine takes on its colour while crossing through the place of digestion, so it is coloured in the kidneys. The experimentor should take the urine after the first sleep because then digestion has been accomplished, and he should take care that it is not variegated, that is with disease and thick nutriment.

There are three regions in the urine, the first of which is the upper, and which we examine for the superior members, such as the cerebrum and the head. The second is the middle region, where the central members such as the kidneys and heart are considered. In the third, or lower region, the testicles, loins and womb are inspected. Thus the text says that the seed always appears on the bottom because of its heaviness.

Note that when a woman has her menstrual period, humours ascend to the eyes, because the eye is a porous part of the body, and experiences things immediately. At this time the woman becomes pale in the face and loses her appetite because her cerebrum and sense of smell are affected. It is harmful to have sexual intercourse with these women, because children who are conceived tend to have epilepsy and leprosy because menstrual matter is extremely venomous.[2]

Commentary B

There are still other ways to tell if a virgin has been corrupted. If a girl's breasts point downwards, this is a sign that she has been

2 For the idea that intercourse during menstruation could cause leprosy, and for the role of *De Secretis Mulierum* in transmitting this knowledge, see Jacquart and Thomasset 1988: 183ff.

corrupted, because at the moment of impregnation the menses move upwards to the breasts and the added weight causes them to sag. If a man has sexual intercourse with a woman and experiences no sore on his penis and no difficulty of entry, this is a sign that she was first corrupted. However, a true sign of the woman's virginity is if it is difficult to perform the act and it causes a sore on his member. This is only true, however, if she did not cause her vulva to contract by using an ointment or another medicine so that she would be thought a virgin, as many women are in the habit of doing. Another true sign of virginity is if the man feels the woman's seed flow abundantly. And there are many other signs that make use of herbs and stones which are known to those who perform these experiments.

MEDICAL WRITINGS ON LOVE

79 Avicenna, *A Treatise on Love*

This is a treatise on love, *Risalah fi'l-'ishq*, by Ibn Sina (Avicenna). This extract is from the section entitled 'On the Love of Those who Are Noble-minded and Young for External Beauty'.

Further reading: for Arabic influence on the 'courtly love' tradition, see Boase 1977. Wack 1990 discusses Avicenna's influence on medical writings about love.

Text: Emil M. Fackenheim (1945) 'A Treatise on Love by Ibn Sina', *Mediaeval Studies* 7: 208–228.

[. . .] We can now make the statement that it is part of the nature of beings endowed with reason to covet a beautiful sight; and that this is sometimes – certain conditions granted – to be considered as refinement and nobility. This disposition is either specific to the animal faculty alone, or it results from a partnership [of the rational and animal faculties].[3] But if it is specific to the animal faculty alone, the sages do not consider it as a sign of refinement and nobility. For, it is an incontrovertible truth that when a man expresses animal desires in an animal-like fashion, he becomes involved in vice and is harmed in his rational soul. On the other hand, [this type of love] is not specific to the rational soul alone either, for the endeavour of the latter requires the intelligible and eternal universals, not sensible and perishable particulars. This [type of love], then, results from an alliance between the two.

This is obvious also from another angle: If a man loves a beautiful form with animal desire, he deserves reproof, even condemnation and

3 This is the Aristotelean idea of the human soul being composed of the vegetative/animal/rational souls.

the charge of sin, as, for instance, those who commit unnatural adultery and in general people who go astray. But whenever he loves a pleasing form with an intellectual consideration, in the matter we have explained, then this is to be considered as an approximation to nobility and an increase in goodness. For he covets something whereby he will come nearer to the influence of That which is the First Source of influence and the Pure Object of love, and more similar to the exalted and noble beings. And this will dispose him to grace, generosity, and kindness. For this reason, one will never find the wise – those who belong to the noble and learned, and who do not follow the way of those who make greedy and avaricious demands – to be free from having their hearts occupied with a beautiful human form. Therefore, if a man acquires over and above those perfections which humans have in addition [to those possessed by other beings] the excellence of a harmonious form – which derives from the integrity and harmony of nature and from the exhibition of a divine impression – then that man has the strongest claim to receive the very kernel of the fruit of the heart and the very essence of the purest kind of love. Therefore the prophet says: Seek ye satisfaction of your needs in those of beautiful countenance, the plain meaning of which is that beauty of form is to be found only where there is a good natural composition, and that this good harmony and composition serve to improve the internal disposition and to sweeten the character. It does sometimes happen, however, that a man is ugly in external form and beautiful in internal disposition. In such a case only two explanations are possible: either his external ugliness is not due to an ugliness of harmony within lying in the very essence of the composition, but to an accidental external damage; or else the beauty of his internal disposition is not due to nature but to long habit. Similarly it sometimes happens that a man who is beautiful in external form is of an ugly disposition. In that case, again, only two explanations are possible: either the ugliness of his character is something that has happened accidentally to his nature after the completion of its composition, or it is due to a strong influence of habit.

Three things follow from the love of a beautiful human form: (i) the urge to embrace it, (ii) the urge to kiss it and (iii) the urge for conjugal union with it.

As for the third, it is obvious that this is specific to the animal soul alone, and its hold on the latter is very strong, so much so that it maintains the position of a steady companion, more, of a master, and certainly not of a tool. It is very hideous. Rational love can, therefore, not be pure except when the animal faculty is altogether subdued. With respect to the desire for conjugal union, it is fitting that a lover who entices the object of his love with this purpose in mind should be suspected, except if his need has a rational purpose, i.e., if his purpose was the propagation of the species. This is impossible with a man, and with a woman who is forbidden by religious law it is abominable. It is permissible and may find approval only in the case of a man with either his wife or female slave.

As for embracing and kissing, the purpose in them is to come near to one another and to become united. The soul of the lover desires to reach the object of his love with his senses of touch and sight, and thus he delights in embracing it. And he longs to have the very essence of his soul-faculty, his heart mingle with that of the object of his love, and thus he desires to kiss it. These actions, then, are not in themselves blameworthy. However, feelings and actions of excessive lust happen to follow them frequently, and this makes it necessary that one should be on guard against them, except if the complete absence of physical appetite and immunity even from suspicion is beyond doubt. For that reason it is not reprehensible to kiss children, although this is in principle open to the same suspicion, on condition that its aim is to be drawn near toward each other and to be united, without secret thought of shameful corrupting things.

Whoever is filled with this type of love is a man of nobility and refinement, and this type of love is an ornament and a source of inner wealth.

80 Constantine Africanus, *Viaticum*

Constantine (d. *c.*1087) was an African-born monk at Montecassino, the translator of several Arabic medical works. These two extracts are from an influential chapter on lovesickness in his *Viaticum* (eleventh century), where he discusses the nature of lovesickness and its symptoms. The treatise is an adaptation of a tenth-century Arabic medical handbook, and the discussion of lovesickness here is indebted to the notion of *'ishq*, or passionate love, in Arabic writing.

Further reading: there is a discussion of *amor hereos* in Jacquart and Thomasset 1988: 84–86, Wack 1990.

Text: Mary Frances Wack (1990) *Lovesickness in the Middle Ages: The Viaticum and its Commentaries* Philadelphia: University of Pennsylvania Press.

(I)

The love (amor) that is also called 'eros' is a disease touching the brain. For it is a great longing with intense sexual desire and affliction of the thoughts. Whence certain philosophers say: Eros is a word signifying the greatest pleasure. For just as loyalty is the ultimate form of affection, so also eros is a certain extreme form of pleasure.

(II)

Since this illness has more serious consequences for the soul, that is, excessive thoughts, their eyes always become hollow and move quickly because of the soul's thoughts and worries to find and possess what they desire. Their eyelids are heavy and their color yellowish; this is from the motion of heat which follows upon sleeplessness. Their pulse grows hard and does not dilate naturally, nor does it keep the beat as it should. If the patient sinks into thoughts, the action of the soul and body is damaged, since the body follows the soul in its action, and the soul accompanies the body in its passion. 'The power of the soul,' Galen says, 'follows the complexion of the body.' Thus if erotic lovers are not helped so that their thought is lifted and their spirit lightened, they inevitably fall into a melancholic disease. And just as they fall into a troublesome disease from excessive bodily labor, so also they fall into melancholy from labour of the soul.

81 Gerard of Berry, *Glosses on the Viaticum*

This and subsequent extracts are from commentaries (1180–1200?) by other authors on Constantine's text. The first extract here discusses lovesickness's similarity to melancholy, and the way that the disease affects human judgement. The second produces a fanciful etymology for the word *heros* and discusses the way that this love affects heroes in particular.

Text: Mary Frances Wack (1990) *Lovesickness in the Middle Ages*, Philadelphia: University of Pennsylvania Press.

(I)

Love that is called heros. The disease is called a melancholic worry by medical authors. It is indeed very similar to melancholy, because the entire attention and thought, aided by desire, is fixed on the beauty of some form or figure.

It is difficult to understand what the cause of this disease is, by which the faculties are hindered. The cause, then, of this disease is a malfunction of the estimative faculty, which is misled by sensed intentions into apprehending non-sensed accidents that perhaps are not in the person. Thus it believes some woman to be better and more noble and more desirable than all others.

(II)

Love that is called heros: Heroes are said to be noble men who, on account of riches and the softness of their lives, are more likely to suffer this disease.

82 Peter of Spain, *Questions on the Viaticum (Version A)*

In the first extract from *Questions on the Viaticum* (1246–1272?), Peter of Spain (*c.*1210–1277), later Pope John XXI (1276–1277), asks which part of the body is affected by lovesickness, the heart or the brain. The second asks whether men or women are more often affected by lovesickness.

Text: Mary Frances Wack (1990) *Lovesickness in the Middle Ages*: *The Viaticum and its Commentaries* Philadelphia: University of Pennsylvania Press.

(I)

It must be said that lovesickness can be spoken of in two ways: first, insofar as it is love, and thus it is a suffering of the heart, but in this way it is not a disease. The second way is to speak of lovesickness insofar as it is accompanied by these circumstances, which are melancholic worry with depressed thought and a damaged estimative faculty, which judges something to surpass all others, and in this way it is a suffering of the brain and also a disease. And thus the first argument is solved, since we readily concede that love is a suffering of the heart, which type of love is not a disease. But a failure or damaging of the estimative faculty, which judges one thing to be superior to all others, is the reason why lovesickness is a disease and a suffering of the brain itself.

(II)

It must be said that lovesickness is more quickly and frequently generated in women on account of their weak hope and because they are more frequently stimulated to intercourse, although not so strongly. But in men it is more difficult to cure, because the impression of any desired form in the brain of a man is stronger and harder to erase than the impression of a form in the brain of a woman, because a man has a drier brain than a woman, and an impression made in the dry is harder to erase than that made in the moist. In this the answer to the arguments is evident.

83 Bona Fortuna, *Treatise on the Viaticum*

Bona Fortuna's[4] fourteenth-century treatise offers a variety of suggestions for curing lovesickness here: some he takes from previous writers, including Constantine, but others are his own suggestions.

Text: Mary Frances Wack (1990) *Lovesickness in the Middle Ages: The Viaticum and its Commentaries* Philadelphia: University of Pennsylvania Press.

Then we come to those things that concern the mind. Note therefore that these people who suffer this illness are either people who have some discretion and are corrigible, or people who have no discretion and are incorrigible. Then they are to be treated as we do boys whom we first teach the ABCs without blows but with all gentleness, and whom we promise nuts, apples, and other things. In such a fashion with all caution we should proceed with them. We ought to promise them something, and join them with companions and with their equals, and promise them honors and benefices if they are scholars and if they delight in this. In this way sometimes they desist from their madness; sometimes they do not, but grow madder. Whence these are not universal recommendations but particular, and also those which the author suggests are not universal, for he says that songs and the sounds of instrumental music are beneficial.[5] This, however, is not universal. And because of this let the physician by

4 Possibly the same person as Bernard de Bona Hora, a master of medicine at Montpellier in the early fourteenth century (Wack 1990: 129).

5 'The author' referred to here is Constantine Africanus, who suggests that music may offer a distraction for the lovesick.

his efforts administer those things that he sees will be useful for the cure. Indeed, this is best, that he have intercourse with other women, and also with different ones. If indeed the patient is in any way corrigible, then we ought to discuss the beloved object with its filthy and loathsome qualities, and relate all the vicious things we can concerning the beloved object. Then we ought to describe to the patient the rejection and hate of his friends that will result from such madness. Also we ought to caution him with a moderate spirit, because he will be upset by this. But these are not universal.

But now note universal recommendations: first is change of locale; second is entanglement in lawsuits; third is necessary business; fourth is intercourse with other women.

84 Geoffrey Chaucer, *The Knight's Tale*

Chaucer's familiarity with Constantine is suggested by two references to him in *The Canterbury Tales*: he appears in a list of medical authorities in the portrait of the Doctor of Physic (I. 433), and he appears again in *The Merchant's Tale* as 'the cursed monk, daun Constantyn' (IV. 1810), author of the book De Coitu, 'On Intercourse'. Many Chaucerian characters show symptoms of lovesickness: Troilus, the hero of Chaucer's long poem *Troilus and Criseyde*, the falcon in the *Squire's Tale*, Dorigen and Aurelius in *The Franklin's Tale*. This description of lovesickness is of Arcite in *The Knight's Tale* (late fourteenth century).

Further reading: Wack 1990, Heffernan 1990.

Text: John M. Manly and Edith Rickert (eds) (1940) *The Text of the Canterbury Tales Studied on the Basis of all Known Manuscripts*, Chicago: University of Chicago Press; my modern English translation.

When Arcite had come to Thebes,
Often each day he grew faint, and said 'Alas',
For he shall never see his lady again.
And shortly to sum up all his woe,
Never had any creature so much sorrow
That is, or shall be, while the world may last.
His sleep, his food, his drink, is taken from him,
So that he becomes lean and dry as a stick,
His eyes sunken and horrible to behold,
His colour yellow and pale as ashes cold,
And he was solitary and ever alone,

And wailing all night, making his moan.
And if he heard a song or instrument,
Then he would weep, he might not be stopped.
So feeble also were his spirits, and so low,
And changed so, that no man could know
His speech nor his voice, if men heard it.
And in his behaviour for all the world he acted
Not only like the lover's malady
Of Hereos, but rather like mania,
Produced by melancholic humour
Beforehand, in his imaginative faculty.
And shortly, everything was turned upside down,
Both physical condition and also disposition,
Of his, this woeful lover sir Arcite.

BIBLIOGRAPHY

Adams, Norma and Donahue, Charles Jr (eds) (1981) *Select Cases from the Ecclesiastical Courts of the Province of Canterbury, c.1200–1301*, London: Selden Society.

Aers, David (1988) *Community, Gender, and Individual Identity: English Writing, 1360–1430*, London: Routledge.

Aertsen, Henk (1994) '*Wulf and Eadwacer*: A Woman's *Cri de Cœur* – for Whom, for What?', in H. Aertsen and R. H. Bremmer (eds) *Companion to Old English Poetry*, Amsterdam: VU University Press: 119–144.

Allen, Peter L. (1992) *The Art of Love: Amatory Fiction from Ovid to the Romance of the Rose*, Philadelphia: University of Pennsylvania Press.

Althusser, Louis (1984) *Essays on Ideology*, trans. Ben Brewster, London: Verso.

Amt, Emilie (ed.) (1993) *Women's Lives in Medieval Europe: A Sourcebook*, London: Routledge.

Anderson, Bonnie S. and Zinsser, Judith P. (1988) *A History of Their Own: Women in Europe from Prehistory to the Present*, 2 vols, Harmondsworth: Penguin.

Anderson, J. J. (ed.) (1996) *Sir Gawain and the Green Knight, Pearl, Cleanness, Patience*, London: Dent.

Appleby, J. T. (ed. and trans.) (1963) *The Chronicle of Richard of Devizes*, London: Thomas Nelson.

Aquinas, St Thomas (1964–1981) *Summa Theologiae*, T. Gilby and others (eds), London: Blackfriars.

Ariès, Philippe (1985a) 'St Paul and the Flesh', in Ariès and Béjin (eds) (1985): 36–39.

—— (1985b) 'Love in Married Life', in Ariès and Béjin (eds) (1985): 130–39.

—— (1985c) 'The Indissoluble Marriage', in Ariès and Béjin (eds) (1985): 140–157.

Ariès, Philippe and Béjin, André (eds) (1985) *Western Sexuality: Practice and Precept in Past and Present Times*, trans. Anthony Forster, Oxford: Blackwell.

Attenborough, F. L. (ed. and trans.) (1922) *The Laws of the Earliest English Kings*, Cambridge: Cambridge University Press.

Augustine, St (1961) *Confessions*, trans. R. S. Pine-Coffin, Harmondsworth: Penguin.

—— (1972) *Concerning the City of God against the Pagans*, trans. Henry Bettenson, Harmondsworth: Penguin.

—— (1999) *Marriage and Virginity*, D. G. Hunter (ed.), trans. Ray Kearney, *The Works of St Augustine* 1: 9, New York: New City Press.

Baird, Joseph L. and Kane, John R. (1978) *La Querelle de la Rose: Letters and Documents*, Chapel Hill, NC: University of North Carolina Department of Romance Languages.

Barratt, Alexandra (ed.) (1992) *Women's Writing in Middle English*, London: Longman.
Bateson, Mary (ed.) (1904–1906) *Borough Customs*, 2 vols, London: Quaritch.
Bawcutt, Priscilla (1992) *Dunbar the Makar*, Oxford: Clarendon Press.
—— (ed.) (1998) *The Poems of William Dunbar*, 2 vols, Glasgow: Association for Scottish Literary Studies.
Bede, St (1990) *Ecclesiastical History of the English People*, trans. L. Sherley Price, R. E. Latham and D. H. Farmer, revised edn, Harmondsworth: Penguin.
Bennett, J. A. W. (1968) 'Gower's "Honeste Love"', in John Lawlor (ed.), *Patterns of Love and Courtesy: Essays in Memory of C. S. Lewis*, London: Arnold: 107–121.
Bennett, Judith M. (1987) *Women in the Medieval English Countryside: Gender and Household in Brigstock before the Plague*, Oxford: Oxford University Press.
Benson, C. David (1984) 'Incest and Moral Poetry in Gower's *Confessio Amantis*', *Chaucer Review* 19: 100–109.
Benson, Larry D. and others (eds) (1987) *The Riverside Chaucer*, Boston: Houghton Mifflin.
Blamires, Alcuin (1989) 'The Wife of Bath and Lollardy', *Medium Aevum* 58: 224–242.
Blamires, Alcuin (with Marx, C. W., and Pratt, Karen [eds]) (1992) *Woman Defamed and Woman Defended: An Anthology of Medieval Texts*, Oxford: Oxford University Press.
—— (1997) *The Case for Women in Medieval Culture*, Oxford: Clarendon Press.
Bloch, R. Howard (1991) *Medieval Misogyny and the Invention of Western Romantic Love*, London: University of Chicago Press.
Bloomfield, Morton W. (1958) '*Piers Plowman* and the Three Grades of Chastity', *Anglia* 76: 227–253.
Boase, Roger (1977) *The Origin and Meaning of Courtly Love: A Critical Study of European Scholarship*, Manchester: Manchester University Press.
Boccaccio (1972) *The Decameron*, trans. G. H. McWilliam, Harmondsworth: Penguin.
Boswell, John (1980) *Christianity, Social Tolerance, and Homosexuality: Gay People in Western Europe from the Beginning of the Christian Era to the Fourteenth Century*, Chicago: University of Chicago Press.
—— (1996) *The Marriage of Likeness: Same Sex Unions in Premodern Europe*, London: HarperCollins.
Brand, P. A., Hyams, P. R., Faith, R. and Searle, E. (1983) 'Debate: Seigneurial Control of Women's Marriage', *Past and Present* 99: 123–160.
Brewer, Derek (1954) 'Love and Marriage in Chaucer's Poetry', *The Modern Language Review* 49: 461–464.
—— (1977) 'Review of Kelly' (1975), *Review of English Studies* 28: 194–197.
Brooke, C. N. L. (1989) *The Medieval Idea of Marriage*, Oxford: Oxford University Press.
Brown, Peter (1988) *The Body and Society: Men, Women and Sexual Renunciation in Early Christianity*, New York: Columbia University Press.
Brundage, James A. (1987) *Law, Sex and Christian Society in Medieval Europe*, London: University of Chicago Press.
—— (1993) *Sex, Law, and Marriage in the Middle Ages*, Aldershot: Variorum.
—— (1995) *Medieval Canon Law*, London: Longman.
—— (1996) 'Sex and Canon Law', in Bullough and Brundage (eds) (1996): 33–50.
Bryan, W. F. and Dempster, Germaine (1941) *Sources and Analogues of Chaucer's Canterbury Tales*, Chicago: University of Chicago Press.
Bullough, Vern L. (1973) 'Medieval Medical and Scientific Views of Women', *Viator* 4: 485–501.
—— (1996) 'Cross Dressing and Gender Role Change in the Middle Ages', in Bullough and Brundage (eds) (1996): 223–242.

BIBLIOGRAPHY

Bullough, Vern L. and Brundage, James A. (eds) (1996) *Handbook of Medieval Sexuality*, London: Garland.

Burgess, G. S. and Busby, K. (trans.) (1986) *The Lais of Marie de France*, Harmondsworth: Penguin.

Burrow, J. A. (1982) *Medieval Writers and their Work: Middle English Literature and its Background, 1100–1500*, Oxford: Oxford University Press.

Cadden, Joan (1996) 'Western Medicine and Natural Philosophy', in Bullough and Brundage (eds) (1996): 51–80.

Camille, Michael (1998) *The Medieval Art of Love: Objects and Subjects of Desire*, New York: Abrams.

Carruthers, Mary (1994) 'The Wife of Bath and the Painting of Lions', in Evans and Johnson (eds) (1994): 22–53.

Cartlidge, Neil (1997) *Medieval Marriage: Literary Approaches, 1100–1300*, Cambridge: Brewer.

Chance, Jane (1986) *Woman as Hero in Old English Literature*, Syracuse, NY: Syracuse University Press.

Chapman, Colin R. (1992) *Ecclesiastical Courts, their Officials and their Records*, Dursley: Lochin.

Cheney, C. R. (1935) 'Legislation of the Medieval English Church', *English Historical Review* 50: 193–224, 385–417.

Clark, Elizabeth A. (1991) '"Adam's Only Companion": Augustine and the Early Christian Debate on Marriage', in Edwards and Spector (eds) (1991): 15–31.

—— (ed.) (1996) *Saint Augustine on Marriage and Sexuality*, Washington: Catholic University of America Press.

Clark, Robert L. A. (trans.) (2001) 'Jousting without a Lance: The Condemnation of Female Homoeroticism in the Livre des Manières', in F. C. Sautman and P. Sheingorn (eds), *Same Sex Love and Desire among Women in the Middle Ages*. New York: St Martin's Press.

Clunies Ross, Margaret (1985) 'Concubinage in Anglo-Saxon England', *Past and Present* 108: 3–34.

Coleman, Janet (1987) '*The Owl and the Nightingale* and Papal Theories of Marriage', *Journal of Ecclesiastical History* 38: 517–568.

Collins, Marie (1981) 'Love, Nature and Law in the Poetry of Gower and Chaucer', in G. S. Burgess (ed.) *Court and Poet: Selected Proceedings of the Third Congress of the International Courtly Literature Society*, Liverpool: 113–128.

Cooper, Helen (1989) *Oxford Guides to Chaucer: The Canterbury Tales*, Oxford: Oxford University Press.

Damico, Helen and Olsen, A. H. (eds) (1996) *New Readings on Women in Old English Literature*, Bloomington: Indiana University Press.

Dauviller, Jean (1933) *Le Mariage dans le droit classique de L'Eglise depuis le Decret de Gratien (1140) jusqu'a la mort de Clement V (1314)*, Paris: Sirey.

Davis, Norman (ed.) (1971–1976), *Paston Letters and Papers of the Fifteenth Century*, Oxford: Oxford University Press.

Davis, Norman, Gray, D, Ingham, P and Wallace-Hadrill, A (1979) *A Chaucer Glossary*, Oxford: Clarendon.

Delany, Sheila (1994) 'Sexual Economics, Chaucer's Wife of Bath, and *The Book of Margery Kempe*', in Evans and Johnson (1994): 72–87.

De Pizan, Christine (1982) *The Book of the City of Ladies*, trans. E. J. Richards, New York: Persea.

Dinshaw, Carolyn (1989) *Chaucer's Sexual Poetics*, London: University of Wisconsin Press.

—— (1992) 'Quarrels, Rivals, and Rape: Gower and Chaucer', in Dor (ed.) (1992): 112–122.

—— (1999) *Getting Medieval: Sexual Communities, Pre- and Post-Modern*, Durham, NC: Duke University Press.

Donahue, Charles Jr. (1993), 'Female Plaintiffs in Marriage Cases in the Court of York in the Later Middle Ages: What Can We Learn from the Numbers?', in Walker (ed.) (1993a): 183–213.

Donaldson, E. Talbot (1970) 'The Myth of Courtly Love', in Donaldson, E. Talbot, *Speaking of Chaucer*, London: Athlone: 154–163.

Dor, Juliette (ed.) (1992) *A Wyf Ther Was: Essays in Honour of Paule Mertens-Fonck*, Liège: Université de Liège.

Dronke, Peter (1968) *Medieval Latin and the Rise of European Love-Lyric*, second edn, 2 vols, Oxford: Oxford University Press.

—— (1984) *Women Writers of the Middle Ages*, Cambridge: Cambridge University Press.

Duby, Georges (1983) *The Knight, The Lady, and the Priest: The Making of Modern Marriage in Medieval France*, trans. Barbara Bray, New York: Pantheon.

Duggan, Charles (1981) 'Equality and Compassion in Papal Marriage Decretals to England', in Van Hoecke, Willy, and Welkenhuysen, Andries (eds) (1981) *Love and Marriage in the Twelfth Century* Leuven/Louvain: Leuven University Press.

Edwards, Robert R. and Spector, Stephen (1991) *The Olde Daunce: Love, Friendship, Sex and Marriage in the Medieval World*, Albany: SUNY Press.

Elliott, Dyan (1993) *Spiritual Marriage: Sexual Abstinence in Medieval Wedlock*, Princeton: Princeton University Press.

Ellis, Roger (1982) ' "Flores ad fabricandam . . . coronam": An Investigation into the uses of the Revelations of St Bridget of Sweden in Fifteenth Century England', *Medium Aevum* 51: 163–786.

—— (ed.) (1987) *The Liber Celestis of St Bridget of Sweden*, Oxford: Oxford University Press.

Evans, Ruth and Johnson, Lesley (eds) (1994) *Feminist Readings in Middle English Literature: The Wife of Bath and All Her Sect*, London: Routledge.

Fackenheim, Emil M. (1945) 'A Treatise on Love by Ibn Sina', *Mediaeval Studies* 7: 208–228.

Fell, Christine (1984) *Women in Anglo-Saxon England*, London: British Museum.

—— (1991) 'Perceptions of Transience', in Malcolm Godden and Michael Lapidge (eds) *The Cambridge Companion to Old English Literature*, Cambridge: Cambridge University Press.

Fenster, Thelma S. and Erler, Mary C. (eds) (1990) *Poems of Cupid, God of Love*, Leiden: Brill.

Finke, Laurie (1996) 'Sexuality in Medieval French Literature: "Separés, on est Ensemble" ', in Bullough and Brundage (eds) (1996): 345–368.

Flandrin, Jean-Louis (1985) 'Sex in Married Life in the Early Middle Ages: The Church's Teaching and Behavioural Reality', in Ariès and Béjin (eds) (1985): 114–129.

Foucault, Michel (1981) *The History of Sexuality Volume 1: An Introduction*, trans. Robert Hurley, Harmondsworth: Penguin.

Fowler, Elizabeth (1995) 'Civil Death and the Maiden: Agency and the Conditions of Contract in *Piers Plowman*', *Speculum* 70: 760–792.

Fradenburg, Louise and Freccero, Carla (eds) (1996) *Premodern Sexualities*, London: Routledge.

Frantzen, Allen J. (1993) 'When Women Aren't Enough', *Speculum* 68: 445–471.

—— (1994) '*The Pardoner's Tale*, The Pervert and the Price of Order in Chaucer's World', in Harwood and Overing (eds) (1994): 131–147.

—— (1996) 'The Disclosure of Sodomy in *Cleanness*', *PMLA* 111.3: 451–464.

—— (1998) *Before the Closet: Same Sex Love from Beowulf to Angels in America*, Chicago and London: University of Chicago Press.

Friedberg, E. (ed.) (1879), *Corpus Iuris Canonici*, Leipzig.

Froissart (1968) *Chronicles*, Geoffrey Brereton (ed. and trans.), Harmondsworth: Penguin.

Furnivall, F. J. and Gollancz, I. (eds), Mitchell, J. and Doyle, A. I. (rev.) (1970) *Hoccleve's Works: The Minor Poems*, Oxford: Oxford University Press.

Gaunt, Simon (1996) 'Straight Minds/"Queer" Wishes in Old French Hagiography: La Vie de Sainte Euphrosine', in Fradenburg and Freccero (eds) (1996): 155–173.

Gies, Frances and Gies Joseph (1978) *Women in the Middle Ages,* New York: Harper and Row.

Giraldus Cambrensis (1982) *The History and Topography of Ireland*, trans. John J. O'Meara, Harmondsworth: Penguin.

Goldberg, P. J. P. (ed.) (1992) *Woman is a Worthy Wight: Women in English Society, c.1200–1500*, Gloucester: Sutton.

—— (1995) *Women in England, c.1275–1525: Documentary* Sources, Manchester: Manchester University Press.

Goodich, Michael (1979) *The Unmentionable Vice: Homosexuality in the Later Medieval Period*, London.

Goody, Jack (1983) *The Development of Marriage and the Family in Europe*, Cambridge: Cambridge University Press.

Gray, Douglas (ed.) (1998) *Selected Poems of Robert Henryson and William Dunbar*, Harmondsworth: Penguin.

Green, Monica H. (1996) 'The Development of the *Trotula*', *Revue d'Histoire des Textes* 26: 119–203 (reprinted in Green 2000).

—— (2000) *Women's Healthcare in the Medieval West: Texts and Contexts*, Hampshire: Ashgate.

Greenfield, Stanley B. and Calder, Daniel G. (1986) *A New Critical History of Old English Literature*, New York: New York University Press.

Griffith, Mark (ed.) (1997) *Judith,* Exeter: University of Exeter Press.

Hair, Paul (ed.) (1972) *Before the Bawdy Court: Selections from Church Court and Other Records relating to the Correction of Moral Offences in England, Scotland, and New England*, London: Elek.

Hajnal, J. (1975) 'European Marriage Patterns in Perspective', in D. V. Glass and D. E. C. Eversley (eds), *Population in History: Essays in Historical Demography*, London: Edward Arnold: 101–143.

Hall, G. D. G. (ed. and trans.) (1965) *The Treatise on the Laws and Customs of the Realm of England Commonly Called Glanvill*, Oxford: Clarendon Press.

Hamer, Richard (ed. and trans.) (1970) *A Choice of Anglo-Saxon Verse*, London: Faber.

Hanawalt, Barbara A. (1992) 'The Widow's Mite: Provision for Medieval London Widows', in Mirrer (ed.) (1992): 21–46.

—— (1993) 'Remarriage as an Option for Urban and Rural Widows in Late Medieval England', in Walker (ed) (1993a): 141–164.

Hansen, Elaine Tuttle (1992) *Chaucer and the Fictions of Gender*, Oxford: University of California Press.

Harrison, Robert (trans.) (1974) *Gallic Salt*, Berkeley: University of California Press.

Harwood, Britton J. and Overing, Gillian R. (eds) (1994) *Class and Gender in Early English Literature: Intersections*, Bloomington: Indiana University Press.

Haskell, Ann S. (1973) 'The Paston Women on Marriage in Fifteenth Century England', *Viator* 4: 459–484.

Head, Thomas (1990) 'The Marriages of Christina of Markyate', *Viator* 21: 75–101.

Heffernan, Carol F. (1990) 'Chaucer's *Troilus and Criseyde*: The Disease of Love and Courtly Love', *Neophilologus* 74: 294–309.

Helmholz, R. H. (1974) *Marriage Litigation in Medieval England,* London: Cambridge University Press.

—— (1987a) *Canon Law and the Law of England*, London: Hambledon.

—— (1987b) 'Abjuration *Sub Pena Nubendi* in the Church Courts of Medieval England', in Helmholz (1987a): 145–155 (originally published in *The Jurist* 32, 1972: 80–90).

—— (1987c) 'Bastardy Litigation in Medieval England', in Helmholz (1987a): 187–210 (originally published in *American Journal of Legal History* 13, 1969: 360–383).

—— (1993) 'Married Women's Wills in Later Medieval England', in Walker (ed) (1993a): 165–182.

Herlihy, David (1985) *Medieval Households*, Cambridge, MA, and London: Harvard University Press.

Hicks, Eric (1977) *Le débat sur Le Roman de la Rose*, Paris: Éditions Honoré Champion.

Hill, Thomas D. (1990) ' "Weahlhtheow" as Foreign Slave: Some Continental Analogues', *Philological Quarterly* 69: 106–112.

Holsinger, Bruce (2002) 'Vernacular Legality: The English Jurisdictions of *The Owl and the Nightingale*', in Steiner, Emily and Barrington, Candace (eds) *The Letter of the Law: Legal Practice and Literary Production in Medieval England,* Ithaca and London: Cornell University Press: 154–184.

Horgan, F. (trans.) (1994)*The Romance of the Rose*, Oxford: Oxford University Press.

Horstmann, C (1885) 'Prosalegenden: Die Legenden des ms. Douce 114', *Anglia* 8: 102–196.

Hough, Carole (1997a) 'Alfred's *Domboc* and the Language of Rape: A Reconsideration of Alfred ch. 11', *Medium Aevum* 66: 1–27.

—— (1997b) 'A New Reading of Alfred, ch. 26', *Nottingham Medieval Studies* 41: 1–12.

—— (1999) 'The Widow's *Mund* in Æthelbert 75 and 76', *Journal of English and Germanic Philology* 98: 1–16.

—— (2001) 'Two Kentish Laws Concerning Women: A New Reading of Æthelbert 73 and 74', *Anglia* 119: 554–578.

Hult, David F. (1986) *Self-Fulfilling Prophecies: Readership and Authority in the First Roman de la Rose*, Cambridge: Cambridge University Press.

Jacquart, Danielle and Thomasset, Claude (1988) *Sexuality and Medicine in the Middle Ages*, trans. Matthew Adamson, Princeton: Princeton University Press.

Jaeger, C. Stephen (1985) *The Origins of Courtliness: Civilizing Trends and the Formation of Courtly Ideals, 939–1210*, Philadelphia: University of Pennsylvania Press.

—— (1999) *Ennobling Love: In Search of a Lost Sensibility*, Philadelphia: University of Pennsylvania Press.

Jerome, St (1893) *The Principal Works of St Jerome*, trans. W. H. Fremantle, Oxford: James Parker.

Johansson, Warren and Percy, William A. (1996) 'Homosexuality', in Bullough and Brundage (eds) (1996): 155–190.

Johnson, Lynn Staley (1991) 'The Trope of the Scribe and the Quest for Literary Authority in the Works of Julian of Norwich and Margery Kempe', *Speculum* 66: 820–838.

Jordan, Mark D. (1997) *The Invention of Sodomy in Christian Theology*, Chicago: University of Chicago Press.

Karras, Ruth Mazo (1996) *Common Women: Prostitution and Sexuality in Medieval England,* Oxford: Oxford University Press.

Karras, Ruth Mazo and Boyd, David Lorenzo (1996) ' "Ut cum muliere": A Male Transvestite Prostitute in Fourteenth-Century London', in Fradenburg and Freccero (eds) (1996): 101–116.

Kay, Sarah (1999) 'Desire and Subjectivity', in Gaunt, Simon and Kay, Sarah (eds) *The Troubadours: An Introduction*, Cambridge: Cambridge University Press: 212–227.

—— (2000) 'Courts, Clerks, and Courtly Love', in Roberta L. Krueger (ed.) *The Cambridge Companion to Medieval Romance*, Cambridge: Cambridge University Press: 81–96.

Kay, Sarah and Rubin, Miri (eds) (1994) *Framing Medieval Bodies*, Manchester: Manchester University Press.

Kelly, Henry Ansgar (1975) *Love and Marriage in the Age of Chaucer*, London: Cornell University Press.

Kittredge, George Lyman (1960) 'Chaucer's Discussion of Marriage', in R. J. Schoeck and Jerome Taylor (eds) *Chaucer Criticism*, 2 vols, Indiana: University of Notre Dame Press: I, 130–158 (first published in *Modern Philology* 9 (1911–1912): 435–467).

Klapisch-Zuber, Christiane (ed.) (1992) *A History of Women in the West: Silences of the Middle* Ages, Cambridge, MA: Harvard University Press.

Kooper, Erik (1991) 'Loving the Unequal Equal: Medieval Theologians and Marital Affection', in Edwards and Spector (eds) (1991): 45–56.

Ladurie, Emmanuel Le Roy (1978) *Montaillou: Cathars and Catholics in a French Village, 1294–1324*, trans. Barbara Bray, London: Scolar.

Lampe, David (1996) 'Sex Roles and the Role of Sex in Medieval English Literature', in Bullough and Brundage (eds) (1996): 401–426.

Larrington, Carolyne (ed.) (1995) *Women and Writing in Medieval Europe: A Sourcebook*, London: Routledge.

Leclercq, Jean (1982) *Monks on Marriage: A Twelfth Century View*, New York: Seabury.

Lees, Clare A. and McNamara, Jo Ann (eds) (1994) *Medieval Masculinities: Regarding Men in the Middle Ages*, Medieval Cultures, vol. 7, London: University of Minnesota Press.

Lemay, H. R. (1990) 'Women and the Literature of Obstetrics and Gynecology', in Rosenthal, Joel T. (ed.) *Medieval Women and the Sources of Medieval History*, Athens, GA: University of Georgia Press: 189–209.

—— (ed. and trans.) (1992) *Women's Secrets*, Albany: State University of New York Press.

Leslie, R. F. (ed.) (1988) *Three Old English Elegies: The Wife's Lament, The Husband's Message, The Ruin*, revised edn, Exeter: University of Exeter Press.

Lewis, C. S. (1936) *The Allegory of Love: A Study in Mediaeval Tradition*, Oxford: Oxford University Press.

Leyser, Henrietta (1995) *Medieval Women: A Social History of Women in England, 450–1500*, London: Weidenfeld and Nicolson.

Lochrie, Karma (1991) *Margery Kempe and Translations of the Flesh*, Philadelphia: University of Pennsylvania Press.

—— (1996) 'Don't Ask, Don't Tell: Murderous Plots and Medieval Secrets', in Fradenburg and Freccero (eds) (1996): 137–152.

Lombard, Peter (1971–1981) *Sententiae in IV Libris Distinctae*, ed. Pontificale Collegium S. Bonaventurae Ad Claras Aquas, Rome: Grottaferrata.

Lucas, Angela M. (1983) *Women in the Middle Ages: Religion, Marriage and Letters*, Brighton: Harvester.

Luria, Maxwell S. and Hoffman, Richard L. (eds) (1974) *Middle English Lyrics*, London: Norton.

Luyster, Robert (1998) '*The Wife's Lament* in the Context of Scandinavian Myth and Ritual', *Philological Quarterly* 77: 243–270.

Macaulay, G. C. (ed.) (1957) *The English Works of John Gower*, London: Oxford University Press.

McCarthy, Conor (1999) 'The Postion of Widows in the Later Fourteenth Century English Community and the *Wife of Bath's Prologue*', in D. Mowbray, R. Purdie, and I. P. Wei (eds) *Authority and Community in the Middle Ages*, Stroud: Sutton: 101–115.

—— (2000a) 'Marriage and Mede in Passus 2 to 4 of *Piers Plowman*', *Nottingham Medieval Studies* 44: 152–166.

—— (2000b) 'Love and Marriage in the *Confessio Amantis*', *Neophilologus* 84: 485–499.

McNeill, J. T. and Gamer, H. M. (ed. and trans.) (1938) *Medieval Handbooks of Penance*, New York.

Manly, John M. and Rickert, Edith (eds) (1940) *The Text of the Canterbury Tales Studied on the Basis of all Known Manuscripts*, Chicago: University of Chicago Press.

Mann, Jill (1991) *Geoffrey Chaucer*, London: Harvester.

Manuale et Processionale ad Usum Insignis Ecclesiae Eboracensis (1875) Surtees Society, vol. 63, London: Quaritch.

Menuge, Noël James (2001) *Medieval English Wardship in Romance and Law*, Cambridge: Brewer.

Mews, Constant J. (1999) *The Lost Letters of Heloise and Abelard: Perceptions of Dialogue in Twelfth-Century France*, with translations by Neville Chiavardi and Constant J. Mews, New York: St Martin's Press.

Millet, Bella and Wogan-Browne, Jocelyn (ed. and trans.) (1990) *Medieval English Prose for Women* Oxford: Oxford University Press.

Milsom, S. F. C. (1981) *Historical Foundations of the Common Law*, 2nd edn, London: Butterworths.

Minnis, Alastair J. (1988) *Medieval Theory of Authorship: Scholastic Literary Attitudes in the Later Middle Ages*, 2nd edn, Aldershot: Scolar.

—— (2001) *Magister Amoris: The Roman de la Rose and Vernacular Hermeneutics*, Oxford: Oxford University Press.

Mirrer, Louise (ed.) (1992) *Upon my Husband's Death: Widows in the Literature and Histories of Medieval Europe*, Ann Arbor: University of Michigan Press.

Moi, Toril (1986) 'Desire in Language: Andreas Capellanus and the Controversy of Courtly Love', in David Aers (ed.) *Medieval Literature: Criticism, Ideology, and History*, Brighton: Harvester: 11–33.

Monson, Don A. (1988) 'Andreas Capellanus and the Problem of Irony', *Speculum* 63: 539–572.

Morgan, Gerald (1977) 'Natural and Rational Love in Medieval Literature', *Yearbook of English Studies* 7: 43–52.

—— (ed.) (1980) *The Franklin's Tale from the Canterbury Tales*, Dublin: Irish Academic Press.

—— (1987) 'Langland's Conception of Favel, Guile, Liar and False in the First Vision of *Piers Plowman*', *Neophilologus* 71: 626–633.

—— (1988) 'The Status and Meaning of Meed in the First Vision of *Piers Plowman*', *Neophilologus* 72: 449–463.

Murray, Jacqueline (1996a) 'Hiding Behind the Universal Man: Male Sexuality in the Middle Ages', in Bullough and Brundage (eds) (1996): 123–152.

—— (1996b) 'Twice Marginal and Invisible: Lesbians in the Middle Ages', in Bullough and Brundage (eds) (1996): 191–222.

Muscatine, Charles (1986) *The Old French Fabliaux*, New Haven and London: Yale University Press.

Nichols, F. M. (ed. and trans.) (1865) *Britton*, London: Macmillan.

Nicholson, Peter (ed.) (1991) *Gower's Confessio Amantis: A Critical Anthology*, Cambridge: Brewer.

Noonan, John T. (1973) 'Power to Choose', *Viator* 4: 419–434.

—— (1986) *Contraception: A History of its Treatment by the Catholic Theologians and Canonists*, enlarged edn, Cambridge, MA: Belknap.

—— (1997) 'Gratian Slept Here: The Changing Identity of the Father of the Systematic Study of Canon Law', in John T. Noonan *Canons and Canonists in Context*, Goldbach: Keip.

O'Donoghue, Bernard (1982) *The Courtly Love Tradition*, Manchester: Manchester University Press.

Offord, M. Y. (ed.) (1971) *Caxton's Book of the Knight of the Tower*, Oxford: Oxford University Press.

Olsen, A. H. (1982) 'Inversion and Political Purpose in the Old English *Judith*', *English Studies* 63.

Olsen, A. H. and Raffel, Burton (eds) (1998) *Poems and Prose from the Old English*, trans. Burton Raffel, New Haven: Yale Unversity Press.

Oppel, John (1993) 'Saint Jerome and the History of Sex', *Viator* 24: 1–22.

Owen, Dorothy M. (1990) *The Medieval Canon Law: Teaching, Literature, and Transmission*, Cambridge: Cambridge University Press.

Palmer, Robert C. (1984) 'Contexts of Marriage in Later Medieval England: Evidence from the King's Court circa 1300', *Speculum* 59: 42–67.

Payer, Pierre J. (1984) *Sex and the Penitentials*, Toronto: University of Toronto Press.

Phillipy, Patricia A. (1997) 'Establishing Authority: Boccaccio's *De Claris Mulieribus* and Christine de Pizan's *Le Livre de la Cité des Dames*', in Renate Blumenfeld-Kosinski (ed.), *The Selected Writings of Christine de Pizan*, trans. Renate Blumenfeld-Kosinski and Kevin Brownlee, New York: Norton (reprinted from *Romanic Review* 77, 1986).

Pittenger, Elizabeth (1996) 'Explicit Ink', in Fradenburg and Freccero (eds) (1996): 223–242.

Plucknett, Theodore F. T. (1956) *A Concise History of the Common Law,* 5th edn, London: Butterworths.

Pollock, Frederick and Maitland, Frederic William (1898) *The History of English Law Before the Time of Edward I*, 2nd edn, 2 vols, Cambridge: Cambridge University Press.

Poos, L. R. and Bonfield, Lloyd (ed. and trans.) (1998) *Select Cases in Manorial Courts, 1250–1550: Property and Family Law*, London: Selden Society.

Powicke, F. M. and Cheney, C. R. (eds) (1964) *Councils and Synods with Other Documents relating to the English Church, AD 1205–1313*, London: Oxford University Press.

Rabelais, François (1955) *The Histories of Gargantua and Pantagruel*, trans. J. M. Cohen, Penguin: Harmondsworth.

Radice, Betty (trans.) (1974) *The Letters of Abelard and Heloise*, Harmondsworth: Penguin.

Razi, Zvi (1980) *Life, Marriage and Death in a Medieval Parish: Economy, Society and Demography in Halesowen, 1270–1400*, Cambridge: Cambridge University Press.

Richards, Earl Jeffrey (1992) 'Christine de Pizan, the Conventions of Courtly Diction, and Italian Humanism', in E. J. Richards and others (eds) *Reinterpreting Christine de Pizan*, Athens, GA: University of Georgia Press: 250–271.

Richmond, Colin (1985) 'The Pastons Revisited: Marriage and the Family in Fifteenth-Century England', *Bulletin of the Institute of Historical Research* 58: 25–36.

Rieder, Paula M. (2002) 'Insecure Borders: Symbols of Clerical Privilege and Gender Ambiguity in the Liturgy of Churching', in Anne L. McClanan and Karen Roscoff Encarnación (eds) *The Material Culture of Sex, Procreation, and Marriage in Premodern Europe*, New York and Basingstoke: Palgrave: 93–113.

Rigg, A. G. (ed. and trans.) (1986) *Gawain on Marriage: The 'De Coniuge Non Ducenda'*, Toronto: Pontifical Institute of Mediaeval Studies.

Robertson, A. J. (ed. and trans.) (1925) *The Laws of the Kings of England from Edmund to Henry I*, Cambridge: Cambridge University Press.

Rosenthal, Joel T. (1993) 'Fifteenth Century Widows and Widowhood: Bereavement, Reintegration and Life Choices', in Walker (ed.) (1993a): 33–58.

Ross, Ian Simpson (1981) *William Dunbar*, Leiden: Brill.

Rothwell, Harry (ed.) (1975) *English Historical Documents, 1189–1327*, London: Eyre & Spottiswoode.

Rubin, Miri (1994) 'The Person in the Form: Medieval Challenges to Bodily "Order"', in Kay and Rubin (eds) (1994): 100–122.

Salisbury, Joyce E. (1990) *Medieval Sexuality: A Research Guide*, New York: Garland.

Saunders, Corinne (2001) *Rape and Ravishment in the Literature of Medieval England*, Cambridge: Brewer.

Sayles, G. O. (ed. and trans.) (1984) *Fleta: Volume IV: Book V and Book VI*, Selden Society, vol. 99, London: Selden Society.

Scattergood, John (1987) '*Chaucer a Bukton* and Proverbs', *Nottingham Medieval Studies* 31: 98–107.

—— (1996) 'Misrepresenting the City: Genre, Intertextuality, and William FitzStephen's *Description of London* (*c.*1173)', in John Scattergood, *Reading the Past: Essays on Medieval and Renaissance Literature*, Dublin: Four Courts: 15–36.

—— (2000) 'The "Lewed" and the "Lerede": A Reading of *Satire on the Consistory Courts*', in John Scattergood (ed.), *The Lost Tradition: Essays on Middle English Alliterative Poetry*, Dublin: Four Courts.

Schmidt, A. V. C. (1987) *The Vision of Piers Plowman*, London: Dent.

Searle, Eleanor (1979) 'Seigneurial Control of Women's Marriage: The Antecedents and Functions of Merchet in England', *Past and Present* 82: 3–43.

Sheehan, Michael M. (1963) 'The Influence of Canon Law on the Property Rights of Married Women in England', *Mediaeval Studies* 25: 109–24 (reprinted in Sheehan 1996: 16–37).

—— (1971) 'The Formation and Stability of Marriage in Fourteenth Century England: Evidence of an Ely Register', *Mediaeval Studies* 33: 228–263 (reprinted in Sheehan 1996: 38–76).

—— (1974) 'Marriage and Family in English Conciliar and Synodal Legislation', in J. Reginald O'Donnell (ed.) *Essays in Honour of Anton Charles Pegis*, Toronto: Pontifical Institute of Mediaeval Studies: 205–14 (reprinted in Sheehan 1996: 205–214).

—— (1978a) 'Marriage Theory and Practice in the Conciliar Legislation and Diocesan Statutes of Medieval England', *Mediaeval Studies* 40: 408–460 (reprinted in Sheehan 1996: 118–176).

—— (1978b) 'Choice of Marriage Partner in the Middle Ages: Development and Mode of Application of a Theory of Marriage', *Studies in Medieval and Renaissance History* 1: 1–33 (reprinted in Sheehan 1996: 87–117).

—— (1991) '*Maritalis Affectio* Revisited', in Edwards and Spector (eds) (1991), 34–44 (reprinted in Sheehan 1996: 262–277).

—— (1996) *Marriage, Family, and Law in Medieval Europe: Collected Studies*, James K. Farge (ed.), Toronto: University of Toronto Press.

Sheridan, James J. (trans.) (1980) *The Plaint of Nature*, Toronto: Pontifical Institute of Mediaeval Studies.

Skeat, Walter W. (ed) (1899) *The Complete Works of Geoffrey Chaucer*, 2nd edn, Oxford.

Stanley, E. G. (ed.) (1960) *The Owl and the Nightingale*, London: Nelson.

Stargardt, Ute (1985) 'The Beguines of Belgium, the Dominican Nuns of Germany, and Margery Kempe', in Thomas J. Heffernan (ed.) *The Popular Literature of Medieval England*, Knoxville: University of Tennesee Press: 277–313.

The Statutes at Large (1758), 6 vols, London.

Swanton, Michael (ed. and trans.) (1997) *Beowulf*, revised edn, Manchester: Manchester University Press.

Talbot, C. H. (ed. and trans.) (1959) *The Life of St Christina of Markyate: A Twelfth Century Recluse*, Oxford: Oxford University Press.

Tanner, Norman P. (1984) *The Church in Late Medieval Norwich, 1370–1532*, Studies and Texts 66, Toronto: Pontifical Institute of Mediaeval Studies.

—— (ed.) (1990) *Decrees of the Ecumenical Councils*, London: Sheed and Ward.

Tasoulias, J. A. (1996) 'The Mother's Lament: *Wulf and Eadwacer* Reconsidered', *Medium Aevum* 65: 1–18.

Tavormina, M. Teresa (1995) *Kindly Similitude: Marriage and Family in Piers Plowman*, Cambridge: Brewer.
Trotula of Salerno (1940) *The Diseases of Women*, trans. Elizabeth Mason-Hohl, New York: The Ward-Ritchie Press.
Turville-Petre, Thorlac (ed.) (1989) *Alliterative Poetry of the Later Middle Ages*, London: Routledge.
—— (1997) 'English Quaint and Strange in "Ne mai no lewed lued"', in O. S. Pickering (ed.) *Individuality and Achievement in Middle English Poetry*, Cambridge: Brewer: 73–83.
Wack, Mary Frances (1990) *Lovesickness in the Middle Ages: The Viaticum and its Commentaries*, Philadelphia: University of Pennsylvania Press.
Walker, Sue Sheridan (1976) 'Widow and Ward: The Feudal Law of Child Custody in Medieval England', in Susan Mosher Stuard (ed.) *Women in Medieval Society*, Philadelphia: University of Pennsylvania Press: 159–172.
—— (1982) 'Free Consent and the Marriage of Feudal Wards in Medieval England', *Journal of Medieval History* 8: 123–134.
—— (ed.) (1993a) *Wife and Widow in Medieval England*, Ann Arbor: University of Michigan Press.
—— (1993b) 'Litigation as Personal Quest: Suing for Dower in the Royal Courts, circa 1272–1350', in Walker (ed) (1993a): 81–108.
Walsh, P. G. (ed. and trans.) (1982) *Andreas Capellanus, On Love*, London: Duckworth.
—— (ed.) (2001) *Augustine; De Bono Coniugali, De Sancta Virginitate*, Oxford: Clarendon Press.
Whitelock, Dorothy (1948) 'Wulfstan and the Laws of Cnut', *English Historical Review* 63: 433–452 (reprinted in Whitelock 1981).
—— (1970) 'Wulfstan's Authorship of Cnut's Laws', *English Historical Review* 70: 72–85 (reprinted in Whitelock 1981).
—— (ed.) (1979) *English Historical Documents, 500–1042*, 2nd edn, London: Eyre Methuen.
—— (1981) *History, Law, and Literature in 10th–11th Century England*, London: Variorum.
Wilkins, David (ed.) (1737) *Concilia Magnae Brittaniae et Hiberniae*, London.
Willard, Charity Cannon (1984) *Christine de Pizan: Her Life and Works*, New York: Persea.
Windeatt, B. A. (trans.) (1985) *The Book of Margery Kempe*, Harmondsworth: Penguin.
Wogan-Browne, Jocelyn (2001) *Saints' Lives and Women's Literary Culture c.1150–1300: Virginity and its Authorizations*, Oxford: Oxford University Press.
Woodbine, G. E. (ed.) and Thorne, S. E. (trans.) (1968–1977) *Bracton: On the Laws and Customs of England*, Cambridge, MA: Harvard University Press.
Woodcock, Brian L. (1952) *Medieval Ecclesiastical Courts in the Diocese of Canterbury*, London: Oxford University Press.
Zeldin, Theodore (1994) *An Intimate History of Humanity*, London: Sinclair Stevenson.

REFERENCE WORKS

Bosworth, Joseph and Toller, T. Northcote (eds) (1898) *An Anglo-Saxon Dictionary*, Oxford: Clarendon.
Kurath, Hans and Kuhn, Sherman M. (eds) (1952–2001) *Middle English Dictionary*, Ann Arbor: University of Michgan Press.
Strayer, Joseph R. (ed.) *Dictionary of the Middle Ages*, New York: Scribner.

INDEX